ADVANCE PRAISE FOR
BECAUSE I LOVE HER

"In our daughters' faces, we see different versions of ourselves: early hopes and dreams, years of self-discovery and hard work to chase after our goals, and the rich reality of the compromises, challenges and joys of being a woman and mother. This candid exploration of 'our daughters, ourselves' captures the unique frustrations and delights facing mothers and daughters today."
—Leslie Morgan Steiner, *Mommy Wars* editor and author of *Crazy Love*

"This collection about one of the most complex relationships we have is so rich and varied that you'll want to read the whole thing from start to finish and then dip into it again and again. The essays are, by turns, wry, funny, angry, forgiving, sad, joyous, and a great many of them are all of these things at once. The book is suffused with hope and punctuated by a fierce, fierce love."
—Marisa de los Santos, *New York Times* bestselling author of *Love Walked In* and *Belong To Me*

"I was so impressed by *Because I Love Her*. Much of the honesty in these pages required real bravery from the writers. Some of these essays are hilarious, and some are tragic. They are all thoughtful and compulsively readable; I easily turned page after page, finding solace, understanding, and inspiration."
—Laura Moriarty, author of *The Center of Everything* and *The Rest of Her Life*

"*In Because I Love Her,* Nicki Richesin brings together thirty-four women who venture unflinchingly into the mysterious, emotionally complex terrain of the mother-daughter relationship. Here there is humor, heartbreak, loss, and, above all, love. Intelligent, provocative, and deeply personal, this book will inspire you to call your mother, hug your daughter, and perhaps even reach a deeper understanding of the most important relationships in your life."

—Michelle Richmond, *New York Times* bestselling author of *The Year of Fog* and *No One You Know*

"One of the harsher realities about having a girl is coming face-to-face with how awful you sometimes were to your own mother—how disappointed you could be in her weaknesses, how judgmental of her outfits, how frustrated by her hovering. But, as the poignant essays in *Because I Love Her* demonstrate, gaining that insight and sympathy is one of the many gifts that come with raising a daughter."

—Jennifer Baumgardner, author of *Look Both Ways* and *Abortion & Life*

"Because we are all daughters of mothers, *Because I Love Her* is a necessary and most fizzy tonic."

—Suzanne Finnamore, author of *Split: A Memoir of Divorce*

"*Because I Love Her* is full of heartfelt, often painful, but priceless mother-daughter moments. Anyone who has ever had, been, battled with, feared, or loved a mother will cherish the stories in this book."

—Katie Crouch, *New York Times* bestselling author of *Girls in Trucks*

BECAUSE I LOVE HER

34 Women Writers Reflect on the Mother-Daughter Bond

HARLEQUIN®

BECAUSE I LOVE HER

ISBN-13: 978-0-373-89202-0
ISBN-10:   0-373-89202-0
© 2009 by Andrea N. Richesin

Library of Congress Cataloging-in-Publication Data

Because I Love Her : 34 women writers reflect on the mother-daughter bond/edited by Andrea N. Richesin.
p. cm.
 ISBN 978-0-373-89202-0 (pbk.)
1. Mothers and daughters—United States. 2. Mothers—United States. 3. Women authors—United States. I. Richesin, Andrea N.
HQ755.86.B44 2009
306.874'30973—dc22
2008038744

www.eharlequin.com

Printed in U.S.A.

Naturally, this collection is dedicated to
my mother Debbie Richesin and my daughter Lily Warwick.
And in loving memory of
Debra McClinton
and
Theresa Duncan

I no longer have fantasies—they are the unhealed child's fantasies, I think—of some infinitely healing conversation with her, in which we could show all our wounds, transcend the pain we have shared as mother and daughter, say everything at last.

—From *Of Woman Born* by Adrienne Rich

CONTENTS

INTRODUCTION

What would we tell our mothers and daughters if we could tell them anything? If all our self-doubts were dismissed and honesty was the only option, what would we really say? This is exactly what I asked the contributors of *Because I Love Her* to discover for themselves. Although for some this was a difficult task, surprising depths of love, long-suppressed memories, and real truths were revealed in the telling. We'd give our lives for our mothers and daughters, but sometimes all they truly need is our love and that we share ourselves and all we know.

Because I Love Her explores the most intimate bonds of motherhood by sharing stories and secrets of becoming a mother and grandmother, negotiating generational differences, and learning from our mothers' past mistakes. These writers discover who their mothers truly are, forgive for past wrongs, and ultimately accept they are, indeed, their mothers' daughters.

This collection of deeply personal essays by accomplished mothers with daughters includes exceptional writings by Karen Joy Fowler, Jacquelyn Mitchard, Susan Wiggs, Sheila Kohler, Joyce Maynard, Catherine Newman, Ann Hood and many others. Most of these contributors acknowledge the great debt they owe their mothers and how through their powerful examples, they have decided to raise their own daughters. They have written about what their mothers taught them, what they in turn hope to impart to their own daughters, and finally, what they've learned about themselves as the bridge between the two. These are stories from women with vastly different experiences—from women with mothers who were mentally ill or absent and from those who had the courage to make peace with their mothers along the way.

As both a mother and a daughter, a woman is essentially at the center of a three-way mirror, reflecting on her past by remembering herself as a young girl and now as a mother, seeing her mother for who she once was. As Katherine Center discovers in her essay, "You have to give up the old to get the new. You can't be the child and the mom at the same time. You can't be your young self and your old self at the same time. You can't know what you know now and feel the way you did then." And yet, the truth is, we all do in spite of ourselves.

After all, motherhood is an inheritance if nothing else. We inherit from our mothers and grandmothers endearments or figures of speech; impossible personality traits; folksongs from the old country; our hands, dimples, and eye color; recipes handed down from their mothers; treasured heirlooms; and most remarkably, humor, warmth, and compassion. We pass along the stories, whispers of remembered fragments of a time long ago, beloved books and films, and hope for richer and fuller lives than we have led for our daughters.

We go to our mothers for comfort, advice, support, in tears and frustration, for company, and for an answer to the neverending riddle of our lives. Just as contributor Ericka Lutz's grandmother, the late Tillie Olsen, once wrote in *Tell Me a Riddle*, "Mama, Mama, you must help carry the world."

Perhaps portrayals such as these have made us take notice of what our mothers have done for us and finally honor and appreciate their sacrifices and burdens.

Many women long to discover the mysteries of who their mothers are and how they have lived. As Mary Haug concludes in her remarkable essay, "she took to her grave what I needed most—the truth of her story and the ways that narrative had shaped her. Such truth might have helped us reshape the myth that defined us as mother and daughter; such honesty might have broken the silence." When the unknowable parts of our mothers' lives remain a mystery, we often feel these could be the key to understanding ourselves.

Quite a few of these writers long for the mothers they've lost such as Joyce Maynard, Ann Fisher-Wirth, Laurie Gwen Shapiro, Karen Karbo and Mary Haug, and for some, like Anne Marie Feld and Jacquelyn Mitchard, they have tried to become the mothers they never had. In a few instances, contributors yearn for their mothers of long ago. Katherine Center would like her "Young Mom" to whisk her family away in her Suburban for spaghetti dinner in her childhood home, which of course no longer exists. Despite the nostalgia, she discovers "that we all carry our mothers inside us."

The contributors have inherited many talents from their mothers and grandmothers such as gardening (Catherine Newman's daughter Birdy), bargain shopping (Heather Swain), obsessive tendencies (Julianna Baggott and her daughter), singing (Susan Wiggs) and a profound love of reading (Sara Woster and Laurie Gwen Shapiro). Gayle Brandeis tells of how her mother taught her the power of the written word through her "poison pen" letters. She has tried to teach that to her own daughter in turn—to teach her to use her voice when something is troubling her personally or in a larger context. Sheila Kohler learns through the challenges of raising her deaf daughter along with her two other daughters how to accept rather than change her children. Her daughter Cybele teaches her how to truly listen to others.

A number delve into the multiple-generational aspect of the

mother-daughter bond such as in Ericka Lutz, Catherine Newman and Laurie Gwen Shapiro's essays. Lutz inherited from her grandmother and mother the self-knowledge that creativity for them is not an option: it's their very life force. One of the ways Laurie Gwen Shapiro and her mother communicated was as a three-way process through children's books. When Shapiro's mother was diagnosed with ovarian cancer, she remained amazingly upbeat until her death. But it wasn't until she was reading about the spiders born after Charlotte's death in *Charlotte's Web* that her daughter, Violet, finally asked her first questions about death.

This collective experience of mothering and often finding mothers in unlikely places shapes us as moms. For Katrina Onstad, she looked to mothers of her friends who quietly influenced her throughout adolescence: The Mean Mom, The Single Mom and The Dying Mom. These mothers altered her perception of her own mother; they terrified and thrilled her; and thus she finally saw herself as her daughter's mom. Barbara Rushkoff's friend's mother, the saucy Mrs. Schwartz, seemed daring and exciting compared to her buttoned-up, sensible mother. Although she is not biologically related to her daughter, nor to the woman who taught her what it means to be a mother, Calla Devlin defined her own parenting style in opposition to her own mother's mistakes.

Offering some measure of forgiveness in *Radical Promises* and *In the Offing,* Anne Marie Feld and Tara Bray Smith come to terms with the emotional legacies they have inherited from their mothers. By the time Feld reached her teen years, her mother had become a ghost in their suburban home. Her eventual suicide was just a formality. Twenty years later, Anne, a mother herself, faces a question posed by her young daughter: "Where is your mommy?" Her story explores her struggle to find an answer to her daughter's question, as well as to the questions of who her mother was, and what kind of mother she herself hopes to be.

Tara Bray Smith played a kind of hide-and-seek dance with her mother for years—trying to help her and to know her. She has been more of a guardian—taking on the role of mother to her many times—than a daughter. In the end, she recognizes that "adulthood is realizing that we all are deficient, and after a certain point no one is accountable for that but ourselves."

Many commend their mothers for their loving examples. As a devoted mother, Ann Fisher-Wirth writes about her close relationship with her mother and daughters. Once separated by Ann's divorce and second marriage, they managed to form a bond, among many things, through their mutual love of poetry and activism. Ashley Warlick sings her mother's praises for her "sure-handed" ways and "her faith in fragile things, in risky love, her willingness to let the good outweigh the bad and weather the consequences." Of all the gifts Catherine Crawford gives her daughters, comfort and ease with respect for their bodies are among the greatest—and looking around at young women these days, among the most rarely bestowed. In *Mother Hunting*, Kaui Hart Hemmings is comforted by the thought that she and her mother would have been friends had they known each other in high school.

After Elise Miller had kids, her mom extolled the virtues of letting go, whether it comes to potty-training or potty-mouth. Her story reveals the new bond that has developed now that she needs and wants advice from her mother. She will impart to her daughter the wisdom her mother has shared with her in the last three years, including forgiveness. Heather Swain wants her daughter to "question her desires, to learn the difference between wants and needs, and to be comfortable opting out of socially mandated 'must haves'" to become resourceful like her mother. Amanda

Coyne's essay takes the form of a letter to a daughter whom she's currently trying to conceive. She describes what it was like to be raised by a woman who eventually served a twelve-year prison sentence for dealing drugs. She explains to this daughter that, because of this and all the ensuing chaos, when her body was most ready for her, life wasn't. But now, things have calmed: her mother is free, Coyne has learned so much from that former chaos.

During my own childhood, from the time I was ten years old, I dreamed of one day having a daughter. I could have neither a true idea of what motherhood for me would eventually entail nor how complete my transformation would be. For it is only once you have become a mother that you can fully recognize your own mother for the sacrifices she has made on your behalf. Once recognized, you remain in complete awe that such a sacrifice is ever made.

In June 1971, two summers after the "summer of love," my mother was married in a white jersey-knit minidress and I was right there—under her daisy bouquet, just waiting to emerge seven months later. I owe a great deal to my mother's example as she had me at what I now consider a very young age and as a result sacrificed much of her youth to take care of my sister and me. I'm sure she wouldn't see it quite that way. In fact, she claims her happiest memories are of our baby and toddler years. I believe her, but I can't help but wonder if she ever felt pangs of envy or regret when my sister and I went on to have our own adventures in our twenties.

As a young stay-at-home mom, my mother was president of the PTA; delivered meals on wheels; served as a school nurse or teacher's assistant twice a week (my schoolmates would run toward her screaming with delight "Miss Debbie!"); baked homemade cookies and hosted gourmet dinner parties; sewed dress-up clothes and a trousseau of doll clothing for my sister and I; and created Halloween costumes so inventive I actually felt sorry for the children dressed in cheap plastic renditions. She cuddled me amidst a stack of books and read to me until she would grow hoarse. Huddled in her arms and listening intently, I felt important and loved by her sharing this glorious world of books and imagination with me. She did all of this with the aplomb and joy of a young mother in love with her girls. In short, she was an indomitable force and a hard act to follow. She was not a mother for whom one enters motherhood lightly.

When I became a mother, I quite suddenly found this new role thrust upon me. Now the person coming to me, calling me "Mommy" in fear after a nightmare with her tear-soaked blankie, expects me to have all the answers. Through giving birth to my daughter, I found myself face-to-face not only with a little girl and woman-to-be, but also with my own unresolved conflicts from the past and my hopes and dreams for our future together. A whole world of trust is exchanged in the transformation from daughter to now mother-and-daughter.

I realize this is just the beginning. I will have to prepare my daughter for countless unpleasant episodes—her first spat with her best friend, the wrath of a disapproving parent or fickle teacher, her first heartbreak, college—life. She will need my support as a sudden depth charge to catapult her into her life. I will have to be brave, too—just as I was four years ago, when she came bursting into my life, a helpless yet brave voyager.

In Mary Oliver's gorgeous poem "In Blackwater Woods" she explains that to live in this world you must do three things—"to love what is mortal; to hold it against your bones knowing your own life depends on it; and, when the time comes to let it go, to let it go." My daughter is teaching me every day these lessons of letting go, letting her fall and make her own mistakes, and letting her grow away from me. This will be my hardest job—the letting go. For even now, I follow her steps cautiously—every ledge, edge, mean hole lurking to swallow her and take her away from me. I would love for Lily to remain as curious and adventurous as she is now. I hope I can encourage her to take risks, and not let my need to protect her hinder her. More than anything, if I can instill confidence and encourage her to love herself, I will feel that my job as a mother is well done.

We've learned many things from our mothers—directly, and more frequently indirectly—as an observer of their lives and choices. As much as we love them, it's true that we're often frustrated by them and afraid of turning into them. However, loving our mothers despite their faults and frailties empowers us to become better mothers and stronger women. I suppose some part of learning to be a mother and a daughter is to forgive yourself for your own foolish blunders and to echo that same forgiveness to the ones you love. By showing compassion for the mother who has made mistakes and seeing her for whom she really is, we can teach our daughters how to live and to grow.

All of the writers in *Because I Love Her* attempt to understand the circumstances, challenges and choices that were made available to their mothers. They confront the rivalries that exist between them and their fears of repeating the same negative patterns. Their mothers are their role models, their biological and emotional road map, and their daughters are an extension of their selves. Their moving stories have taught them much about the true meaning of what it means to be a mother, a daughter and a family.

Andrea N. Richesin
San Rafael, California
August 2008

BECAUSE I LOVE HER

THE MOTHER LOAD
Jacquelyn Mitchard

Hundreds of dewdrops to greet the dawn,
Hundreds of bees in the purple clover,
Hundreds of butterflies on the lawn,
But only one mother the wide world over.
—From "Only One Mother" by George Cooper

I take good care of myself—working out at least five times a week, flossing like it's a religion, avoiding secondhand smoke and even a second glass of wine. My grandparents lived well into their eighties and nineties. So, why do I treat my life every day as if I were making graduation scrapbooks for my daughters, who are only nine and twelve years old, filling each hour I spend at their sides with visual and emotional impressions—in the hope that half of them will stick?

I'm mother-loading.

Just in case.

And why?

I know it's crazy. Each of my seven kids has a baby book Proust would have admired—when, among my friends, even the most devoted mothers barely got the baptismal certificate and the footprints stuck into the album if they had more than one child. Of course (and the seven kids might be your first hint) I'm over-compensating. I'm being the Ubermom.

I have my reasons.

There's a look. You know that look? It's the look people get when their mothers or mothers-in-law are about to arrive for a visit. *That look* is always the same. And so is my response. My friends get those rolling cue-ball eyes, and tell me that—even though they love their mothers and mothers-in-law *dearly*—they just can't bear the thought of that upcoming visit, that the three days that will feel like three *months* because of all the unsolicited childrearing advice and teensy criticisms about everything from diet to demeanor to decor.

I can't help it.

I get weepy.

I don't have the slightest idea what it's like to be an adult and have a mother or…really, a mother-in-law.

I don't know what it's like to be nagged and nurtured, treasured and tortured as though I were still in pigtails. I scarcely even remember my mother—who had many friends, hobbies, a job and an active social life—who thought, I'm sure, she'd be getting ready for my eldest's college graduation by now and rocking my two-year-old. But it didn't go that way.

When I was nineteen and my brother fifteen, my mother died a swift and vicious death from a brain tumor that robbed her first of her exquisite beauty and then of her considerable wit. Her illness was detected at Thanksgiving and by Valentine's Day, it was all finished.

As a half-grown woman who had to spend the rest of her life without the considerable force that had propelled me to whatever achievements I'd attained, I remember asking myself, *now whom will I try to impress for all the life I have left?* My mother was exacting. She had requirements: Straight As were expected. I had to be terrifically literate and nice-looking, too, using acne scrub by age eleven and doing sit-ups by thirteen. Always remember, she said, that it was no accident that I had the same name as Jacqueline Kennedy Onassis. When I was a tiny child, I can remember her saying, "Jackie Kennedy will be famous all her life. She's famously thin." Mama set the same high standards for literacy (and concavity) for herself: A high-school dropout educated by reading our textbooks, from Latin to Russian literature, she could translate any tombstone and called *Anna Karenina* a book that took "all the fun out of adultery." If she'd had an education, she probably could have run a corporation—or a small country.

As a grown-up mother, she might not have been so great, and I freely concede that. She drank too much and she smoked as though it was a vocation—which was probably why her generation outwitted her parents' heritage of longevity. She was bold to a fine point—still able to do cartwheels at fifty. She was funny and charming and gallant and occasionally cruel.

But even before she got sick, I always had the distinct feeling that we never had enough time. In fact, I have only two delicious memories preserved entirely like dioramas under glass. My mother once picked me up from second grade and drove with me deep into the forest preserve behind the zoo, where a developer who ran out of money had once planned a ritzy neighborhood. There were sidewalks back there and streetlights and even park benches. Best of all, from those benches, we could see the hidden part of the zoo, where mother giraffes nursed their babies and elephants got their baths. For hours, we watched the kind of animal care that little kids in the sixties, long before *Animal Planet,* never glimpsed. And then, one other time, when I was as grown as I would ever get during her lifetime, she came to my first apartment. While I was at work, she put up curtains made from brightly striped bedsheets and made grilled-cheese-and-tomato sandwiches. I take out and hold those memories against my stomach when I ache for the smell of her sweaters (that curious, fetching cocktail of smoke-and-cologne) and the sound of her singing her favorite song: "My Buddy."

You might wonder, at this point, where my father fits in all this.

He doesn't. Although my brother and I certainly tried, my father once told my brother and me that he simply was not "a family man." Although he died when I was forty, he was living with a woman with whom I'd gone to high school. And he died of Bright's disease, the kidney ailment that "ginnies" among the poor in Victorian England got—which could also be achieved in twenty-first century America by dint of a fifth of gin a day. After I was widowed in my thirties, a grief counselor told me that the relationship with my father that I described sounded like what people said about men who married their moms when they were already adults.

Not surprisingly, I envy my friends their mothers, even the difficult ones.

I'd give my molars for someone who smelled of Chanel No. 5 or My Sin to come to my house and point out that I would never have been allowed to back talk *my* parents that way, to knit me funny-looking sweaters I'd actually have to wear, to rearrange my drawers, to make me grilled-cheese-and-tomato sandwiches with Velveeta and buy my kids foolishly expensive boiled-wool coats.

For years, I wanted a mommy so bad that I searched for mothers wherever I could find them.

My first husband was another orphan, whose parents both died by the time he was twenty-one. We learned to change diapers from *Dr. Spock's Baby and Child Care*. But four years after he died, also of cancer (I know this all sounds terribly bleak; but we had a good run, fifteen years and three wonderful little boys) I married a man who had a mother who was just absolutely ducky. She was smart, beautiful, fashionable, bookish and adoring. The only problem was, my husband is more than ten years younger than I and his mom was a teenage bride. In the sweetest possible way, she made it clear that she wasn't interested in being a mother to someone who could have been her younger sister. Becoming a grandmother at fifty was a shock to her system. When it came to a contretemps between my husband and me, and inevitably over time, it did, my mother-in-law made it clear that she couldn't side against her son in any situation that didn't involve a penitentiary. Though I longed to form the word *mom* with my lips, I made her happier calling her by her first name.

And then, what was my choice?

For my daughters, I became the memorable mom I couldn't ever have.

Now, don't get the impression that defines a "smother mother." I'm the one who cheers them on to try rock climbing and scuba diving and to come parasailing with me. I encourage them to take emotional and physical risks—although not, obviously, the "fall in love with the local rehab kid" kind.

I encourage their independence.

But also, I tuck their ordinary days full of Mommy-stuff—mushy notes in their field-trip lunches, movie festivals in the big bed when Dad's out of town, sharing the books I loved as a girl and reading the ones they love now, going out for "coffee" with twelve-year-old Francie and shopping for "makeup" (lip balm) with nine-year-old Mia. We three go on girl dates to musicals, and when I can justify an out-of-town business trip as educational, I take one of them along. Until they all but threatened to strangle me with them, I bought them matching sundresses. I still sing them the songs that my mother sang to me, as well as the ones I love best: They can identify everything from Freddie Mercury to "Un Bel Di Vedremo." I tell them extravagantly that I had to adopt them because there were so many brothers and I couldn't live without a daughter of my own and when one daughter came, I loved her so much I couldn't wait to have another.

Next to my bed, I keep a special diary made from handmade paper in which I have written down the things they said as little children and the things I feel about the two of them. I know they will find it one day and the diary will make them cry. (It already makes me cry.) But it's not some vine that will cling to them from the beyond. The only piece of my mother's handwriting I have is a grocery list. They will have all this: When two-year-old Francie learned we were going to have another sister (from what she called the "so-so" worker who came to our house) she cried, "My darling-drop Mama, you're getting me another me!" And I wrote that down. I wrote down how much Mia loved the game that she called "hide-and-secret" and how, when she was four, she asked me, "When will my feet get high so I can wear high heels?" I paste in photos that the girls took—all with one thing in common. They all depict views that are clearly framed by someone three feet tall. The interesting bits are always near the ground, even if it means any human beings in the photo are visible only as torsos.

None of this effort is meant, even subtly, as a guilt trip.

My girls frankly expect me to live forever. They cheerfully offer me rooms in their attics when they marry (I wonder how cheerful they'll be if I ever take them up on that). They don't get misty when they ask me which of my belongings each of them can have when I'm dead. But more precious than the ruby ring or the ruby slippers will be the mother load—the scads of stories and words and images that say, "Get a load of me" because you never know when you'll need it and when you need it, you can't imagine how glad you'll be that you have it. Francie and Mia won't have a few faded photos and a wedding picture. (They ask, often, about the woman in the gilded frame they call "the princess.") If I shouldn't get a chance to meet their daughters, at least I won't be a myth. There'll be the stories that were published, the recordings of our voices (somehow, much more intimate than any home video), an album of ribbons and traditions and even recipes. Even though I'm no great shakes as a cook, I get up at least once a week before dawn to make muffins from scratch as a breakfast surprise, so that the scent will curl up the stairs and waken them before I do. Mia once told her best friend, "Promise not to tell your mom about how my mom makes French toast. It's award-winning." I make big rituals out of baking the Christmas cookies, letting everyone use the cookie press and assemble the four hundred or so ingredients it takes for the traditional Italian cookies called *Tu Tu*. They'll have a tactile imprint of the times I plumped one of them on either side of me and, although they're quite able to read on their own, read them chapters from *Where the Red Fern Grows* and *Anne of Green Gables* and poems about the landlord's black-eyed daughter twining a dark red love knot into her long black hair.

If I weren't to return from the business trip on which I'm writing this, both Mia and Francie would have not only a very good or at least very real map for *being* mothers (including potholes and cul-de-sacs), but more importantly, they'd have the best legacy I could leave them: a solid and indelible sense of having *been* mothered, an umbrella that will always be a shelter between them and the clouds. Perhaps it would be an invisible umbrella, only a relic of recollection. But as a writer friend of mine said not long ago, the consolations of the imagination are not imaginary. They may be the realest things we keep.

THINGS TO REMEMBER NOT TO FORGET
Katherine Center

No wonder the moon in the window seems to have drifted
out of a love poem that you used to know by heart.
—From "Forgetfulness" by Billy Collins

At our house, for our kids, who are two and five, everything is better with a big side order of Naked. Jumping on the bed is good, but Naked Jumping is better. Hiding in the closet is good, but Naked Hiding is better. Every good thing is better as a Naked Thing: Naked Hide-and-Seek, Naked Running in Circles, Naked Tooth Brushing, Naked Breakfast, Naked Zoo Animals.

The only thing, in fact, that's not better naked is bathing, which is far better done with socks on.

Still, bath time excepted, as often as they can remember to, my kids strip down and enjoy the particular tickle of delight you can only get from being just plain nude. I don't know where they get it from.

But I do know I should be recording it on video. Just like I should be recording birthday parties and trips to amusements parks and all our official moments of happiness—and even, on occasion, our moments of sadness. Just to keep things real. Though I will confess that when my daughter Anna was a baby, just as she was learning to roll over, I videotaped her rolling across our living room, over and over, until, as she got close to me with the camera and lifted her head way up to smile, she lost her balance and clonked over, smacking her head on the hardwood floor. The camera hit the sofa, and, then, there was only the floral pattern out of focus, my muffled voice shouting, "Holy shit! Oh, holy shit! Shit, shit, shit!" and the baby crying an endless, unsootheable river.

That moment, I recorded back over. Now, in the video, she rolls and rolls and rolls, with never a hint of the injury to come. Just at the precipice of disaster, we cut to a new scene of Anna in the Baby Bjorn, strapped safely to her daddy, who is hopping around and singing a little rhyming rap ditty about her toes and her nose and a red, red rose. Whenever I go back to watch that section of our early recordings of Anna's baby life, I squint with dread as she rolls. And then, when it cuts, I relax. Crisis averted! She's safe with Daddy. As if it never happened. As if the video is somehow truer than the moment itself.

There's so much I should be recording. Especially the things I will never remember: Anna inking her entire body with a green stamp pad. Thomas wearing his sister's Tinkerbell costume along with a tool-belt holster and announcing he's Bob the Builder. All the little moments that break like waves on the surface of our lives and then disappear.

But I'm not recording nearly as much as I should. Even though I know that one day these nutty little people, whose inquiries about ladybugs and Lowly Worm populate almost every minute of my waking life, will be gone. Not gone, exactly, of course. Still here, still my children. But grown-up.

Someday the objects of their little selves will be replaced, and I know it as well as every parent knows it. And so, the video recorder. The digital camera. The albums. The baby journals. The storage tubs full of outgrown pj's and macaroni-encrusted artworks. What else can you do but to hang on to anything you can?

But I forget things so easily. Like charging the camcorder batteries. I've never been great at planning ahead. And anyway, another part of me says there's some tension between recording a moment and actually living that moment. Some part of me says it's better to see everything firsthand with my actual eyes than through the flip-out screen of the camcorder.

I forgot, for instance, to charge the battery before my daughter's third birthday—possibly one of the best days of my entire life. We had a butterfly party in my mother's backyard on the cheeriest spring day a birthday-throwing mama could possibly wish for. The air was cool, but the sun was warm. The grass was bright green, and we had a machine releasing hundreds and hundreds of bubbles from a balcony above the yard. A friend painted all the children's faces like butterflies—bodies on the noses, brilliant red and blue wings on the cheeks, and tall, curled antennas on the foreheads.

That day is still absolutely vivid for me. And I can't help but wonder if it would have been the same if I'd been messing with the video camera or panning the faces in the crowd instead of just drinking them in. Maybe it's best to just be there. To live it and to let it go.

I go back and forth. There are, of course, so many moments that you spend with your children. It's not like missing a few of them will suddenly mean missing the whole thing. Parenting, as I'm more and more aware every day, is a long-haul kind of thing. So long-haul, in fact, that your eyes, and even your mind, can glaze over. It's so easy to check your e-mail compulsively or flip through some magazine. How is it possible that I ever, even for one minute, felt more interested in reading about a celebrity than watching my kids make a stew in our igloo cooler out of grass clippings and a whole bag of cat food? It is not possible. It just can't be.

My own mother had a Super 8 camera that she carried around in her big purse when we were little. For Christmas a couple of years ago, my parents put those movies on DVD for my sisters and me, and for many months afterward, my kids and I watched them every single day.

At first, I was tickled to see us all again, at the beach, our chubby legs stomping the sand. Or riding the monorail at Disney World, our hair fluttering. Or hunting Easter eggs in our old backyard. I'd point at the screen and try to explain everything to my little ones. "That's Baby Mama! And that's Baby Aunt LaLa! And that's Young Nana!" They loved to hear about it, but those people didn't mean anything to them. Who is that again? Which one is she? Where is the *Real* Nana?

After a while, it started to make me sad to watch the movies. I found myself calling my mother every time we turned them on. "They're making me watch the movies again," I'd say, and then I'd ask her any question—"What are you eating?" "How did you sleep?" "Where are you headed?"—just to get her talking. Just to remind myself that even though the Young Nana was gone, the Real Nana was just across town. Even if my kid-chasing, booty-wiping life didn't really allow me to talk with her the way I used to. She was there, still. Anyway.

I never imagined how all-encompassing having children would be before I did it. In my mind, if I'm really honest, I guess I imagined that my mother was going to raise my kids, somehow. She knew all about it, after all. She was the mom. I'd never even changed a diaper! I imagined that having children would be a kind of return to my own childhood. When, in fact, of course, it has only taken me further away.

That's what just hit me: How you really can't have everything. You have to give up the old to get the new. You can't be the child and the mom at the same time. You can't be your young self and your old self at the same time. You can't know what you know now and feel the way you did then. You can't, you can't, you can't.

But I still find myself keeping an eye out for things that are already gone. As if they might reappear somehow. As if my Young Mom—the mother I knew when I was growing up, the person who is my definition of what a mother is—might pick us all up one afternoon in her Suburban and take us to my childhood home for a spaghetti dinner.

If my mother were watching me type right now, she would argue the pointlessness of even thinking about it. There is no point in longing to be back in that house. It doesn't exist anymore, and neither do those people—not in the same way. I can't be there. So I might as well have somewhere else to be.

And so I do. Of course I do. I don't mean to say that one house is better than another. Just that some funny part of me keeps expecting my redheaded mother from 1977 to show up and take over. Because I certainly don't know what I'm doing. Maybe she didn't, either. Now that I'm the age she was then, I wonder about that a lot.

But she must have. She's still a thousand times better at the mechanics of life than I am. She can always find the sock I can't find, or get out the stain I can't remove, or solve the algebra problem that I've messed up three different ways in three different tries. And despite everything I know now, I still believe, as I did when I was little, that there is an entire universe of things that she knows that I don't. I still believe that nothing truly bad can ever happen if my mother is around. I know it's not true. But still. It is true.

Here's the thing: I don't believe in myself in that same way.

Last Christmas, my kids got the flu. The Influenza flu. And after our lengthy quarantine was over, I took them to the mall, to a bookstore, to celebrate. I'm not very brave about taking my kids to crowded public places, especially since Thomas is not only the King of Running Away From Parents and the King of Running Into Traffic, but also the King of Getting Lost. For our mall excursion, I strapped him into the stroller and then listened to him fuss and writhe and beg to get out for the next thirty minutes.

When we finally hit the bookstore, I unsnapped him, and he took off running (since he is also the King of Pulling Books Off Shelves) just as my daughter announced that she needed to pee "like crazy." I don't think I'd ever let her go to the bathroom on her own like that, but I was triaging at that point, and her brother was heading for the stacks. I let her go, which she did with confidence, as I ran to get her brother—and then, just as I grabbed him by the arm, I heard a scream. In public places, all screaming children sound to your ears like your own child. But when I turned toward the sound, this screaming child, this time, was in fact, my own—with her pinkie caught in the hinge of the massive, self-closing bathroom door.

I ran over and pushed the door open, remembering to *be cool*—knowing that I could not, under any circumstances, panic. "Okay," I said, pushing the door open. "It's okay."

And that's when I saw that, actually, it wasn't okay. Her fingernail on her pinkie had come off. I mean: Off. In its entirety. It was just hanging by a piece of skin, flapping open like a shutter.

Now, when I think back to that moment, I always think about my mother and how she handled it on the day I slipped on gravel in the street and came back with a knee that she describes as "hamburger meat." She had to pick the pieces of gravel out of it with a pair of tweezers, and she was so woozy doing it, she says, that she called our next-door neighbor to come and stand beside her.

I know how I should have handled that moment in the bookstore. I can imagine my Better Self calmly guiding us all with confidence from crisis to recovery. But my Better Self was not there that day. Just my Regular Self. Or, more truthfully, my Insanely Freaked Out, Flapping Like A Chicken Self.

Because once I pieced together that our car was parked five floors up in a garage packed with post-holiday traffic, and that I had no Band-Aids and no Neosporin, and that I—nobody but me—was going to have to decide what to do next, I lost my cool. Should I pull the nail completely off? Should I try to stick it back on? Should I rinse the meat of that finger under the faucet in a bathroom that was easily a petri dish for flesh-eating bacteria? I didn't have the answers, and I didn't know how to get them. And, yep: I lost it. In a big, bad way. My nine-fingernailed daughter was calmer than I was. She sat, crying and shaking, on the side of a sofa while the bookstore staff went off to look for a first-aid kit. But I was so hysterical that one spectator even leaned in and said, "Your panic will make it worse for your daughter." To which I responded, right in her earshot, "She *lost* her bleeping *fingernail!*"—as if this injury were so off-the-charts horrible that all parenting bets were off.

This would not have been a camcorder moment for me.

On the drive down the five parking-lot ramps, my son cursed like a sailor, trying out a vast new lexicon of naughtiness, as my daughter held her throbbing and bandaged finger above her head, and I honked at a guy in a Datsun who was driving one mile an hour.

"How did that work out?" My husband teased me later, after we'd been to the doctor, built an enormous, splintlike nail bed protection device out of bandages and foam, and put everyone to bed.

"Not too well," I said.

14

My husband went on. "He didn't move politely to the side?"

"No," I said. "He slowed down to point-five, straddled the lane so I couldn't get around him, and gave me the finger out the window."

"Nice," my husband said.

Yeah.

In a moment like that, all you can hope for is to rise above your limitations. I would have given anything for my mother's steady resolve, her rocklike, we-can-handle-this quality. On the day I skinned my knee, my mom just handled it. In the way that she always handled everything. In the way that she got baked potatoes and salad and flank steak on the table every night when I was a kid. In the way that I always used to fall asleep to the sound of her adding machine rattling on her table in the kitchen. In the way things were just taken care of. There was food in the fridge. There was gas in the car. Doctor's appointments were made, dentist appointments were kept. On her carpool day, she was in the carpool line. No matter what, it was done.

I'm terrified that I won't be able to make my children feel absolutely safe and cared for in that way. I am the Queen of Forgetting Things. I can forget an appointment I made five minutes earlier. Activities, deadlines and birthday parties bob around in my brain, disappearing and then surfacing at random intervals. I make lists and lose them. I keep a calendar and forget to check it. I worry constantly about carpool and whether or not I've forgotten a carload of weeping children at the school gate. How on earth does anyone do it? How did she make it look so easy? Or maybe time makes everything seem easy. Or maybe I am really terrified that I'll never become enough like her to keep her with me. I know that we all carry our mothers inside us. But that doesn't seem like enough.

It's possible that preserving things just makes us more aware of what we've lost. Maybe the past is supposed to fade—and that's actually a kindness of human memory. So many of my memories from childhood are lifted directly from my mother's home movies that I sometimes wonder at the few that are my own.

But some do stay vivid, all on their own.

When my daughter was a baby, I remember my mom rocking her to sleep one night and singing a familiar song over and over. I didn't remember the song, but I knew it, somehow. As I listened to her in the other room, I started singing along.

"What is that song?" I asked my mother, when the baby was down.

"It's just something I used to sing to you."

"But what's it called?"

She didn't know, but we Googled the lyrics. It turned out to be a song that had topped the charts in the forties, when she herself was a baby. Her mother had sung it to her. Then, when I was born, she and her mother had sung it to me. Then, when my kids came along, she and I sang it to them.

Maybe that's the only way mothers can hold on to things—in echoes, through generations. It's not enough. But it will have to do.

RADICAL PROMISES
Anne Marie Feld

Do it for the living, do it for the dead,
Do it for the monsters under your bed
Do it for the teenagers and do it for your mom,
Broken hearts hurt but they make you strong
—From "Loose Lips" by Kimya Dawson

"Where is your mommy?" my daughter asks over her shoulder. Her hair is up in a sloppy bun. Damp tendrils form loose letters against her neck: Ls, Js and Cs. Her baby brother, Liam, is asleep in his sturdy white crib in the next room. These are nice times for us, when we sit alone together in the bathtub, in limbo between day and sleep, when nothing interrupts us, nothing intrudes. Except now, my mother's ghost is hovering. Again. What exactly do you tell a preschooler about a grand-mother she will never know, a woman lost to suicide more than twenty years ago?

There are things I can tell her about my mother—about how she was a gifted carpenter and mathematician. That she was the hardest working person I've ever known. That she was tall, and per-fectly proportioned, and still wore a bikini (two that I can remember, one in white satin, and the other in navy cotton that she made herself) after having two children. She cut her own hair—short—and wore slacks with bootlegs, but never boots. She liked to draw.

I'm less inclined to tell Pascale that when my mother drew, she drew strange faces, oddly proportioned, part human, part frog. Or that she smoked fiercely, filling the air above the kitchen table with swirling blue clouds. Or that she thought that our house was bugged by her former employers. Or that she killed herself on my birthday—especially that, because for Pascale, birthdays are all goodness topped with vanilla frosting and candles. But more so, because at this phase in Pascale's life, mommy is the center of all things. And she has no idea that I won't always be here.

In my most vivid memory of my mother, we are home, spending time together, which is rare. I'm fifteen. We've just watched a talk show segment on the proper application of blush, which must go, we are told, on the apples of the cheeks. When the commercial cranks up, my mother offers to try it out. We sit on the couch, a couch she has reupholstered with her own rough, wide-nailed hands, in a wooly brown-and-cream striped fabric. In front of the sofa sits the coffee table she has also made—solid and heavy, stained almost black, topped with an excruciatingly practical rosewood laminate.

My LeSportsac bag sits on the table, brimming with makeup, and my mother strokes a soft brush onto the hollow below my cheekbone. This moment stands out because my mother and I didn't do things together. We didn't have shared hobbies—hobbies in general were dismissed. When I told my mother that I wanted to learn the violin, I was told that I didn't have the ear. When I told her that I wanted to be a photographer, I didn't have the eye. Over time, I learned not to like my mother, to expect only silence punctuated by discouragement. And I was always looking to get even.

"That's the wrong spot," I say.

"It's not."

"It is! You're doing it all wrong!" In seconds, we're wrestling for the brush.

"You'd better not lay a hand on me, or I'll call child protective services and tell them that you're abusing me." I think I may have gotten this idea from an episode of *Good Times*. It enraged Janet Jackson's mother on the show, as well.

"Child abuse," she says, between her perfect teeth, "I'll show you child abuse," and she lunges for me. Something feels very wrong, like a record skipping, then ripping across vinyl to scratchy silence. Circling the sofa with my mother at my heels, I run up the stairs three at a time, adrenaline rushing through me, making my arms and legs vibrate. I slam the door to my bedroom, flip both locks and reach for the desk chair to wedge underneath the knob. She didn't knock or try to open the door. We never spoke of it again.

A few months later, I pushed open a different door, and found her hanging, lifeless. There was no note. Months, maybe years later, I was told that my mother was diagnosed as schizophrenic, and that she had made earlier attempts on her life, but while she was alive, it never occurred to me that she was sick. I thought all mothers worked long days and then spent their nights studying, or renovating the bay windows or staring at *M*A*S*H* reruns on the floor in front of the television after handing the kids their bags of takeout. My father recently gave me a picture of the pair of us, hugging, on what looks like a hiking trail. Our arms are wrapped around each other and we look happy. I still find it perplexing when I look at it. I don't remember doing anything with her that wasn't a necessity.

In my memories, my mom is always working, doing all the things required to keep a family going. She put in long hours as a computer scientist, made good money, kept a spotless house. We went to the dentist and to restaurants to pick up food, but I don't remember seeing movies with her, or laughing or lingering over a good meal. She taught us no songs, nothing about the place she grew up, nothing about her family, people I met only once or twice during her life. I have no memories of playing with her, of going to a school event or community gathering. She offered no advice, no lectures. I didn't tell her about what happened in school, and she didn't ask. When I needed tutoring, my father ran the flash cards. When we took our first splashy family vacation— a trip to the Bahamas when I was fifteen—my mother didn't join us, and none of us found it odd. At sixteen, I didn't know my mother's religious affiliation, but I could recite the entire network television lineup, from 3:00 p.m. to 3:00 a.m. by heart.

My father supplied the warmth in our family; he was the one who liked to splurge, liked to dance, liked to make us treats out of lemon juice drizzled on top of pyramids of white sugar when we begged for sweets. It's with him that I remember playing house, and doing the twist and swinging like a clock.

On my father's most recent visit, my husband, Dave, and I show him the bamboo we planted along the side of the house. Tall black spears had shot up, seven feet in places, doubling in size within a few months. Growth was perceptible between morning and night. In the back garden, Liam, still wobbly on his chubby legs, pops the flowers off the cosmos plants and eats the sand out of the box. Pascale hovers over the plants with our little green watering can until fast streams of muddy water slip down the hillside and I beg her to move on to the next one. When I ask my father about the garden in my childhood home he says, "Your mother would never have let you work in the garden. She wanted it to be perfect."

And there it was. She wanted things perfect—one of the many things you can't ever hope to attain in the messy world of family relationships, especially when children are involved. When I was little, my mother made me beautiful clothes, and I see from the pictures that she took pride in how I looked—white shiny

shoes and flowered dresses with angel sleeves, little orange rain-
coats with matching boots. On school picture day, she'd take out
the bun form, brush out my long brown hair, coil it through and
around, until it looked like I had a factory-made cupcake on my
head. Perfect. But the things that weave a family together? Like
screeching "Take Me Out to the Ballgame" at the top of your
lungs at dinner, unable to stop laughing? Jumping on the bed to
Bob Marley on a sunny weekend morning? Pretending to be a
wicked pirate, and throwing imaginary drunken sailors off the
kitchen table? Just talking? Not even part of the equation.

In my tiny house in San Francisco, my kids can't escape me.
I'm with them for almost every meal, every kiss good-night.
Pascale's artwork is framed and hanging in most of the rooms.
Liam, well past a year, has never gone to sleep at night or for a
morning nap without nursing down. I'm sure that someday, they'll
both be on a therapist's couch, moaning about how I was on them
too much, but I'm driven to let them know with my presence,
my words, my touch, how vital they are to me. A few weeks ago
at Pascale's school, I watched her run around with the older kids,
playing a game we made up at home, warding off monsters with
imaginary repellent. I had painted her face and the faces of all of
her friends like kitties. I love knowing that she shares the things
we make up together. I love knowing her friends and watching
her play. I could watch the parade of her naked emotions—
loving, angry, litigious, thrilled—for hours. This doesn't mean that,
at times, I don't find mothering staggeringly difficult, or that I
don't wake up in the middle of the night, awash with fears that
I'm not doing a good enough job, or that the kids aren't getting
enough whole grains. But my other goal is bigger. I need to
ensure that Pascale never knows how lonely and confusing the
world is when your mother sees you only peripherally.

With Pascale, as with Liam, I feel like my job as mother is twofold. And while both probably seem obvious, they're things I practice with intention and some insecurity. My primary job is to love her, to know her inside and out—the good, the bad, the ugly and the pretty—to celebrate the good things in her nature and help her compensate for her challenges. My other job is as tour guide to the world, to show her the good stuff, make her laugh, help her find what she loves, teach her the customs and set up the big orange warning signs around the pitfalls. It's her job to decide what she likes, what she'll keep with her. For Pascale, this should not be a problem. She's always known what she wants. When she finally burst into the world after four days of labor, the nurses sped her off to the exam table to insert a tube into her lungs to extract the meconium she'd swallowed. She was seven pounds and two ounces of muscle, her skin the color of a drugstore hot-water bottle. She flailed her little arms fiercely, nearly stopping the nurses. Thirty seconds in and she was already feisty, already sure of herself, and she's been like that ever since. It's her best and worst quality. Before she was born, I had no sense of the unmapped areas of my heart, of all the tenderness that hadn't seemed to exist, because it hadn't been traversed—or of the cup-runneth-over feeling of watching her sleeping, or victorious or just happy. I didn't know how our lives would knit together to make something bigger and better than both of us alone. Before she was born, I had no idea how much she'd change the way I saw my mother.

In the early 1950s, before my mother turned ten, her own mother did the unthinkable. She abandoned her family, leaving a child to cook and clean for an angry, silent father and brother, who believed that women were vastly inferior to men. For the first time, I could see this deeply wounded, motherless little girl, promising herself that her children would never suffer the way she did. She kept that promise, showing me and my sister that women can do anything a man can do. We had no real chores; we were allowed to be kids. But a lifetime of selflessly working to make things run smoothly domestically and, later, financially, came at the price of really knowing her children. There was simply too much to do to connect. She just kept checking things off of her list without noticing—without anyone else noticing—that she was stumbling into madness. Deficits of love, relatedness and understanding accumulated until they brought her to her knees, and then down for good.

I didn't see this right away, of course. When I saw how intently Pascale looked at me to interpret the world for her, how vulnerable she is, I began to seethe at my mother for abdicating that job, for being too sick to really be a mother. All the old hurts—the ones that I had papered over with interesting work and a happy marriage came back with a force that I didn't have a container for. Though I had been warned, I didn't know that having a child would force me, face-first, into the ashes of my own childhood, which seems blacker now that I have a clearer view into what's possible in a life with kids. It's taken a couple of years to get my balance back, and I still have moments when I want to climb back into the thick torpor of hatred and reclusiveness I inhabited at sixteen. But my life and the people in it don't fit. Once you've replaced the things you hate with the things you love, it's hard to go back. But I didn't know that then.

After my mom died, I swung wildly between timidity and recklessness. Late at night, my sister and I would car surf, climbing onto the hood or the roof of our car, speeding along the smooth black asphalt near our house. I'd hitch rides or cut through the woods behind the Temple after school, and streak across six lanes of freeway to get to the shopping center faster. I'd chase men who didn't like me much more than they liked themselves, which is to say, not much. I drank Scotch in quantity, wrote tortured love songs and played them badly on my guitar, and tried on and discarded lifestyles and people like jeans. All of these things are gone now, and the thought of picking them up again is laughable. But they're only laughable because other things came along to fill the void. Work that I love, people that I adore; and I believe all of that came because I had the luxury to make stupid mistakes, and the time to look hard at how I wanted to live, constructing ideas of the way things could be—first at a safe distance, through books and movies and music, and then by examining my life and those of others to smoke out the values I wanted to live by. I was able to choose a loving, emotionally rich man, and a life where I look at things, and when they're broken, I have enough help and enough self-respect to try to fix them, even when it hurts, even when it's hard. The process is still imperfect, and it took time, time I had because I didn't have my kids, as my mother did, at the age of twenty-three.

As I write this, I'm a few months older than my mother was when she died. Her legacy is still cautionary, but now, I can also see it as sacrificial. She was demolished by her circumstances. She swore, I feel sure, that the mistakes made with her as a child wouldn't live on in her own children, and in some ways, they didn't. When Pascale was born, I looked into her blue eyes, eyes not unlike my mother's, and I made my own promises to the universe. My promises began with ideas about how to build love and connection, and with images of the things we would do together, things we have since done—gone ice-skating, taken art classes, thrown parties, made friends, dipped our toes in two oceans, cried, laughed. With luck, in a few decades, when Pascale looks down into the face of her own baby and dreams of the mother she wants to be, she won't feel like she has to make any radical promises.

THE HEART SPEAKS
Sheila Kohler

It has memory's ear
that can hear without
having to hear.
    —From "The Mind is an Enchanting Thing"
    by Marianne Moore

I am sitting, talking to my daughter, Cybele, her gaze fixed intently on my face, when she puts her hand on my arm and glances around the room. "Where is Masha?" she asks, referring to her eldest daughter.

"Have you seen Masha?" I ask Charlotte, Cybele's middle daughter, who is playing with the Lego set, but she bites her lip and shakes her head and opens her brown eyes wide. My daughter has three daughters, like the three princesses in a fairy tale. Masha has been named after one of the characters in Chekhov's *Three Sisters*. We are a literary family, you see. Words have always been important to my husband and me.

Cybele scoops up the baby and strides fast through the rooms of our West Side Manhattan apartment, calling her child's name. My daughter takes after my husband's side of the family. She has endless legs, a graceful neck. When I see her walk in my door, she looks to me, despite the babies in her arms, like a medieval queen.

"Masha, are you hiding somewhere?" I ask, my voice rising with panic as I go through the rooms, looking under beds, behind armchairs, the standing mirror.

Masha, at four, likes to play hide-and-seek. She likes to dress up. I open closet doors and hunt behind dresses, behind my shoes. Cybele peers behind shower curtains.

"I hope to goodness she hasn't gone outside," I say, imagining my grandchild taking the elevator into the lobby and stepping out into the dangerous New York street.

"She wouldn't have done that," my daughter reassures me, as she has so often in my life.

Still, it is not until I open the front door that I find Masha, tears running down her face. She is wearing her yellow fairy costume, though it is long past Halloween, and she has lost her wand. She has locked herself outside and has been standing there while we were hunting for her. I kneel down and gather her up in my arms. "But, Masha," I ask, "why on earth didn't you just ring the bell?" She sniffs and gazes at me blankly with her gray-green eyes, almost the same color as mine, as I abruptly understand and hold her to my heart.

"If you ever get shut outside like this again, you must ring the doorbell, and I will hear it ringing even if Mummy cannot, and I will come," I explain.

It was my mother-in-law who discovered Cybele's deafness one holiday at the sea. It is hard now to believe that our daughter was already a year old and that we had noticed nothing—or almost nothing. I remember mentioning to our distinguished elderly physician that Cybele seemed to have a high-pitched voice. "Is that normal?" I asked him. He looked at me disapprovingly through thick glasses and said solemnly, "What does the word *normal* mean?" I didn't dare ask anything else.

My husband and I were just twenty years old and did not notice much except ourselves. We had married, for love, while he was still a student at Yale studying French literature, and had come that summer to visit his mother, who lived on the Italian coast. One hot morning, the three of us sat on the beach in the sun, as one did in those prelapsarian days. I sat on my husband's lap, my arms around his neck, gazing into his eyes.

Draped across a deck chair, my mother-in-law, a long, lean lady from Kentucky, watched Cybele playing with her green bucket near the water. The calm sea glittered. Nothing moved in the still air. My mother-in-law called out to Cybele, who went on playing in the sand; she clapped her hands loudly three times. It was then that my mother-in-law put a hand on my arm and said, in her Southern drawl, "Do you know, I don't believe that child can hear!"

I remember thinking, *That woman, that woman, she is always looking for the fly in the ointment*. I picked up my little girl, clutched her to my heart, and carried her down to the edge of the sea. I waded in up to my knees, up to her toes. I swung her around and listened to her laugh and watched her bare feet rise and fall and the drops of water glisten in the bright air, and realized, in spite of myself, that I would never see the world quite like that again.

It was August and very hot when we returned to New York, and it seemed the doctors had all left town. I sat on the living-room floor and flipped through the yellow pages with my sticky fingers. There was no air-conditioning in the brownstone where we had rented rooms.

When I finally found a specialist, he told us that, had we each married someone else, it would not have happened. We must both carry the same recessive gene. Perhaps we had a common ancestor? Even at that moment, as he did not himself use the word *deaf*, I continued to deny the obvious. Much later, when it broke through upon me, and I once found myself weeping, my husband said, "That's not going to help." So I stopped.

What the doctor did tell us was to talk to our daughter, as if she could hear—no, more than we would have if she had been able to hear. "You can at least teach her to use words," he said encouragingly.

"How can you teach a deaf child to use words?" my husband asked with his logical mind honed on French literature. As for me, I did not ask questions of that kind. I did as I was told. It seemed the easiest thing to do, being, as I was, diligent, or perhaps just stubborn.

"You must make her as aware of sound as possible," the doctor explained.

There were few people entirely devoid of hearing. Hearing aids might help at least to modulate the quality of her voice, even if they did not make her speech intelligible to her. He fitted Cybele with two heavy rectangular gray boxes, worn on her body, containing microphones that amplified the sound and sent it by wires to small speakers in her ears. Then he had given her a lolli-pop, telling me, "Talk to her. Don't give her ice cream until she can say the words *ice cream*."

She wore these bulky hearing aids in a cotton bodice under her smocked dresses, her plump body weighed down, so that she tipped forward like a teapot as she tottered along.

Next, I was introduced to a speech therapist, a good lady with orange curls. "Follow me," she said, and I followed her into the freight elevator, with my daughter clutched in my arms. We went down into the bowels of the hospital, down a green corridor with thick pipes along the ceiling, past an open door where vast women in white, who stood ironing sheets, cooed at my child. The thera-pist ushered me into a small, airless cubicle where we sat together with Cybele on my lap under the soundproofed ceiling, and she demonstrated how to teach my child to speak.

This was the sixties, and no one spoke to me about signing. Indeed, I was told not to use my hands to make words. "You must be firm to be kind," the therapist had said. "You must give her a lesson every day."

So, every day, I sat my screaming daughter in her high chair and gave her lessons. She did not want to be confined, to be instructed, to practice anything; she wanted to play in the sand with her bucket and spade. It was a battle of wills. While she kicked her little red lace-up shoes against the steel tray and waved her fists in the air and wailed loudly at me, I held up the animals in the puzzle. "The pig says oink, oink. The duck goes quack, quack. The lamb goes baaahhh," I bleated at her, opening my mouth wide, while she opened hers to yell back at me.

We sweated in the New York summer heat, and we screamed, we hit, we grappled with each other, fighting over the animals as though they were prizes. She grabbed them, put them in her mouth, chewed them and tried to swallow them. I stuck my fingers into her mouth and down her throat, extracting them, damp and tooth-marked, and put them back in their places, covering the puzzle with my splayed fingers. I would not have skipped an animal if my life depended on it. She would not have stopped screaming to save hers. We were relentless, locked in a battle to the death.

I had no real understanding of what my child must have been feeling at moments like that, her inability to comprehend my words, or the reason I was saying them to her. And she, of course, could not understand my own wounded pride, my determination, but could feel only fury at being forced to do something that gave her no pleasure and whose purpose she could not fathom.

For what I was determined to do was not merely to teach my deaf child to use words, as the specialist had encouraged me

29

to do; I was determined to teach her to speak just like all the other little girls, whatever the cost. She was determined to kick a hole in her tray, a hole in my knee, a hole in the dumb and uncomprehending world.

No matter how loudly she screamed, I kept up the whole routine: "The dog says woof, woof." We fought through the summer and into the fall and winter. Every day we did exactly the same thing, as though we were two characters in a fairy story, condemned to repetition. I believed that if I altered one word, all the magic would flee and Cybele would never become the perfect, fairy-tale princess I needed her to be.

Brought forth by the screams, my husband would wander into the kitchen to suggest I might vary things, change a word here or there, liven it up a bit. Could I not?

But I, a would-be writer, after all, and blessed with imagination, would not, or perhaps I could not. There was security in the sameness of the words I repeated. Despite my English background, I began, my husband told me with some dismay, to sound like the speech therapist who hailed from Brooklyn.

Every day the plastic nesting cups, which came in different colors and sizes, had to be fitted into one another and put "up, up, up." How else could one teach a child a preposition? But Cybele was determined they would go "down, down, down," and with a scream, rather than a word, at that. Her mother went down with them, scrambling around on the sticky, black linoleum floor to pick them up and start all over again. The end of the lesson, the final insult, was my showing her the photograph of the perfect pink-and-white baby, while mouthing the words *Mummy, Mummy, Mummy,* as my deaf daughter screamed at me in a paroxysm of rage.

My daughter's first word though, when it came, was, of

course, not "Mummy" at all. It was no animal sound, either, no bleat or quack or woof. It was a word which I had never pronounced, and it was not said to her screaming mother or to her logical father. My daughter's first word was said to a little boy she played with in the sandbox at the park.

It was a cool spring morning when, exhausted from one of our daily battles over the animals, we were staggering to the park. All the trees were in bloom, and the shadows shifted on the pavement. We were crossing a wide, windy avenue when Cybele caught sight of the little boy. He waved from his stroller and called out, "Hi" to her, and she waved back and said quite casually and extraordinarily, "Hi."

This victory was, of course, a Pyrrhic one and not the end of the war. Though the words continued to come, each one was fought over like a piece of terrain in some endless campaign. It seemed, at times, as if the English language were not Cybele's mother tongue, but rather a foreign one, some secret, esoteric and hermetic tongue, like Sanskrit. Though she learned to speak in complete sentences before she was three, her voice remained that of one who has come to a language from a great distance. The voice was that of a foreigner, I suppose you might say, and her understanding came from that most impossible of arts, which she practiced with great expertise: the reading of lips.

Though Cybele continued to learn more words and could understand almost anything I said, what I feared now was that she would have no one with whom she could speak. In my heart of hearts, what I dreaded was her being ostracized, left out, left alone, shut up and shunned in her silent world.

All this, you understand, took place in the days when women still had the time and the inclination to invite one another to tea. I would dress my child up in her elaborate smocked dresses and matching pants and nervously adjust the little Dutch cap I had bought in a vain and absurd effort to cover the earpieces of her hearing aids, and we would sally forth to visit. I would watch her rush off eagerly with the child of the house, my teacup trembling in its saucer on my knees, smiling stiffly, asking polite questions and pretending to show great interest in my hostess's chatter but listening instead for the sounds of disaster. Often the little friend would come wailing back to report some crime—a doll whose eyes had been poked out, a smashed toy, a book shredded—and we would not, of course, be invited again.

Still, I strived to claim a place for my child in the wider world. I learned to cultivate and flatter, and when that did not work, I stooped to the basest bribery and corruption: I offered carousel and carriage rides, elaborate teas at Rumplemeyers and extravagant presents to the startled women and children I was able to cajole into these outings.

Then there loomed the shadow of school. Though not Catholic ourselves, we thought the nuns might be generously disposed to a child of this kind. The head of the school told us she had to consider her teachers, after all, and there was already a dwarf in the class. The private school that finally accepted Cybele did so with great trepidation. I remember the nursery school teacher, a frail and elderly lady asking me if I could teach my daughter the word *gentle,* and requiring that I come every morning to watch her, a remarkably agile and dexterous little girl, lest she fall as she played on the jungle gym.

I hoped that the privileged children in these places would be kind. But the world, inevitably, behaved as I had feared. On Cybele's sixth birthday we planned a party. I made the cake and decorated it with white icing and jelly beans in all the colors of the rainbow. I think I still have a picture somewhere of the lopsided thing. We laid the table with a starched white cloth and flowers, elaborate party favors, blowers and balloons. There were multicolored jellies trembling in cups, candies in great pyramids, cupcakes. There was a new dress for our daughter with a blue sash and lace around the collar and cuffs. We had invited the entire class for greatest security. We waited eagerly for their arrival. I kept looking at my watch and trying to think of how to distract our child. The afternoon wore on, and the telephone instead of the doorbell continued to ring. One by one the mothers declined. Once, someone rang the doorbell, but it was our doorman delivering a present someone had dropped off. We continued to wait and hope until nightfall, but no one came in the end.

The friends Cybele made on her own, eventually, were friends she has kept ever since, all her life. The intense attention that lip reading demanded helped her develop into a gifted listener—loving, understanding and loyal. Her friends were often children who had been left out themselves, who knew about being different, about solitude, about scorn. There was Claudia, the little curly-headed girl from Brazil, who could speak only Portuguese; Jess, a child with a Botticelli face who was born paralyzed down one side and still walks with a slight limp; and Jeanne, a tall, black student from Haiti, who spoke with a French accent.

I no longer remember what crime she had committed that day to warrant such a punishment. Perhaps she had torn up some book of mine, or one of hers. I never stopped reading to her, her little hand hovering over the pages to turn to the next picture, or to tear out the incomprehensible words. The place I chose for the punishment was the bathroom. I thought it a safe place: there was nothing anyone could break; it did not matter if something was spilled on the green-tiled floor. Also, there was no window. I put her into the bathroom for a moment to calm her down, or more probably, to calm myself down. What I did not think of was the lock on the inside of the door. But when she turned it and trapped herself in there in a misguided effort to escape, we had no way to explain through the door that she had not been left inside in retribution for an act of consummate wickedness. Until the locksmith finally came, hours later, and broke open the lock, we could do nothing to comfort her, and could only listen to her, wailing and beating with her little fists on the wood.

It was then, when the door was finally open, that she said something which I, with my strict English upbringing, had not taught a daughter to say to her mother, and more important, something I had not previously been willing to hear. Her face smudged with tears, she stamped her little foot and looked up at us, her eyes filled with rage, and said, quite clearly, "I am angry with you." It was then that I realized what a terrible burden I had imposed on her, insisting that she become part of my hearing world.

When we have dried Masha's tears and brought her a dish of ice cream, she sits beside her mother and her little sisters, and I tell her a story about how her mother had once locked herself inside a room, as Masha has just locked herself out, and how we could not explain why she was in the room for such a long time, all alone. I tell Masha how we struggled to teach her mother to talk, how she learned despite our lack of understanding of her difficulties. How she went on to the same famous university where her father had gone before her and became the very first deaf student there. I tell Masha how her mother studied art at that university and became an artist, who paints the world for us as she sees it in all its colors, and how she met her husband, Masha's daddy, at the same university and fell in love with him.

One day I will tell Masha that it was her mother's courage and intelligence, her ability to love and to forgive, more than my desperate efforts to instruct her, that helped her to find her way through life. It was not we who taught her to speak, but rather she who taught us to listen.

GARDEN VARIETY MOTHERING
Catherine Newman

Our England is a garden, and such gardens are not made
By singing:—"oh, how beautiful!" and sitting in the shade...
—From "The Glory of the Garden" by Rudyard Kipling

Do you know that children's book *Frederick?* While his fellow mice scurry around gathering food for the coming winter—corn and nuts, seeds and grain—Frederick sits around all dreamy and heavy lidded, reassuring everyone that he's hard at work, too, yes indeedy. ("'I do work,' said Frederick. 'I gather sun rays for the cold dark winter days.'") Come winter, the food eventually runs out, and it's Frederick's poetic reminiscences—all that color and sunshine he's stored up in his memory—that sustain the mice through the remaining dreary days. It's one big shameless apology for the slacker life of an artist—last time I checked, someone's harvest-time recollections weren't exactly getting the hungry fed—and I've always loved it.

Maybe industriousness skips a generation. While my seventy-year-old mother and four-year-old daughter share a thumb so green I could entertain a thousand mice with stories about it, I can barely tend a houseplant. My mother once offered to foster Raul Julia, my Christmas cactus, after noting its dusty failure to thrive in a college dorm room. Twenty years later, come December, it still blooms for her. And when my daughter, Birdy, crouches down to admire those pinkly succulent flowers—well, if a happy, old cactus could smile, it would.

My parents spend much of the summer in an old farmhouse, way upstate in New York, and when we join them for the weekend, Birdy skips directly from car to garden. Even while we're still schlepping in bags of swim rings and string cheese, she's knee-deep in herbs in the blue twilight, munching thoughtfully on a handful of chives. If you watch from the kitchen window when my mother goes out to join Birdy, you might see her hand Birdy a small pair of shears and bend her silvery head to tell her something, then you might see Birdy's glossy curls bobbing happily as she sets to work. Later, in your salad, there will be large, earnest clumps of lovage and mint, basil and lemon balm, and they will be bracingly delicious.

Me? I'm the gardening version of the person who shows up at Tavern on the Green for the broiled salmon after skipping the synagogue portion of the Bar Mitzvah: I will knife down an armload of rhubarb and happily bake it into a buttery crumble; I will pick and shell peas to serve steaming-hot with butter and mint; I will even weed laconically, pulling purslane and lamb's quarters from the asparagus patch with an Old Slugger ale in one hand, just to hang out where my mom and Birdy are. But the hard work of gardening—all that digging and dirt—eludes me. My son's the same way: he might come out to pick a dinner's worth of green beans into the colander, and he'll do a beautiful job, but really what he's doing is listening to himself sing "Elijah Rock" in his tremulously high soprano or telling his grandma a new joke. ("Get it? Shrek the halls?")

Birdy, though—Birdy's the kind of person who's ready to toil in earnest: she steps into her rain boots and snaps up a slicker, or pulls on her down vest and someone's ancient pom-pommed ski hat, and out she trundles with my mom in all kinds of weather to help with soil preparation and the turning over of the compost, with deadheading cosmos and hoeing up the withered tomato plants and preparing beet beds for planting. She may stop for a moment to identify a clump of wild sorrel and cram the arrow-shaped leaves into her puckering mouth—but then it's back to work. I watch the two of them from the kitchen window, where I'm dumping the end of my coffee into the sink, where Ben is yelling from the comfy depths of the living room for me to return to our Monopoly game, and it may be the first time in my life I feel happy to be left out.

Even at home it's like this, although our funny suburban condo, with its concrete patio and clique of towering pines, is hardly a pastoral oasis. But a few flowers do straggle up into the shade—the handful of violets and bleeding hearts planted by the woman who lived here before us—and Birdy dashes out to them with watering can, like some kind of botanical EMT. Every buttercup and dandelion gets an urgent daily sprinkling, even in the pouring rain, when Birdy stands outside in her rubber boots, watering redundantly from beneath an umbrella. (Maybe I should submit the screenplay for a movie sequel called Edward Wateringcanhands.) But not even Birdy can keep alive the fancy perennial I persuaded my mother to buy me when I went with her to the nursery (a gardening outing in the car? Sure! And let's stop for coffee, and at that yard sale we saw, on the way home!): it looks as though it's been set on fire and then extinguished, not entirely unlike a campfire marshmallow. When I bend finally to pull its black skeleton from the ground, I read the common name beneath the Latin *Lamium:* "Dead Nettle." What kind of person cannot keep alive a plant that already has the word *dead* in its name?

The Jews—maybe we're not such a gardening people. I mean, if there's not a spare moment to let the bread to rise, I'm guessing there's hardly time to stop fleeing and germinate the arugula. Maybe paternally inherited Jewishness is like brown eyes or smooth peas in those high school genetics graphs—a dominant trait—despite the fact that my mother is English and as crisply delightful and delightfully no-nonsense as Mary Poppins herself. Even when the children were tiny they couldn't wait to help her. "Birdy, my love," she'd say, kneeling down to talk to my barely walking daughter. "Would you mind awfully doing me a huge favor?" And off Birdy would toddle, proud and competent, to fill a crystal vase with pansies or push sunflower seeds into the ground. My mother always has a lovely little job for everyone: "Would you mind awfully making one of your lovely crumbles?" she says to me; "Would you mind awfully making one of your lovely herb sauces for the fish?" she says to Ben. (This is somewhat different from my father, who gets my husband up on a rickety ladder to trim the top of the hedge with a chainsaw bungee-corded to a broomstick, while he nags him from below.) My mother frets over how hard we're all working or our ruined fingernails, thanks us constantly and insists that we take frequent breaks for the tea and the miniature cheese sandwiches she brings out on a tray. If you confess to screwing something up—maybe you yoinked up all the cukes, mistaking them for weeds—she waves her hand dismissively. "Oh, never mind," Birdy said last week in a perfectly brisk imitation of her, after dropping a plastic string-cheese wrapper to the car floor. "It will turn to compost soon enough."

It's not that my mother's exactly relaxed by nature. ("So it's going to be just the rhubarb, then?" she frets, as I'm putting the crumble into the oven to bake. "You don't think it might be nicer with a few apples in it?") But she's more of a doer than a brooder, and I wish I were more like her. This is partly because her journal is filled with notes about when to dig the Jerusalem artichokes and whether or not the borage kept beetles off of the neighboring tomatoes, while mine is filled with the moody minutiae of my feelings, the angsty, solipsistic musing over this or that vagary of my personality. And it's mostly because she's the happiest kind of person for a young child to be around. Sometimes I succeed, and the kids hum and wash parsley for me in the sink, help me whir it in the blender, and then later devour the green sauce over a frittata they help make. And other times, impatience and boredom leak out of me such that beating eggs in a bowl becomes about as much fun as an afternoon at the sausage factory in an Upton Sinclair book. "Grew impatient and regretted it," I will jot down in the exact same space where my mother would have written "Plant more parsley next year."

Was it always like this? Maybe. My girlhood memories are fragrant with garden-scented happiness, but the details seem less green-thumbed than ham-handed: the time I got it into my head to make chocolate leaves for an elderly neighbor down the road, only instead of sturdy, shiny leaves, I used fuzzy lemon balm, and so the chocolate stuck ("Never mind—they're even lovelier that way!"); the time I got it into my head to make pesto during a sudden summer-storm blackout, smashing basil into oil and dripping the evil, black sauce onto our candlelit plates of spaghetti ("Never mind—it still tastes delicious!"). The way my mother said *yes, yes, yes* even when the picture forming could be interpreted as a big *no*. The way my mother weeded and watered while I curled up in a corner of the Jerusalem artichoke patch with my book—not because I was so enchanted by the garden, but because *The Shining* was too scary to read alone. And because I wanted to be wherever she was. Even if I never learn how to overwinter thyme or prune the forsythia, that's the kind of mother I want to be.

And there's still time for growth, I know. When we pack up the station wagon to leave again, my mother will hand me the rosemary or creeping vinca that she's potted up neatly for me, along with her instructions about how effortless it will be to transplant and care for, and I will be filled anew with hope. "One more chive!" Birdy will cry, and then she'll stand in the garden chewing, and looking wistfully out at the hills, stalling before her beloved grandparents bend down to kiss her goodbye. And later still, when she wraps her striped pajamas around your neck to kiss you good-night, you'll smell the oniony chives still lingering beneath the bubblegum of her toothpaste, and the soft pink of her happy cheeks will look exactly like my mother's.

MY MOTHER AT FIFTY
Joyce Maynard

Thou art thy mother's glass, and she in thee
Calls back the lovely April of her prime.
—From "Sonnet III" by William Shakespeare

I'm looking at a photograph of my mother and myself, when I was eighteen years old and she was forty-nine. My mother was a striking woman, but she looks old in this photograph: tired, a little discouraged, and more than a little melancholy. In this photograph, she is dressed in clothes that would be described as "matronly," and underneath, I know, she would have been wearing a tight and binding girdle. In the picture, her hair is set with beauty-parlor stiffness, where mine hangs straight, well past my shoulders, in the style of my idol that year: Joan Baez. But it's not just an unfortunate hairstyle that makes my handsome mother look old beyond her years in the photograph: It's the sadness that comes through, the look of a woman whose marriage ended years before, except that nobody moved out. There's sadness on my face, too, of course. Because I was the daughter of unhappy parents. Trying desperately to fix things, and unable to do it.

The girl in that photograph—me—turned fifty last year. So I am older now than my mother was then. My own daughter, too, is older than the girl in the picture. As for my mother, she's been dead fifteen years now, making me only a mother now, no longer anybody's daughter.

But after all these years, my mother remains a daily presence in my life, as I know to be true for most of my friends, like me, whose mothers are no longer living. I think of her at all kinds of moments: when something happens in the lives of one of my children that I'd want to tell her about, when I suffer a loss or a heartbreak and when there's good news. I wished she was there to put her arms around me when I went through my divorce, of course, and when my daughter—her only female grandchild— graduated from college, wearing her grandmother's graduation cap, spilling over with flowers.

I think of her at funny little moments, too: when I try to make gravy (and it doesn't work, and I can't call her up to ask what went wrong) or when I reach for the line of a poem, and I know she'd be able to quote me the whole thing. She's suddenly there again, when I hear a passage from *Don Giovanni* (an opera she loved, whose arias she sang along with the record, while vacuuming, in a big, beautiful off-key voice). And I think of her when I pass through the perfume department of a department store, and I see a bottle of Rive Gauche—her fragrance—and feel a need to squirt a little on my wrist, just to breathe her in for a moment.

But lately, I have been thinking about her in a particular new way, too. Reaching the landmark of age fifty, I found myself calling to mind who my mother was at the age I have reached now. With no living mother around to guide me, I look to my mother's life for the lessons it may have for me, at the half-century mark. And I find them, too. I see the similarities between us, and the differences.

My mother grew up in Birch Hills, Saskatchewan, daughter of Russian immigrant Jewish shopkeepers, the only Jewish family in town. For her, the great dream was going to the city, getting an education. Though her parents had very little money, they managed to send her to university in Winnipeg, where she distinguished herself as a star student, winning a scholarship to graduate school in Toronto and then to the United States, where she earned a Ph.D. at Radcliffe. She had fallen in love with my father by this time: a dashing, impossibly handsome painter, twenty years older than she, and not Jewish—a fact that broke her parents' hearts, or close enough.

Then came the bitter lesson: The discovery that the man she loved was an alcoholic. She had a child (my sister) and then another (me), but even in those early years, she told us later, the relationship between my parents was impossibly strained, though she put up a good show.

And then there was a second sorrow: In that small town, my brilliant, educated and accomplished mother was unemployable by the university where my father had a job, for no reason but the fact of her gender. She was supposed to attend tea parties of faculty wives and keep house, not go to work. And so, unable to find regular employment, she got a job selling encyclopedias door-to-door, and another job tutoring French, for a dollar an hour. The Ph.D. she'd worked so hard to earn mattered less, in that world, than the tidiness of her kitchen or the question, "Do you play bridge?" (She didn't.) No career to speak of. Not a lot of loving closeness with her husband. Her family, far away. As the product of a culture virtually unknown in chilly New Hampshire, my mother lived a lonely and isolated life.

And so, for all the years I was at home, my mother's greatest and most ambitious accomplishments, as she would have been the first to announce, were her two daughters, my sister and me. Those were times when a woman defined herself by who her husband was, how many children she had. And who they became.

Later, she would say she had stayed in an unhappy marriage for her daughters' sakes (not words that any child feels good about hearing), and of course we also knew she'd given up her career, her Jewish heritage, even her country (Canada), to make a life in that small town where my father taught at the university, while she exchanged recipes with the faculty wives. (Few of whom would ever have heard of a knish or tasted matzoh. None of whom could quote Chaucer, as she did.)

When you grow up seeing yourself as the repository of your mother's aspirations—her emissary into the world of acknowledgment, success and big-world achievement—you are not simply pursuing your own dreams, but hers. I know that even as a young child I felt it: the burning need to lay at my mother's feet the kind of success and acknowledgment she had deserved and never gotten. Not surprisingly, the weight of carrying around all that responsibility for my mother's happiness, as well as my own, left me with a certain ambivalence. Always love, too; love was always the dominant emotion. But resentment was somewhere in the mix, I know. And so, as close as we had been when I was growing up, I put some distance between us.

I came of age into a different world from that of my mother—one in which young women were taught to view ourselves as no less valuable or worthy than men, and a world where opportunities for women were suddenly exploding. The old model—that the appropriate ambition for a woman was marriage and parenthood—had been replaced by a fierce emphasis on career achievement.

I attended an Ivy League college, once an all-male bastion, and from there, moved swiftly into the world of New York City and a life of publishing success. Early on, I won recognition for the work I did. If there was struggle in my life (and there was) it had less to do with the challenge of making a career than with what happened on the home front, where, as a young mother of three, I had found myself in my own version of a deeply troubled

45

marriage. But like my mother, I kept that part under wraps, presenting only my successes to the world, and to the one whose applause always mattered the most to me: my mother.

She loved it that I had a career, as she loved my sister's successes. Sometimes, I have to admit, it felt almost claustrophobic, how much she loved my accomplishments, how much it mattered to her that I had gotten what she'd been denied.

When my mother was fifty, her twenty-five-year-long marriage to my father had finally ended. With her children grown and gone from home, and no particular reason to stay in our big old house in a town whose college had never seen fit to give her a job, she returned to her native Canada and made a career for herself as a writer. She met a man she truly loved, and at the age where so many people are winding down, retiring, cutting back, she created a whole new life for herself.

It's funny how this works: All those years, my mother had sacrificed herself for my sister and me—cooking special meals, sewing us dresses, knitting a sweater, even, for a doll of mine (so small she had to use toothpicks for knitting needles). All those hours she spent, going over our writing with us, typing our manuscripts, taking us to plays and concerts and museums. All to ensure that our lives would have what hers had not. And yet, there was probably nothing my mother ever did for me, more truly inspiring—nothing that I ever admired more, and nothing that serves me better as I go about my life now, without her—than the model she provided, when she finally stopped living just for us and made her own good, rich and independent life.

The picture I carry of her, in my mind's eye, is not so much the mother bent over the stove, stirring soup, as it is the bright-eyed woman in a ribbon-decked hat (over fifty, by this point) who, shortly after moving to Toronto, decided to throw a party to which she would invite only men. One hundred of them. Many of whom she'd never met. (She just wanted to.) And the best part was: they showed up.

Photographs of my mother, from that final happy decade of her life (she died way too young, at sixty-six) show a far happier woman than the one who looks out at me now, from that photograph of the two of us, as she was closing in on fifty. It's clear to me, from looking at her face, that in the last years of her life she found a kind of joy that was mostly absent from her forty-eight-year-old face.

I think it was having witnessed my mother's joyful rediscovery of her independent self—her great talents, her ability to make her way in the world without a husband at her side—that brought me greatest comfort when, shortly after her death fifteen years ago, my own marriage ended. My mother had been fifty-one when she divorced; I was just thirty-five. And the fact that my marriage ended sooner than hers did was due, I think, in no small part, to the summer I spent in Toronto, helping to care for her as she was dying. That handful of months I spent sitting in her garden with her, talking over our lives, had revealed to me, finally, the source of my long-held resentment I'd felt towards my mother, over nothing more than the guilt her own unhappy marriage had left me to bear.

That summer, as my marriage crumbled away, I saw myself repeating the old pattern of self-sacrifice for my own three children, saw how I'd substituted the creation of a life that looked good for a life that was truly happy. I looked in the mirror and saw the same tight, strained expression I remember on my mother's face when I was young. I did not want my daughter, one day, to look in the mirror and see the same thing—didn't want to pass down, one more generation, the legacy of mothers living only for their children and weighing them down, as they did, with a heavy sense of obligation.

What came to me, finally, the summer of my mother's dying, was the futility of trying to keep alive—for the sake of the children—a union that had died long before. Child, myself, of parents who stayed together in that kind of marriage, it came to me that no parent can truly protect her child from the pain of an unhappy marriage.

I'm no advocate of divorce. In fact, there's nothing like having lived through divorce to make a person understand, as I do, that two people in a troubled marriage should do everything they can to work things out, make things better, stay together, so long as they can do it in a way that is true to themselves, and not simply out of fear for the alternative, or a belief that they somehow owe it to their children to remain under the same roof.

For my parents, it was simply not possible in the end. And for my children's parents, the same was true. The same year of my mother's death, in fact, my marriage ended. And that is not entirely a coincidence, I know.

My mother, in her later years—the years after her marriage—finally revealed to me what her face looked like when she was happy. Not all the time, of course. But more so than at any other time in her life.

And actually, the same is true of me. I look at photographs of myself when I was thirty, and though I may feel a certain stab of regret that I no longer possess that unlined skin or those knees, the woman I see in the pictures looks anxious and unhappy, often. Not that I don't feel that way now sometimes, still. But the face my children see when I greet them now is more my own than it has been at any other time before.

I like to think that whatever sadness my children experienced over their parents' divorce (and there was plenty), this much at least has been a good thing for them. They are the children, at last, of a mother who no longer depends on them for her sense of well-being, any more than they depend on me for theirs. They've seen me mourn my own mother, mourn my marriage. But they have also seen me become, at last, a woman who is true to herself, the same as my mother became one, in the end.

It is a part of my mother's legacy, I think, that a year beyond the half-century birthday now, I can truly tell my sons and daughter that their mother is a happy woman. The only happiness they are responsible for creating now is their own.

BEYOND THE FAMILY PARTY FACE
Ericka Lutz

I am the family face;
Flesh perishes, I live on,
Projecting trait and trace
Through time to times anon,
And leaping from place to place
Over oblivion.
      —From "Heredity" by Thomas Hardy.

We were in an old-style movie palace and the whole family was there, my aunts and my parents, my cousins, my husband, Bill, my daughter, Annie…and down on the left, there was Ronnie Gilbert of The Weavers, and right in front of us, wearing a cap tiled with political buttons, an old veteran of the Lincoln Brigade who fought the good fight against Franco. Old lefties and literati overfilled the eight-hundred-seat theater; floor-sitters crammed the side aisles. The energy was wild with reunions and introductions and laughter.

Then the movie palace darkened. And the movie came on, and there was my dead grandmother come to life, telling the stories she always told; there was our family history spilling out on the screen, my mother making her big-screen debut, the audience laughing and crying. Behind me, an aunt sobbed, my husband and I leaned against each other's shoulders, my fifteen-year-old daughter grabbed my hand, and her hand was cool and smooth like my mother's hand. Like my grandmother's hand. And this was not some strange dream—this really happened, a few months ago.

I'm a fourth generation "Red Diaper Baby," born into a

family—on my mother's side—of atheist, culturally Jewish, Marxist, Feminist, West Coast lefty union leaders. I come from a family of creators and artists, musicians, jewelers, dancers and, most of all, writers. My grandmother, who died at the beginning of 2007, was the author Tillie Olsen, well-known in literary, feminist and political circles. The movie was a documentary about her life, and the screening was its debut.

A couple of years ago, just being in that movie theater would have felt unbearable. I would have arrived home exhausted and had to go to sleep *right away* to wake up at three in the morning to begin a postmortem. *Who said what? Who looked at me like that? Did they turn away when I approached? Who am I with these people— my family—and who am I without them?* And above all, I would have fretted about my daughter's reactions: to the event, to seeing me first with a thick mask of pretense on my face—my Family Party Face—then seeing my collapse as I removed the mask.

It was different this time: my family diminished, my grandmother dead, the movie on the screen somebody else's version of my family history, of my grandmother's life. And though I came home tired from the emotion swirling around me, I was intact.

I am the Oldest Daughter of my grandmother's Oldest Daughter, which makes my daughter Annie the fourth in a line of Oldest Daughters. And during my childhood, until I was in my midthirties—until roughly the time I began establishing my identity as a writer—my grandmother and I were very, very close.

It is an amazing family and a stunning legacy, and yet it is a family where I've never felt good enough just being my own flawed self. When I was little, we had family parties for every holiday, every birthday. I remember sitting on my grandmother's lap, my younger sister and I groomed impeccably by my nervous mother. I'd wear a beautiful and serious face, my Family Party

Face. My grandmother's cool hands stroked and stroked me. My aunt Julie played the guitar, my dad the banjo. We'd sing the family songs: "Union Maid" and "De Colores" and "Drill Ye Tarriers Drill." "Let's sing 'Nellie Gray' and watch Ericka cry," somebody would suggest.

> There's a low green valley by the old Kentucky shore
> Where I whiled many happy hours away
> Just a sitting and a singing by that little cabin door
> Where I first met my darling Nellie Gray

…and I'd cry. For the injustice of Nellie Gray, sold to another plantation to slave her life away and her lover never to see her again. And I'd cry because they wanted me to, and because of the feel of my grandmother's hands holding me, and the warmth of her lap. I remember that feeling of wearing the Family Party Face—"Sensitive Ericka, Brilliant Ericka, Ericka Who is Destined for Great Things."

Twenty years later, and the dynamic hadn't shifted. Three weeks after Bill and I got together, I took him to a family party. This was unusual. I'd only let The Family meet one of my too-many boyfriends, and then only after we'd lived together for a year. This was a Labor Day picnic-slash-birthday-party for a great-aunt, a well-known San Francisco labor activist. Before we went, I drew Bill a family tree of my mother's side of the family. "Here," I was saying, "here is what you are getting into, here is how I'm going to woo you. Look at my impressive lineage."

Besides Aunt Reeva, I told Bill, we'd meet my great-uncle Leon, one-time head of the printers union who went to jail with Cesar Chavez in the seventies. "I was at that march, too," I told Bill. "And I got arrested at Livemore for antinuke stuff, once." I really liked Bill—his vivid blue eyes, his strong opinions, his passion for justice. I was laying it on thick.

And my parents would be there: Dad, still with a ponytail, a precision machinist who sold hand-wrought jewelry at crafts fairs; Mom, a professional dancer. My grandparents would be there, I told Bill. Grandpa Jack was a local labor leader and sage. Grandma Tillie was a famous writer. He'd also meet my aunt who ran a college child development department, another aunt who lectured nationally on immigrant education rights, and their husbands, the archaeologist and the Maoist musician. And some of my cousins would be there: Karl, a First Amendment attorney; Margaret, who used to go by "Darooda" and take me to Sufi dances; Baby Joshie; Little Jesse; Rebekah, the brilliant poet.

On the way there, my body began to tense and my face began to tighten, a familiar sensation, so that by the time we got to the picnic, I'd transformed from the punkish art student he was dating to somebody else—a good child, a gracious and graceful child, a pretty child, a child who was smart and sensitive and poetic, a child who aimed to please. I was still wearing the Family Party Face.

Bill studied the family tree I'd drawn. He internalized it—and he kept everybody straight. At the party, in a green meadow in Golden Gate Park, we ate potato salad and sang Spanish Civil War songs. My cousin Rebekah and I danced "Tzena, Tzena, Tzena" to the applause of the crowd. Bill was dazzled. "What an amazing family you have!" An ex-hippie communications teacher, my lefty "Red Diaper Baby" family credentials were not wasted on him.

"Yeah, they're amazing," I muttered as we drove back to his apartment in the Mission District, wiping the Family Party Face off and reverting to myself. I had pink streaks in my hair then. I was twenty-five, and my sullen reaction could still pass as late-model teenage rebellion. But it wasn't rebellion—it was deep ambivalence. I loved my family, and I hated them.

I wore that Face for them all, especially my grandmother, who I tried so desperately to please. I wore it through my childhood, my teen years, and into my twenties and thirties. Deep into my forties, I was still struggling with the public face and the private, my need to carve a place for myself in my mother's family of offbeat achievers.

Creative work is in my blood. My mother danced into her seventies. I grew up with thick, flesh-colored tights and faded black leotards hanging on the drying rack in the bathroom; her bedroom was filled with yards of billowy translucent chiffon for her belly-dance outfits. She affixed jewels to her navel and long black eyelashes to her eyelids with medical adhesive from my dad's work at UC Medical Center. Her costume bras were covered with sequins. She had long, straight brown wigs to cover her shorter hair, and she changed her name (professionally) from Karla to Karima.

She taught belly dance, she studied flamenco, she left us once to go to Salt Lake City for a couple of weeks but came home early. In her fifties, with me and my sister gone, she began to travel, always alone, first to study dance and Spanish in Southern Spain for six months, then to stroll the Swiss Alps. She was a dancer and a teacher and a caregiver. She took care of my daughter twice a week until Annie turned thirteen, and the last year my grandmother was dying, she spent hours with her every day, doing her hair, helping her walk, bringing her special food.

My relationship with my mother is a combination of tenderness and irritation. She's impossible. She's never heard a joke she understands; she falls asleep at the dinner table with her mouth open; she eats as much as a teenager and goes on food fads; she spends sleepless nights for months fretting over small slights. Never go to a restaurant with her, because she never orders on the menu, she always asks for something special. Yet she supports my writing life utterly, loves hearing about our lives, fights fiercely for what she believes in. Cats curl around her legs when she walks down the street. She feeds the wild deer in her yard apples from her bare hands.

My relationship with my grandmother was more fraught. Like many outside the family, as well as inside, I worshipped her. She was my hero, the one I idealized most, the person I struggled against most. I wanted to emulate her. I wrote her dozens of love letters, and she lavished me with praise and gifts and compliments. But even as a young adult, I realized the tyranny of that worship—for I could never get enough of her, and yet she was difficult and judgmental, and she never had enough time for me. My worship of her she took as her due, and she loved me in the cracks of others. I don't know when or why she stopped supporting my writing, but I resented the years when every stranger who yearned to write got her attention and support, but not me. And there were miscommunications, misunderstandings, dementia (hers), stubbornness and fear and denial (mine), rebellion (also mine). And finally, when I was in my mid-thirties, we stopped seeing each other, except for rarely, at family gatherings. And since she was the matriarch of the family, that meant I rarely saw my extended family, as well.

My daughter, Annie, was still very young when we stopped going to most family parties. Some I refused to go to, many we stopped being invited to. But I can still see her, a little girl on my grandmother's lap, mesmerized by my grandmother's intense blue eyes and firm, smooth, stroking hands. I was uncomfortable having my daughter see me act like this around my family, to see her mother wearing a false face, now weathered by time and sorrow into almost impassiveness.

From across the room, I would watch them together, wild wavy hair matching wild wavy hair, my grandmother's voice raised in song, *"Tumbala tumbala tumbalalaika!"* and I knew what it felt like to be the object of my grandmother's love and charisma. But I also knew what it felt like to have that love taken away, that charisma no longer available to me. My heart ached. As a fierce mama, I didn't want that to happen to Annie.

Time passed. Bill and I celebrated our twentieth anniversary. Once the older generation became too old to register or express outrage at my behavior, I began to write about my experiences within my family, breaking a huge taboo. Even unconventional families still have their unspoken rules; like most families, my entire family wears a public Family Party Face. We present the honorable and hide the hard, private parts away. "I was angry at you for writing about this," an aunt said to me recently, about reading one of my pieces in a literary magazine. "But it was fair." And in the process of finally writing about my family, I began to see myself without the Family Party Face for the first time.

My older relatives—first Grandpa Jack, then Reeva, Leon, and finally my grandmother—aged and died. When Tillie died, I entered and passed through a grief made more rocky by remorse and confusion.

Yet a few months ago, I sat in Oakland's Grand Lake Theater, in a situation like something from a life-after-death fantasy (surrounded by loved ones, the dead come back to life) and I realized something had changed. I was appreciating my grandmother. I was loving her without guilt or anguish. I was listening to her tell

the old stories of her father's escape from White Russia, and I was laughing along with her. And I could feel her hands on mine. *No.* That was real, and it was the hand of my daughter, sitting next to me, linking us down through the generations.

I had changed. There was no sudden epiphany to this—outside of fiction, people don't change in an instant, though the recognition that they've changed can hit full force. My grandmother was dead; *she* hadn't changed. So it must be me. Sitting in that movie theater, both separate from and part of what was happening on the screen, I recognized that no matter how I feel about my family's dynamics, I am of them, *I am them.* And for me, it was the perfect closure to a relationship fraught with love and grief.

It's taken me decades—and a lot of really good therapy—to arrive at Myself and, in that process, to feel my own place in my extraordinary family. I am my family. They are me. And there's no mask on my face anymore.

Watching my dead grandmother come to life on the screen, my mother talking about mother-love—I felt my daughter's pride at her membership in this family. She's fifteen now, my Annie, a beautiful girl-woman with wise eyes, pointed ears and a vivid imagination. She's a dreamer, like me, like her grandmother, like her Great-Grandmother Tillie. I hope she gains from her dancer grandmother, her writer great-grandmother, and her shadowy revolutionary great-great-grandmother, the beauty of music, nature, emotion, the resilience of the human spirit, and the belief that it's important to work for justice for all. I hope that, as my contribution to her legacy, she learns the importance of authenticity. Of seeing and telling her truths, and wearing, not some Family Party Face to please those around her, but her own.

I wonder what she will take of this proud heritage of politics and creativity. How she will separate from it so she can be herself. And whether she will come back to it, as I have, full circle.

MOTHER-DAUGHTER THERAPY: AN ESSAY ON NEUROTIC, CONTEMPORARY PARENTING
Julianna Baggott

Neurotics build castles in the air, psychotics live in them.
My mother cleans them.
—Rita Rudner

My daughter and I are driving home from her therapist's office. We have just touched dog puke. This ranks as a glowing success, according to Dr. Jennifer who is young and still believes in, well, One: The curative powers of touching dog puke. Two: Most of the things she learned in graduate school, and, Three: That she can change the world with most of the things she learned in graduate school—one overwrought kid at a time.

But Phoebe and I are having a hard time *internalizing* the success. We have the joyless, beaten air of people who are slowly realizing they've been talked into touching dog puke.

"I feel like Benny Ogden," I say.

"Who's Benny Ogden?" my daughter asks, piping up from the backseat. She's ten—an earnest kid with mussy hair who wears her zip-up boots sockless. She has enormous blue eyes and light freckles. She's recently started using a lavender-scented conditioner that makes her smell like a teenager, and she's become afraid of going to the movies, birthday parties and a place called Fun Station—which, according to her, should call its parking lot a *barfing* lot because of all of its germs. She has a fear of germs and of barfing. Which is why we're seeing Jennifer.

"Benny Ogden was the kid growing up in our neighborhood who would do anything." If ten or more kids gather, one of them is bound to become the kid who'll do anything, and one is bound, I suppose, to be the one to dare him to do anything—it's a childhood society standard. Benny Ogden couldn't stand up to simple taunts accompanied by chicken-bocking. "Benny Ogden would do anything a bully would ask him to. He made a naked snow angel and ate cat food. He moved the neighborhood dog poop, bare-handed, into Mr. Hoffman's yard."

"Was that the mean old man who made his wife sell her afghans door-to-door and was always retarring his driveway?"

"Yes, him." It dawns on me that I tell too many stories about my childhood. I should be handing over real information, things that will be important later in life, or at least more relatable than Mr. Hoffman, the compulsive re-tarrer of my childhood. Have I told her about Napoleon, Lincoln, Betty Ford? No. And I feel guilty all of a sudden about this.

"I feel like Benny Ogden, too," she says. "But I'm glad you touched the dog puke with me."

"Of course, absolutely. I wouldn't let you touch dog puke *alone*." What kind of mother lets her kid touch dog puke alone? Not me! And I didn't *have to* touch the dog puke, either. It wasn't part of the plan. But when Dr. Jennifer told me how things would go, I volunteered. At first she'd looked at me skeptically. I was figuring that around the same time in graduate school when you learn how to get a dog to puke and then scoop it up, you're also learning how to look at people skeptically.

I said, "I've got issues, too—as you know." She likes when I admit my culpability. "I mean, this is mostly my fault so I should model, at least, good things like this."

Good things like this? Certainly it's dawned on me that the desensitivity training is idiotic. Certainly it's dawned on me that I prefer the question: "What kind of mother lets her kid touch dog puke *alone?*" to the question: "What kind of mother lets her kid touch dog puke *at all?*" Well-intentioned—that's the most I can hope for here. But my decision to touch the dog puke showed a glimmer of forward-thinking intelligence on my part. I know how these things go down…as a parent. If you don't touch the dog puke and only the kid touches it, and the kid becomes a memoirist—which is a possibility every parent should prepare for—then the mother has scarred the child. But if you do touch the dog puke, you were just stupid. In the grand scheme, I'll always opt for stupid. In most cases, it's the best I can do.

"It's all going to work out," I tell my daughter now, with a grand sense of authority. "I mean, I think things are getting better. If you can touch dog puke, you can touch the joysticks at Fun Station, right?"

"I think it's pretty rare for people to catch sicknesses from dogs." Since we adopted two dogs from the Humane Society earlier in the year, my daughter has been watching *Animal Planet*. Occasionally, she'll say things like: "Whale nipples are retractable." I've learned not to question her random knowledge of animal life. Plus, our neighbor is a vet, and Phoebe spends a lot of time over there.

"Oh," I say.

"Plus," she adds, "if we're Benny Ogden, then Dr. Jennifer's the bully. And you know what you think of bullies."

Unfortunately, I've lied about what I think of bullies. I've told the kids to stand up to bullies, that they usually back down. But I'm pretty sure this isn't true. Bullies are bullies because they have a history of bullying and are likely, based on that history, to bully again. And I realize that I'm terrified of Dr. Jennifer. Her youth, her conviction! Give me the old doctor who just shrugs and says, "Have it your way."

Dr. Jennifer is supposed to call me this week to discuss the next step in the process, and now I realize that I'm going to have to stand up to her, and that the reason I'm going to have to stand up to her is twofold. One: Because she is a bully. Two: Because my daughter is playing me.

For good measure, she adds, "Next time she'll have us picking up dog poop and putting it in someone's yard—with our *bare hands!*"

"Right," I say. "Right."

"She has to be stopped."

"Of course."

Here is the real issue: I don't want my daughter to turn out like my mother. Glenda Baggott is an overly anxious, OCD matriarch, who doles out equal doses of love and worry, and I'm her baby, still. She has spent her life trying to keep us all alive and intact, which, to her mind is no simple task. She believes that the world is out to get us. She's not content to warn against drinking from germy water fountains, sitting on public toilets, eating foods past their sell-by dates.

No.

Her fears are much wider in scope, including, but not limited to: dented canned goods, unscrubbed fruits, flea dips, sushi, doctors' offices, gas fumes, idling cars, microwave ovens, household cleansers, the waxy edges of bologna, elastic waistbands that could compromise the circulation of young children...

Et cetera!

My mother takes her medication now—off and on—so that she doesn't scrub pots until her hands crack and bleed. But sometimes the medicine itself seems too poisonous to ingest, and sometimes the medicine makes her too tired. It seems that not having enough energy to scrub pots until your hands crack and bleed can be worse than scrubbing pots until your hands crack and bleed.

There are plenty of other quirks and phobias—some of which she's handed down to me, and some of which I've unwittingly handed down to my daughter. If there's anything I can do now to spare my daughter this fate, I will, which is how we wound up in the clutches and bullying effervescence of Dr. Jennifer.

The truth is, though, germ-phobes don't have a chance in today's market. There's too much money to be made in single-use wipes. Marketers have learned not only how to attract germ-phobes, they've also learned how to create them in order to sell more products. How sad. How very sad.

Dr. Jennifer called on a Monday, midday. I was in the middle of things and picked up the phone without looking at the caller ID. I was surprised to hear her voice—her chipper condescension. I wasn't prepared, but she certainly was. Her speech was poignant and savvy and cluttered with scientific backing. She had data.

The plan was simple. In the upcoming session, she wanted to get Phoebe closer to the feeling of throwing up without throwing up. Dr. Jennifer explained that she'd introduced this idea to Phoebe already. In fact, she'd invited her to try it by drinking a big glass of milk in the session before the dog puke touching—when I was out of town.

"And what did she do?" I asked.

Dr. Jennifer paused. "Is Phoebe lactose intolerant?"

"Not really. I mean, I think she thinks she is because our babysitter was and she kind of liked the idea of it—the way kids this age like glasses and braces and casts—but she eats ice cream happily. So she isn't."

"Well, she said she was lactose intolerant and couldn't. She's very...*clever.*" She said the word *clever* like it was a bad thing. She went on to explain that this week she was planning on having Phoebe drink a big glass of water—to avoid the lactose argument—and then spin around to show that she can feel sick without throwing up, and that she was then to practice this at home, twice a day.

"Really?" I asked. "But what if she throws up?"

"She won't."

"She won't? I thought psychologists believed in the power of suggestion. I mean, if you tell her she's going to feel like throwing up, she might very well throw up."

"If she does, she'll realize that throwing up isn't that bad."

"But it is."

"No, it isn't."

"Throwing up sucks. It makes you feel completely out of control."

"She needs to see her therapy through."

"But, you see, I want her to say no to people who make her drink things that make her feel like throwing up. I mean, we're heading into the teen years. I can tell her to do what you say because you're in authority, but in a few years her peers are going to be the authority. And I want to teach her to say no."

"Look, I know that you may want to back out, because, well, you have enabling issues, but I really think you should see the program through to its end."

"I think I have commonsense issues. I don't want her to be afraid of throwing up anymore, but I don't want her to associate drinking water with throwing up. We've got enough associations with throwing up."

She responded to this. There were more facts. There was

more data. It was all really compelling. "It's a controlled environment. It will be fine."

"Well, I don't want her to develop a bad association with controlled environments, either. I mean, I mean…" I wasn't being articulate. I was being bullied by the chicken-bocking of data and facts—with my family's history clanging in the background. I decided to deflect. "How did you get that dog to throw up anyway?"

"It wasn't really dog vomit," she said. "It was a mixture of cottage cheese and vinegar and some other ingredients."

I was totally disillusioned. "Do you even have a dog?"

She didn't answer at first. She just asked me if Phoebe and I were coming in for our next session.

"That depends," I said. "Do you have a dog or not?"

"I don't understand your logic…"

"Do you have a dog or don't you?"

"No. I don't have a dog."

"Did you have a dog as a child?"

"I didn't need a dog for Phoebe's session to be a success. You touched what you thought was dog vomit, and…"

"Did you have a dog as a child?"

"No."

"Did you have a little brother or someone who would let you pretend he was your dog—crawling around on all fours and barking?"

"What?"

"Did you have a little brother or someone who'd pretend to be your dog?"

"No. I was an only child."

"Did you always want a dog as a child? And was your childhood lacking because you never had one?"

"Maybe a little."

"Okay, then."

"Okay what?"

"We're not coming in."

My logic was simple. All childhoods are lacking in something. All childhoods are difficult. All childhoods are held together by painful joists. And, I'm not sure, but one of the main things we can hope for is a true expression of that pain—an honest expression of what's going wrong and why. We need to find out why we try to avoid that pain and why we're afraid of that pain, and maybe that can only be done in real life—not in a controlled environment at all.

That afternoon before my daughter comes home from school, I drink a big glass of water and spin around. I sit down on the sofa and watch the room churn. I'm reminded of a time when I was on a high school beach trip, dating the guy who powered the spinning boardwalk ride where the floor drops out. I drank a lot of peach schnapps and was spun, and I haven't had peach schnapps since. I feel like throwing up, but I know I won't, and I don't.

I ask myself, "What did I just learn?"

I answer, "The contemporary suburban human being of a high-strung nature and mediocre intelligence has been force-fed the obvious masquerading as insight for so long that they no longer know the obvious."

And then I burp, and the burp's a little high in my throat, and I gag.

A few minutes later, my daughter comes home from school and finds me on the sofa. She plops down her backpack and sits next to me. "You look weird."

"I talked to Dr. Jennifer."

"Do we have to go back?"

"We don't if you'll do one thing…"

"What?"

"You have to go to Fun Station and touch all the joysticks in the place."

She eyes me, gauging my seriousness. I'm serious. "Okay," she says.

"And you're not lactose intolerant. You know that, right?"

She rolls her eyes. "I know."

"And I'm not an enabler."

"I don't even know what that is."

"If it comes up later, in your memoirs or something, just remember that I wasn't an enabler."

"Okay."

We sit there on the sofa, looking out over the backyard where the dogs are lying in the sun.

"She doesn't even have a dog," I tell Phoebe. "It was fake puke."

"I thought so," Phoebe says.

"You did?"

"Yeah," she says. "I've been thinking about Dr. Jennifer and about bullies." She gets up and walks to the window at the yard, rutted with dog paths and dug-up holes.

"What about?"

"I've been thinking of Benny Ogden, too. And I was thinking that one day, we could bring dog poop over to Dr. Jennifer's yard. Like proof."

"Proof of how healthy we are? Proof of how we're glowing successes?"

She smiles and nods.

"Bare-handed?" I ask.

"Of course not. That would be crazy."

CUTTING THE PURSE STRINGS
Heather Swain

Empty pockets never held anyone back.
Only empty heads and empty hearts can do that.
—Norman Vincent Peale

The other day, my two-and-a-half-year-old daughter, Clementine, raced up the stairs from our den shouting, "Mommy, I just saw a gorilla on *The Muppet Show!*" In the next breath, she ran to our craft box and began pulling out scraps of paper and a glue stick. "Let's make a gorilla costume!" she exclaimed. Two things made me very happy about this situation. First, that she loved *The Muppet Show* DVD circa 1982 I had picked up at a clearance sale, and second, that she asked me to help her make a gorilla costume instead of asking me to buy her one.

I was in the middle of cooking dinner, so I told her that we didn't have enough time to make a costume right then. "But," I said, "Grammy is coming tomorrow and she can help us."

"Oh, yeah," said Clem, tossing aside the paper and glue stick. "Grammy is good at that." And she's right.

My mother grew up in a working-class, immigrant family in which money for frivolities such as toys and new clothes was virtually nonexistent, so she and her eight siblings imagined and improvised their way toward fun. They had an impressive repertoire of outdoor group games such as kick the can, Red Rover, freeze tag, statues and hide-and-seek. On rainy or cold days they stayed inside and made clothes for their homemade, shirt-board paper dolls or played "secretaries" with pretend typewriters made from pieces of paper hanging halfway out of books (that make an impressive clacking noise when one pretends to hammer away at the keys) and telephones made from tin cans and string.

Since they were left on their own quite frequently, they discovered some other interesting ways to entertain themselves, many of which were not strictly legal—or if not illegal, not exactly ethical anyway. They got pretty good at carting off cold sodas, bags of chips and occasionally, buckets of fried chicken from family reunions or company picnics in a large, leafy park near their house. The only problem was, they weren't related to anyone at those family reunions, nor did their parents work for the sponsoring corporations. They also knew how to shimmy through the fence after hours at a local trampoline park and jump to their hearts' content, sometimes naked. They had peeing contests off the roof of the shed in their backyard—and my mom and aunts swear girls can do it just as well as, if not better than, boys.

As children, my cousins, brothers and I loved nothing better than huddling on top of my grandmother's washer and dryer in the corner of her kitchen to listen to our parents regaling one another with their childhood stories until they were all laughing so hard they cried and our stomachs and cheeks hurt from matching their hilarity. Some people might call the antics of my mom's childhood "delinquent behavior" and by today's standards those people would probably be right. As a parent now, I find myself wondering what was going on in that household to allow nine children to run amok all over town without any parental supervision. I know the answer, of course. My grandmother was either pregnant or caring for an infant continuously for a dozen years while my grandfather worked three jobs. It's amazing that nobody died or at the very least went to jail, yet somehow all nine of my grandparents' children grew up to be good people with respectable jobs and nice families of their own.

As a result of a lifetime of improvising, my mom, like all the women in her family, is very crafty. She cooks, she bakes, she sews and paints, shellacs and macramés, refinishes old furniture, and is an excellent potter with a devoted clientele. She is also the consummate bargain shopper and a champion Dumpster diver, but that doesn't mean she doesn't like nice things. As a kid, she fantasized about being a member of the Anderson family from the TV show *Father Knows Best* with their perfectly pressed new clothes and fine furniture. When it was her turn to raise a family, having a nice house and children that always looked good was a high priority. However, given my parents' tight budget coupled with my mom's inbred frugality, she had to develop a nearly preternatural sense for a good deal to reach these goals.

She became the kind of person who can walk into a major department store, sniff out a totally hip, past-season designer winter coat marked down seventy-five percent, then hit a few rummage sales on the way home where she'll uncover a hardly worn pair of vintage leather boots for ten dollars that match the coat perfectly. Plus, she'll talk the seller down to parting with the boots for five bucks and throwing in for free a scratched-up end table with a wobbly leg sitting next to the garbage cans. Then she'll take that table home, strip it down, fix it up, and hand paint it so it matches her family room furniture perfectly. Growing up watching my mother work her peculiar magic of turning a little money into plenty of stuff meant that I learned the art of opting out—that most mainstream spending is silly because fads don't last and desires will pass, that paying full price means you're a sucker, and that you should never be too proud to use other people's cast-offs.

I got through my teen years and early twenties with those principles about spending, always hunting for a bargain and priding myself in my ability to live on a shoestring budget, until I met and married a guy with some money. (What can I say? I'm a lucky girl.) It's not as if my husband and I have so much money that we can light Cuban cigars with hundred-dollar bills, but we're lucky in that we don't have to worry about making ends meet every month and there's always a little something left for a splurge. That's when I discovered the illicit thrill of buying in and spending money just for fun.

I still remember the first time I paid full price for a dress, and not just any dress—a gorgeous black wrap dress that I had been coveting in the window of a little boutique near my house for months. As I slipped the clingy fabric of my dream dress around my body I felt woozy, a little sweaty, sort of naughty. It's probably the same feeling some people get buying porn or shoplifting. Until that moment, nearly all of my clothing had come from clearance racks and discount stores. I wasn't simply buying this dress on a whim, though. I was shopping for something special to wear to the first reading and book release party for my debut novel. Sure, I had plenty of suitable clothes in my closet, or I could've even spent a third of what I paid for that dress had I searched through my old shopping haunts. But that wasn't the point. I wanted to celebrate with something out of the ordinary and to do that, I chose to spend money on myself, something my mother would never do.

During the early years of my marriage, I had purposefully wriggled free of my mom's absolutism about thriftiness, but once I had my daughter I began to reconsider how I spent money. My preparenting days of extravagant dinners at fancy Manhattan restaurants to celebrate birthdays and anniversaries, or my occasional shopping sprees at trendy Brooklyn boutiques for special events no longer held the same appeal for me. For one thing, I was too exhausted from not sleeping to sit through three-hour dinners and too ravenous from around-the-clock nursing to tolerate the precious portions of chic dining. Plus, I knew every piece of my clothing would wind up spewed with various bodily fluids by the end of the day, so why bother with anything other than T-shirts and indestructible fleece pants?

On another level, I was trying to work out the intersection of my attitudes about spending money with my attitudes about raising children. Once I became a parent, I found it harder to justify tossing money around frivolously when I had a tiny person counting on me to provide her with a good life. And therein lies the rub. What is the good life for a child? Love, devotion, affection, time and attention were all things I could provide without question. It was the material goods, services and privilege that money can buy that had me stumped.

I knew for certain I didn't want to spend extravagant amounts of money while raising my daughter. Before I became a mom, I taught third grade in a posh private school in downtown Brooklyn and I was loathe to rear the kind of entitled little New Yorkers I encountered there. Then again, I knew I couldn't raise my family on the kind of tight budget I grew up with, since I was no longer willing to impose it on myself. And yet, I was drawn back toward the familiar notions of simplicity and ingenuity that governed my childhood.

As Clementine approached her first birthday, I began to see where the lines I was drawing about spending money differed from the families around us. We would not be renting a carousel for dozens of guests to celebrate her birthday or letting her scale a tiny mountain of brightly wrapped presents only to discard the contents for the boxes. Her birthday would be celebrated at home, in the garden with homemade cupcakes, a few close friends and some modest gifts. Nor would I be filling out private preschool applications when she hit eighteen months to insure her space in an elite learning institution. We planned to roll up our sleeves and dive into the local public school when she turned four. Like anyone, I was making choices for my daughter based on beliefs deeply ingrained from my childhood. My paradigms about parenting and money intersected in such a way that I prioritized fostering a lifelong sense of resourcefulness in my child.

The deeper I get into parenting, the more I realize that there are two types of resourcefulness: one born of necessity and one born from choice. My mom came from a family where there was no money left over after meeting basic needs, so she had to make her own fun and find her way in life. When I was a kid, I assumed I didn't have the same things as my peers because my parents couldn't afford them. We drove to state parks for vacations instead of flying to Florida. We went to the local public pool or friends' pools because we didn't have one of our own. We didn't have cable TV, a stereo or new cars. Later I realized that my parents had enough money to purchase the kind of lives I saw my friends' families leading, only my parents chose to spend money differently. They were diligent about staying out of debt, paying off their mortgage, and putting money aside for college and retirement. Though I'm now in a position to indulge my daughter and still save for her future, I've learned that she doesn't need the latest and greatest of everything even if I can afford it. That having less can make you feel like you have more because you appreciate what you do have, and often, making do is more rewarding than buying new.

Looking around my house, it's clear that we place a high

priority on making do. Clementine's bedroom furniture is all used, but hand painted by my mom and me. I knit her sweaters from yarn I buy on sale and my favorite part of Halloween is making her costume. Clementine loves to create her own holiday cards and thank-you notes and her favorite gift for people that she loves is baking cookies or bread. When my mom comes to town, she and Clementine spend hours doing art projects, dressing up and pretending. (Most recently as the gorilla from *The Muppet Show* with a wonderful mask my mom made out of a piece of leftover poster board she found in the craft closet and a fuzzy old brown sweatshirt that hung to Clementine's knees.)

My mother, my daughter and I happen to enjoy these artsy activities, and I hope Clem is learning that using what you have on hand can make material possessions more meaningful because they are imbued with personality. Even better, it pleases me that making our own fun is usually a lot cheaper than going shopping. On a deeper level, I hope that, by limiting her material possessions, I'm teaching Clementine to be resourceful—a character trait I believe will serve her far better in life than any object I could purchase for her.

Despite my respect for my mother's thriftiness, I see that it has a downside. For my mom, money is always the object, no matter how much or how little she has. Money must be battled, tamed and constantly negotiated. When she was young, these habits were necessities, but at some point there was a subtle shift where she had the material wealth but not the self-worth to spend money on herself. As a result, I think she's missed out on some fun in life. She's never been out of the country, never had a pedicure, never bought exactly what she wants but always settles for what's a little bit cheaper.

Now in their early sixties, my parents are so conditioned to not spending money that, even with a comfortable retirement ahead of them, they won't loosen the purse strings. They believe that every purchase should be maximized, whether it's trolling the aisles of Big Lots to save ninety-eight cents on shampoo, cleaning out the gutters themselves rather than paying someone else to do it, or spending hours and hours online searching for the absolute cheapest plane tickets to visit their grandchildren. Someday, I swear, they'll show up at my door wearing Kleenex boxes for shoes and newspaper hats, not because they can't afford anything better, but because they refuse to spend money on themselves.

We've all heard that you have to have a healthy relationship with money, and part of that relationship is knowing when *to spend* it. What I'm learning as I negotiate my life as a mother, a wife, a friend, a writer and a daughter is that at times there are perfectly good reasons to dole out the cash. When my time is more scarce than my money, I'll pay for services such as two-day shipping for some online purchase because I can't get to a store before an upcoming birthday party. When I'm completely overwhelmed by my life, I'll gladly shell out a few bucks for take-out food, a baby-sitter, or on rare occasions, a cleaner to get our house back from the depths of filth to a place of general sanitation that we can maintain. When it comes to things I value greatly, such as buying plane tickets to visit family scattered all across the country or providing good healthy food, I don't hesitate to use money to get what I want. And then there is the occasional, unapologetic good old-fashioned splurge because sometimes it's simply fun to spend money on something special. I'm the first to admit that a really great pair of boots can brighten up a long, dull winter. (But go out and buy forty-seven new pairs of boots and you'll quickly experience the lesson of diminishing returns. The more you have, the more you want, and the less special each individual thing becomes.)

So, while I hope Clementine is learning that she'll usually do fine without spending much, I also hope to teach her how to spend money wisely—how to bargain shop, how to haggle, how to spot a good deal even if you're buying something expensive. I also want her to understand the awesome responsibility of having money and spending it well. That far from being evil, money can do some remarkable things in the world and many times, giving it away is the most rewarding thing one can do.

Despite the power, prestige and privilege money gives, I don't want my daughter to be afraid *not* to have money. My husband and I could lose all of our assets tomorrow. That's the nature of the stuff. Just watch the stock market for a week and it's clear that wealth can be fleeting and unpredictable. Tornadoes can knock down houses, insurance claims can be muddled, a sudden illness can wipe out a family's savings. Although I know my life would become considerably more complicated if we lost it all, I know we'd get by with less because I've done it before. I know that we could still be happy, healthy, and live fulfilling lives.

I want my daughter to be bold in life. To take risks and go out on limbs. I want her to never be afraid to try something potentially rewarding because it may disrupt the status quo of her life. To do that, she's going to need to be self-sufficient, ingenious and have healthy relationships—with people, with food and with money. While she's young, I want my daughter to learn to question her desires, to learn the difference between wants and needs, and to be comfortable opting out of socially mandated "must haves" and expensive fads. In short, I want her to be resourceful like my mom, but I also want her to know when it's okay to cut the purse strings and let loose a little.

Now, as the daughter of a mother and the mother of a daughter, I am sandwiched between the two most important girls in my life. I reach out and hold their hands, bridging their worlds, passing back and forth what I've learned from each. "You'll get by," I can tell my daughter with confidence, because my mother before her has done it. And to my mother I can say, "Come, let's splurge a little to celebrate life because we're worth it."

A WILLING SACRIFICE
Mary Haug

*I am becoming confident in my mother's ability
to stand in the light
and I feel strong enough to join her there.*
—From *Riding the White Horse Home*
  by Teresa Jordan

The summer my mother died, I sorted through old pictures and letters, in hopes I might find some wisdom she had intended to share with me. But I really didn't expect success. Here on the Great Plains, where the vast space and emptiness make us feel exposed and vulnerable, we protect ourselves by drawing inward, as animals will curl up to protect themselves from predators. This instinct inhibits honest conversation, and so we take our secrets to the grave. My mother was no exception.

I peered at a faded and grainy photo of my mother as a small girl, most likely taken around 1920. In the picture, she sits on a tricycle, her back to the camera. She rests a large framed mirror against the handlebars and studies her reflection. Her dark, bobbed hair curls under at the nape of her neck and hugs her skull like a helmet. The bodice of her dress is smocked and the wide collar is trimmed with rickrack. The skirt drapes over the narrow metal wheels; her chubby, bare feet stick out beneath the hem and rest against the pedals. Her tiny body and the mirror are the only objects that break the line between the immense sky and the vast central South Dakota grasslands that surround them, except for a cluster of shadowy leaves that cascade down the right side of the frame.

Until that summer, I had never really noticed that the face reflected in the mirror was strangely mature and vaguely recognizable. Suddenly, I felt a chill. I was looking at my face in the mirror: my pug nose, heavy-lidded eyes and sweep of thick bangs across a wide forehead. It was a surreal sensation, as if the camera had captured my mother looking in the mirror at the face of the adult woman I would become while I looked back to the child my mother once was.

The photo captured the time warp women travel as mothers and daughters. We study our small daughters' faces seeking clues to the women they will become. At the same time, we imagine our mothers as small girls so we can understand the children they once were.

Knowing my mother as a child might have helped me to better understand this complicated woman I found so difficult to pin down. The mother who is clearest in my mind is the one who played boogie-woogie on the piano; cooked and baked for family, farm workers and neighbors; held court at family gatherings with her quick wit; and thrived on the clutter and chaos of five children. But there was this other mother, the one who lay on the green velvet sofa, one arm flung across her eyes, in a living room made dark by drawn curtains in a silent house. She is a shadowy figure in my memory, a woman spoken about in whispers. And then there was the mother of my middle years who shriveled me with her sharp tongue and her silence.

The photo also illustrates the time warp between the pre- and postfeminist eras, a period of transition and revolution during the several years when I now think I came of age. In my early adolescence, two women dominated television, delivering polar opposite images of women into our homes. The zany Lucille Ball brought chaos to her family with her childish schemes until finally being rescued by Desi. And the serene and beautiful Jane Wyatt manipulated Robert Anderson by letting him believe he was in charge.

Through the 1960s and 1970s, the media brought us new images of women. Bella Abzug stood in front of a bank of microphones, her enormous hats and presence filling the screen, and talked about abortion, equal pay and the absence of women in politics and business. We saw women burning their bras and waving banners that called for a sexual revolution. And later, the Boston Women's Health Collective published *Our Bodies, Ourselves* which encouraged me to become intimately acquainted with my body. If I could not define myself as a childish schemer or a manipulative saint, neither could I see myself as revolutionary or primal. I struggled to navigate as wife, mother and professional in a culture where the rules seemed to shift and slide.

In 1973, when I was pregnant with my daughter, Maura, the women's movement was gaining steam, and mothers could dream of a future for their daughters without the limitations imposed by gender. As I rocked her at night, I would study her tiny face and wonder what wisdom I could offer that would prepare her for a future that had been unimaginable for me.

But if the feminism opened doors for Maura, it closed the door between my mother and me. I suppose she, too, felt confused by the shifting social order, and so Mother blamed the women's movement for destroying families, for encouraging women to neglect their children out of selfish ambition, for demeaning men.

Mostly her barbs were aimed at women in general, but every now and then, she focused on me in odd ways, like criticizing the books I read. Once she picked up a copy of *To the Lighthouse* from my coffee table and snapped, "You can't even read books by men."

Another time she told me that "men worry that if their wives make too much money they will leave them because they don't need them financially anymore."

I said, "Look, Mother, I don't make enough money to support myself. And besides, staying married because I couldn't afford to leave would be a crummy basis for a marriage, don't you think?"

She clammed up and stared at the floor as she did whenever I challenged her. Our conversations were like negotiating a minefield studded with bombs that didn't explode, but rather fizzled like cheap fireworks into silence. Over time, I grew weary of dodging and weaving around topics that would provoke the silence, and so I limited our talks to hometown gossip, weather and grandchildren.

As our relationship withered, her connection with my daughter blossomed. Every summer, my daughter and her five girl cousins spent a week at their grandma's house. She broke all rules during their visit. She stocked the freezer with ice cream sandwiches and Sara Lee cakes, filled the kitchen cupboards with M&Ms, potato chips and bubble gum, and treated them to fast-food meals three times a day. They stayed up all night, slept late, watched soap operas and read *National Enquirer,* which she bought by the dozens in preparation for their stay.

Her house became a monument to those visits. She pressed carnations and baby's breath from bouquets they had given her into the books she kept by her recliner. She taped their penciled drawings, block-printed notes and scrawled letters to the walls and door frames of the living room and covered the refrigerator with their pictures. One year, they gave her a balloon bouquet, which she tacked to the archway in the living room. In time, only a single, shriveled red balloon remained. It hung there for years until she moved into an assisted-living facility and my niece Sara framed it for her apartment.

When Maura came home from her week with Grandma,

she was cranked up on sugar and trash and the certainty that her grandmother adored her. And she, in turn, adored her grandmother. As Maura matured, my mother ignored the signs that her granddaughter was becoming an assertive, opinionated and liberated young woman. At the same time, Maura detached herself from her grandmother's condemnation of women, giggling at her ludicrous comments and teasing her about being "a crazy lady." Mother would laugh at herself, call Maura a "silly girl," and slip her twenty dollars. On my good days, I was happy that their relationship was based on total acceptance because it fostered Maura's confidence. But there were dark days when I resented and envied their bond and felt confused by Mother's anger at me.

I realize now that Mother was most often angry when she was afraid of something. Her first argument with my father came when he told her a truth she was afraid to know: that her brother took to his sickbed because he was passed-out drunk, not suffering from migraines. She was so furious that she didn't speak to him for weeks. She only yelled at us children when we did something dangerous like climbing the windmill, standing too close to the power takeoff or leaning over mountain cliffs. The night my father died, she came home from the hospital carrying a plastic bag with his glasses, bridgework and billfold. Without a word, she walked to the garage, threw the bag in the garbage and went into the house to make coffee.

Being widowed at fifty must have terrified her. Overnight, she became responsible for budgeting the household accounts, buying insurance, managing home repairs, dealing with a ranch, raising a teenage son and living with loneliness. After my father's death, I never again saw the mother who lay on the couch in a dark living room. Anger was Mother's weapon against her fears, and feminists, who she saw as hypercritical of men and scornful of the traditional family life, were her necessary target.

And anger gave her hope—as long as she was angry, she was still alive. Until the last five days of her life, she never quit hoping to live through another medical crisis. In her last hours, her anger gave her the courage to face death on her own terms. When the hospital chaplain, a skinny and unctuous man, visited her in hospice, he first talked about how busy he was but then promised that despite his lack of time, he would be back.

She was so weak that she could hardly lift her hand. But she dismissed him with a wave of skeletal fingers and said, "I wish you wouldn't." He read a quick prayer from his little black book and bolted.

She could never see herself in me when I was outspoken or assertive and she was puzzled by my pluckiness. But in the last years of her life, we had both mellowed and grown comfortable with one another. I would take her out to lunch and then to shop at Younkers for lipstick and face creams. She would tell me funny stories about her family, my father and my childhood; if she had regrets or secrets, she kept them to herself. And I, too, kept my secrets. The old instinct to curl inward and protect ourselves was still too strong.

I regret my silence. I should have tried to explain to her that Maura had a happier childhood because I never felt trapped by society's choices for me. In her book *Riding the White Horse Home,* Teresa Jordan writes with admiration of her mother because she had "decided not to make sacrifices she couldn't make willingly" and so was free to "marry and mother free of martyrdom or guilt." When we read Jordan's book in my literature class, the young women said they wished their mothers would make fewer sacrifices for them so they might not feel burdened by their mother's martyrdom.

I could have told Mother that I made an essential sacrifice for my family when I chose not to pursue a doctoral degree because I didn't want to split up my family. My choice meant I would be granted neither tenure nor promotion to full professor. Yet, I have never resented nor regretted my decision because it was a "willing sacrifice."

And I wish Mother had understood that although feminists helped me define my career and my place in public life, it was images of her that guided me as I learned to be a parent—her cool hand on my feverish forehead and her worried face in the nightlight's glow; her long fingers on the steering wheel as she drove me around town while I sobbed over losing the cheerleading election; her slender shoulders and straight back as she led her children across the brittle grass of a prairie cemetery to bury our father.

Today, my daughter is a bright, aggressive businesswoman who has traveled the world, assumed a mortgage at age twenty-six, entered marriage expecting nothing less than an equal partnership in which her husband would cook, clean, change diapers and support her career goals, who has confidence about her place in the world. She has become the woman I imagined when I held her tiny body years ago.

But I want her to remember that her life might have been different. Before feminists undertook the battle to change women's lives, we had only three career choices—four for a Catholic girl like myself who could enter the convent—secretary, nurse or teacher. I became a teacher because my father told me it was "a good career for a woman to fall back on should something happen to her husband." It was only blind luck that I found teaching so gratifying.

Before the women's movement, I had no financial independence. When I began my teaching career, I went to a local women's shop to replace my jeans and sweatshirts with polyester pantsuits and skirts and was told that my husband, Ken, would have to open the account because a woman couldn't charge in her own name. Before feminism, I was expected to see my career as a gift from my husband. Women often said to me, "You're so lucky your husband lets you work outside the home," and they praised Ken for being helpful around the house.

That was my experience; my daughter's is different, in large part because she has benefited from all the women who came before her. In her is the manifestation of these words spoken by Matilda Joslyn Gage: "The women of today are the thoughts of their mothers and grandmothers—embodied and made alive. They are active, capable, determined, and bound to win. They have one thousand generations back of them…"

Now that my daughter is herself a mother, I hope she will know what sacrifices she is willing to make and those she cannot make. I also hope she will understand the difference between mothering and smothering. I loved my daughter with ferocious mother love, but sometimes the demands of motherhood seemed so consuming that I felt as if I couldn't breathe. When I went back to teaching, I hoarded that part of my life from both my daughter and my husband because I needed a bit of the world that was mine alone. But at the end of the day, I came back willing and happy to enter their world. Too many women cast their shadow over their children and then are devastated when their children step out into their own light. And other women stand forever in their children's shadows. Shadows are dark, musty places; they are no place for women.

It's been three years since Mother died, and I think often about the small inheritance she left me—her lotus-and-dragon carnival glass bowls, a teapot with pink roses, her collection of bone china cups and saucers, and the picture of her sitting on the trike. And I am especially grateful that she bequeathed me her love of music, her sense of humor, her spunkiness and irrepressible irreverence. But in an uncharacteristic act of selfishness, she took to her grave what I needed most—the truth of her story and the ways that narrative had shaped her. Such truth might have helped us reshape the myth that defined us as mother and daughter; such honesty might have broken the silence.

THE WHOLE POINT OF MOTHERHOOD
Barbara Rushkoff

My mother had a great deal of trouble with me,
but I think she enjoyed it.
—Mark Twain

Rhonda Schwartz's mother used to smoke thin, ladylike cig-arettes and say curse words (the bad ones) while she made lunch. She would ask point-blank about how far I ever went with a boy while simultaneously rubbing gel blusher on my twelve-year-old cheeks. It was shocking, daring—and I kind of liked it. Mrs. Schwartz would also get undressed right in front of us, and model scanty clothes, asking earnestly our opinion of her new hot pants outfit or tight metallic sweater that she wore with no bra. She would take hour-long bubble baths in the afternoon and chain smoke while heating up frozen egg rolls for us. Everything she did was in full makeup. I had never seen a mother like her before. I wondered, could mothers even do that?

When I would come home from Rhonda's house after a sleepover, my mother would ask me what Mrs. Schwartz cooked for us at dinner and at breakfast the next morning. The answer would always be the same: Burger King and McDonald's. My mother would scowl and I would wonder why because, duh, both of those meals were delicious. Then my mother would go to the phone and dial her cousin who lived across the street from the Schwartz's to hear *the stories*. Apparently, Mrs. Schwartz stood at the window—topless—puffing on her cigarette. A lot. She also *made eyes* at my cousin's husband. My cousin didn't like her, which meant my mother automatically didn't like her.

My mom wore plain clothes in muted shades of blue and black, had short, no-fuss hair and spent most of her time chauffeuring us around to various activities. We had home-cooked meals every night and clean clothes folded neatly on our beds every day. The house was always tidy and my mother always seemed to be doing something, in some room somewhere that involved lemon fresh Pledge. However, Mom did own a silver sparkle pantsuit for Bar Mitzvahs and a fancy gown with a tiger made out of rhinestones on the bodice, but she didn't wear those things during the day. There were times that I wished she would dress a little more swingy, a little more hip, a little more, you know, not so Mom-ish.

As I got older I had one main wish when my mother would come to pick me up from school. *Please stay inside the car.* I was almost a teenager and whenever I saw my mother standing outside of the car waiting for me, it made me feel about four years old. It was embarrassing. And why did she want to talk to me about exactly what happened today at school the second I got into the sedan? While it was sort of cool that she had put on the rock station for me, I'd cringe when songs like "Feel Like Making Love" played. *Please, Mom, don't ask me about this song, and please do not sing along with it.* When I got home, I would immediately call Rhonda and beg to go over to her house. My mother always obliged, even though it was clear that she did not approve of the Schwartz lifestyle. I always felt relieved when the car sped away and I could sit in the rec room with Rhonda and her mom and dance *Soul Train* style to "Keep on Truckin'" by Eddie Kendricks.

I haven't spoken to Rhonda in over twenty years. I have no idea if her mother still has her fire-engine-red hair or if she remembers telling me that she got her wide-whale corduroy pants dry cleaned, a request that I asked of my own mother and was met with arched eyebrows, a deep sigh and a call to the cousin about such nonsense. I don't know if she herself is a mom or if Mrs. Schwartz would even own up to being a grandma. I picture Rhonda's mom in full botox mode, in the same exact clothes she wore in the seventies. I have a feeling I am not too far off in approximation.

It might seem too weird to think of these people from my childhood, but now that I have a daughter, I tend to examine mother-daughter relationships past, present, future—and television. If I didn't have a daughter I might think that the *Gilmore Girls* would be my ideal in mother-daughter rapport. The mother is young and cool and pretty, and the daughter is smart and nice and gorgeous. They watch bad TV together while eating ice cream, bantering back and forth witty barbs about obscure indie rock music and fashion styles of the sixties. They're like the coolest of the cool. Before I had my daughter, I imagined that to be the quintessential relationship, that is, *the young mother.* I always wanted to be the young mother. Granted, my mother was a young mother, but she felt old to me. She had three kids by the time she was twenty-nine. At twenty-nine, I was still sleeping on a futon in a studio apartment in a bad part of town. Mrs. Schwartz was a young mother, but maybe she was a little *too* young. But really, is age all that relevant? Or am I saying that because I'll be pushing sixty when my girl enters college?

Growing up, I always thought my mom was a great mother. She was a mom. Not a friend. Instead of connecting on a deep level after three-hour talks about life, we spoke in riddles to one another. I recall hiding my birth control pills, like every nice Jewish girl, in my pajama drawer. Magically a few days later, my mother told me that she happened to have a discussion with her lady friends about birth control; about how if *her daughter* ever went on the Pill she would be happy that she was taking care of herself. I took that as her way of letting me know it was okay that I was using contraception. (For the record, I wasn't even having sex. I had the pills just in case. I wouldn't use them for years.) It was the whole messy sex part that was left out. I shouldn't complain, but when people ask me how my mother told me about sex, I just tell them how Ellen-from-around-the-corner, the one with the "Up Against The Wall, Motherfucker" record filled me in while we drank our cherry-cola Slurpees one summer night.

When my mother and I weren't talking in conundrums, we were covering up my many mishaps by vigorously lying to my father. See, I had strict parents. They were the kind of people who needed to know everything about where I was going. They didn't want to know what I was going to do; they just wanted to know everything was going to be fine. I am surprised they didn't energetically cover up their ears and start singing "Oklahoma!" whenever I mentioned something unpleasant to them: non-Jewish boys, multiple ear piercings and not wanting to become a nurse ("you'll meet doctors!").

I got a lot of freedom, yet that same liberty could be yanked by either of them at any time for no given reason. So when I begged for the car one particular snowy night to go to a punk club downtown, it was my father who told me to be extra careful. I countered back with "it will all be fine" and I was off in my thrift-shop angora sweater with the price tag still stapled on. The night was fun. The night was cold. I even met a nice non-Jewish boy. At 3:30 a.m. when we got to the car, I saw that it had been broken into. The contents of the car were scattered all over the street and all I could think about was how I would never be allowed out again.

I got home at 4:30 a.m. I didn't have a curfew for some

reason. My parents didn't mind that I stayed out ridiculously late, they just wanted to know *exactly when* I would be home. My mother was waiting up for me because she had a sixth sense about these things. She told me that she had a bad dream about me and had decided to wait up. I was really glad she did, even though I knew I was going to get yelled at pretty badly. When I told her what happened through tears and stale Aqua Net, she echoed my sentiments about my dad banning me from car use forever. She had a plan though. Mom asked me if there was still broken glass in the car. When I said yes, she told me to go outside to the car and distribute the glass over the sidewalk.

"We have to make it look like it happened here," she said.

So I did. Then I went to my room and waited for my mother to rouse the dog into a barking fit.

"Someone has bashed in the windshield," she said loud enough for my father to hear.

I heard my mother give some account of a "man in a blue coat" terrorizing our Honda Civic. To my shock and amazement, my father bought it and when I woke he told me that he was glad it happened here instead of downtown. I guess if it happened downtown it would have been all my fault, but since it happened at home, it wasn't. I wasn't going to argue with that kind of logic.

I think of this story a lot, because I know girls and I know how crafty they can be with the truth. And I know my daughter is going to lie to me. I know she will smoke cigarettes and most probably pot. I know she will meet horrible boys behind my back and lie to me about whose house she is sleeping over that night. I know that she will buy clothes that I don't approve of and change into them as soon as she meets up with her friends. I know she will do all kinds of things that I will want to know about, but

91

that I don't want to know about. I can't blame my folks too much for wanting to be out of the loop.

But that's the difference. I *do* want to know. The difference is I am not going to judge. I am going to let my girl be herself. I probably won't like everything she does, but I don't want to inhibit her or hold her back from expressing herself. I think it's possible to effectively mother a child without crushing their spirit. I want things to be open between us. Whether she confides in me or not is her option. That is my intention.

While it would be super awesome cool, just like the mom on the *Gilmore Girls,* to be able to hang out with my daughter and her friends and play punk rock from 1979, I don't expect that to happen. I don't expect to be the cool mom. Will I be bummed? No, I really won't. That's what friends do with each other. And I'm her mom. Sure, it would be great if she wants to go shopping with me for new clothes, but I won't fault her for preferring to do that with one of her girlfriends. I want to be a mother to her first, and for me, being a mother means knowing when to step back and *not* be a friend. Will it make me sad if she shrinks down when I drop her off at school? Sure. But that doesn't mean I am going to be like my mother was with me and wait outside of the car in *a white pantsuit.* That, I've learned.

There is a medium between my mother and Mrs. Schwartz. I know there is, because that's where I'm writing this from. There's a fine line between being a loving mother and *being available* to my daughter as a friend. I want the choice there, for her to decide. If you ask me today, I'd say that I want to be both, but I know that can't be.

Ask me again in ten years.

IN THE OFFING
Tara Bray Smith

It was difficult to realize his work was not out there in the luminous estuary, but behind him, within the brooding gloom.
—From *Heart of Darkness* by Joseph Conrad

It was July 2003, month of the Lahaina Noon, when the sun is directly overhead like a lamp, casting no shadows. Downtown, the drunks were out of the bars and the air along Hotel Street toward the river smelled the wrong kind of sweet. My sister, Layla, and I had been looking for our mother for a few days and finally had learned she was at a mission called the River of Life—and there I was.

Doors opened at nine for breakfast—men in a queue on the left, women on the right. One of the women in line wore only a bra; another wheeled a large suitcase. For Christmas the previous year, when Layla and I had been so crazed to find her, get her into treatment, help in any dumb way we could, I had bought Mom a similar kind of suitcase, though smaller: a weekender. She had seemed so burdened, carrying those backpacks around. Layla gave her a fifty-dollar gift certificate to Safeway. When she got caught drinking cough syrup—or was it mouthwash?—in an aisle of the Pali Safeway, she spent her first night in jail. I don't know what happened to the bag.

That's what kind of year 2003 was. What had seemed a temporary horror—she had relapsed into heroin addiction in 2001 and ended up on the street—had stretched into a life. Mornings meant packing up her knapsacks early, before the cops came in on their sweeps, or the cleaning ladies showed up to mop the breezeways of the office buildings where she and Ron, her husband, occasionally stayed. For a while it was the Prudential building where her father had worked when he was alive. She said she often dreamed about him when she was staying there. She and her siblings were younger and growing up in Nuuanu, across from Jackass Ginger, on the banks of the Nuuanu Stream.

When I think of my mother, I think of that stream, which cuts through downtown Honolulu and is the source of the city's modern name. The natural harbor that formed at its mouth, known as Kou or Mamala after an Oahu chiefess who surfed there, became Honolulu, "sheltered bay," following the arrival of European ships in the 1780s. My mother's great-grandmother was there the day the first shots of the Hawaiian revolution were fired in 1893, signaling the end of the Hawaiian kingdom and the islands' eventual annexation by the United States. Her grandfather's sugar plantation offices were right down the road. She and her three siblings were born at Queen's Hospital a quarter mile away, and when she married my father in 1970, it was at St. Andrew's, across the street. Her sister's ashes are interred there. I think she's even slept on those steps. And though the stream's banks are concrete now, laced by bridges and sidewalks, crossed over by highways, and though the water is polluted and plastic bottles float along its green length, it is still the same stream that she grew up next to, privileged among her grandmother's gardenias.

That the river downtown is one of the scariest, scuzziest, lowdown places in all of Hawaii is chilling. How can things so close be so lost to us?

By way of an answer: the River of Life. You could get breakfast at the mission, and though it was hot outside and there was vomit on the sidewalk, inside, order and sober friendship ruled.

Mom said she liked it because of the air-conditioning and the community. You can take a shower after breakfast at the River of Life, or choose an outfit from the donations room upstairs. The day I accompanied her there, Mom got a pair of chinos. Then we left and went to the post office, where Ron's disability check was supposed to be.

"This is what people do every day," she said. We were sitting outside on the rough edge of a concrete planter. "They eat. They walk around. They go back to the River of Life. They find a place to sleep."

I felt sullen and mistrustful. "So why are you doing it? You've got a fascination with the dark side?"

She scowled. "No, I don't. I had a hard time and now I'm paying for it. I was tired. Taking care of everybody. I wanted to say 'Fuck it,' and so I did and here I am. Being out there," she was fussing with the dirt now, making furrows with a rigid finger. "It wasn't so bad. Yeah, I wanted to *see*. I think all of life should be *felt*. I didn't know what it was like to walk into a *mission*. Then I did and I was, like, '*Whoa*.'"

She looked at me—her eyes are a light shade of gray-blue, and just the slightest bit tilted—then back at the planter.

"God! Look at this earth! Look at how beautiful it is!"

It was a characteristic pronouncement: the beguiling mix of experience and innocence that is my mother. But at that moment, there was something wrong with its insouciance. She lived on the street. The "earth" we were talking about was not underfoot along a ginger-scented hiking trail, but in a cruddy planter in front of a post office down by the river, a last bid at tidiness in an otherwise squalid scene. But, *ah,* she was my mother and I loved her. She was trying to be brave. What did it matter, anyway? As long as she seemed happy.

When I used to look for her, it always seemed so scary there down by the river. Up Nuuanu, down Sun Yat Sen Mall, across Hotel, past the pimps and the dealers and the gamblers and the whores. That particular whore I thought was my mother. But this last time, sitting by the post office, it didn't seem so bad. The water was the blue-green of corporate park ponds, the stone walls guiding it and the bougainvillea setting it ablaze. I could see the boats in the harbor and beyond that a hyphen of horizon. It wasn't horrible. It was even sort of pretty.

Fascinate, from *fascinare:* to cast a spell on. When I was young, I dreamed of a witch in a tunnel of fire. Or did I make myself dream about the witch, as I willed myself to sleepwalk because it seemed exciting, a habit I can't, to this day, seem to shake?

My grandmother once mused that maybe my sisters and I drained my mother, took the best things she had when we were born. As in a fairy tale. Of course, it's my grandmother who should take the most responsibility for how my mother turned out, but things don't work like that in my family. In my family, as in fairy tales, it's the witch that's responsible, or the mean-spirited little girl who speaks in phrases of toads and worms. But they are just born that way, and come to horrible ends, and when they die, no one is actually sad.

A long time ago, I was with my mother. Beaches were involved, and sand, and the waves shushed at night. I didn't have to go to school when I didn't want to. A Yami Yogurt truck played its tune in the afternoon and I ran down a dirt lane that smelled like oleander to meet it.

I barely knew my father as a young child. They had met in Honolulu when my mother was nineteen. He was a surfer kid from California, and she was, as he told me, charming. They married after she got pregnant, and moved to the North Shore, to a defunct sugar plantation where my mother said she kept a garden and learned from a neighbor how to make bread. He left when I was not quite two. By the time I was three, he had a new girlfriend. She would become my stepmother.

But Mom was the leading actress, director and cinematographer. She also collected the tickets. It never occurred to me to want anything different than this. It was a chaotic, impressionistic, and exciting life, with no lack of love but a serious lack of a plan. We moved—all the time. Houses were measured in weeks, not years. During the months we lived in Kahala, down the street from my grandmother, her husband used to see Mom in her nightgown, walking me to school. He told my grandmother he was worried, but Mom was young, twenty-six or so. No one knew how bad it could get.

Eventually my father provided the exit. She was at the grocery store one day. He came on a plane and poof, I was gone. I was seven. She was twenty-seven. I never lived with her again.

When I left, I missed her. I cried. I saved every letter she sent me from Houston, where she moved with my new half sister, Layla. Later, she moved to Monterey, where I visited her after she'd given birth to another girl, Lauren. I got to know my father. I got to know my stepmother. I played soccer after school and got grounded and learned about the perils of dishonesty. I went to school, then college. I became an adult.

Sort of. Whatever continuity my father and stepmother provided was limned by the breathless drama that was Karen. When she called, when she cried, when a sister was left at an airport, I came running. I obsessed about incidents in my childhood. I wrote about her, refining every story I could remember, until what was on the page replaced what actually happened. She got better for a while, and then didn't.

When she fell out of her apartment in Honolulu and on to the street, I was crushed. For five years she was homeless, addicted, in and out of jail, the horrible list goes on. I wrote a book about it. I cried, I yelled, I felt wrecked, but only in my dreams did I really scream at her.

Then in the fall of 2005, she got sick with MRSA, a kind of staph. She started coughing blood. She had developed ATP, an autoimmune disorder in which one's body destroys one's platelets. The blood can't stick together, and internally you begin to bleed, which she was doing a day after I arrived in Honolulu from Germany, where I had moved.

Her hematologist told us to prepare for the worst. We were all there, my grandmother, my sisters, my aunt and me. At a diner one night, I told my sisters to prepare themselves for the possibility that she'd die. She had brought herself here, I said. Life was less important than her drugs. These were all things I had heard from other people, or read, or picked up from TV or from the letters I had received after my book came out. I even thought that the psychotherapist who had reviewed my memoir *West of Then* for the *New York Times* might have been right: I was "addicted to Mom," and her death would at last relieve me. I told my youngest sister to "live her own life." I told my mother that I loved her and that she'd soon get better, but I did not believe she would.

She stayed in the hospital for three weeks. Then she recovered. "Of course she's still alive," my father said over dinner the last night I was there. He was laughing. "Pure bitchiness kept your great-grandmother alive. What was she, a hundred and two?"

My father, my black-haired, black-humored dad, who'd been there all along. My consolation, my savior, the reason I had turned out okay.

"You can do a sequel. Four women, four different destinies, come back to face their dying mother. You can call it *Daughters of the Moon*.... It'll be great!"

I laughed, too. It would continue. She would continue. It could only go up from here.

He died on Superbowl Sunday, 2006, a sad day in my memory as that was also the day, twenty years earlier, that he and my stepmother told me they were getting a divorce. He had a heart attack while surfing at a spot off Waikiki called Paradise, fell off his board and drowned. It was around three o'clock. My mother, miraculously healthy by then, was at a bar, somewhere in Wahiawa, with Ron. She said she was drinking a soda and watching the game.

I was in Madrid when I got the call. There was a quality of panic in my father's girlfriend's voice that I knew the exact timbre of. I was absurdly relieved that it hadn't been a shark. I flew to Honolulu and fell ill during the trip. The second day I was there, still sick in bed, my mother came to visit. She was three months out of the hospital, and she'd just gotten the federal housing for which she had waited five years, a Section 8 apartment in Wahiawa, up the road from where the plantations used to be.

Scattering his ashes, we went to the spot where we thought he might have been surfing that afternoon, a week earlier. His stepmother and stepsister had come, and his two sisters and brother. My fiancé was there; and his girlfriend, Audrey; and his best friend. I didn't know where Paradise was; none of us did. The papers had called the spot "Populars," or Pops, which I always thought stood for Grandpop, because I knew older men on their longboards surfed there. I looked into the water and was comforted by the shade of blue that would receive him: what I like to think is a peculiarly Waikiki blue, a dense turquoise under which is the blue of the deep ocean rather than a sandy Caribbean floor.

I unpacked the box. His ashes snaked into the sea and flashed white for an instant and then were gone. The flowers that we tore off the leis and scattered in after him were all that was left.

Though a picture of me sitting on the edge of the boat, my toes just missing the ocean, shows a woman lost in her thoughts, a bit disheveled but not terrorized by grief, inside the only thing I could think to do was to throw myself in. I didn't want to die, or follow him to the afterworld; I just wanted to be in the ocean.

My father slipped under, my mother slipped out. Both left before I was ready for them to.

The offing is the part of the sea that is farthest from the shore but still visible. Spying a ship in the offing meant that it would dock soon; whatever that ship was bringing would soon be manifest. It is the space of potential, the cresting moment, what one looks for day after day standing on the shore. Should you miss something in the offing, you won't know how to prepare, for war, for gifts, for a homecoming or news.

Growing up with my mother, I learned to memorize the features of a landscape so as to be able to stay safe and find an exit when I needed to leave. That was thirty years ago. Still, when I was looking for her, I'd go down to the river, run home, try to recollect every detail of what had just happened: the stoned fights, the disorienting hiking trips. The damned mission was called the River of Life and my father died in Paradise. I still have little ability to discern the small, meaningful details. Daily objects, not yet analyzed, not yet made into part of the tale, have been so obscured by the dramatic that I have a hard time finding the thread as to why it all played out the way it did. This lack of talent for meaning-making happened partially because the need for my mother replaced my desire to make sense of things (it would change tomorrow, so why bother?), but also because of the forest-for-the-trees thing.

My mother's things are in storage, and I am dreading the day that I have to go through that mess. Packing up my father's belongings and sending them to myself in Germany was awful. Yet there is something in all of this about the storage of the self in the parent. The release—though release is too pleasurable a word for what it feels like—the ripping open and taking out the compartment that is you (I) happens when the parent dies. It feels like not having a skin, losing a parent. It is disorienting, and you don't know where to put your eyes.

At some point you have to take your eyes off them. It is better to do this while they are alive, so that when they die, they can go knowing that they raised you and that you grew up. My father knew that, and it lessened the pain of death that is the implacable pain of regret and things unspoken. I don't know why I think my mother knows this, but it is an instinct and I do.

I learned from my mother how to go with the flow, how to make a mango cheesecake, that children should not be overcoddled. How to make Kokee plum jam and swim out far, even when you're scared. I learned that you keep going until you don't anymore. But I also learned from my mother about the power of meaninglessness. I don't underestimate the pull of meaninglessness in a life. Though it seems somehow wrong here to elucidate what's broken—what's painful and confusing about being alive, when there is so much need for good in the world—loss is also our inheritance.

I think about what the last seven years have been like: losing my mother, then my father for good, writing a book about her, getting married and moving to Germany. The image that comes into my mind is of a river in the woods, a stream shallow and wide, the color of the tea they serve in Chinese restaurants. I can see the individual stones at the bottom. A stick is in the current and it is being carried fast downstream.

But my metaphors are getting screwed up here: am I talking about a river or the horizon? I always liked the image of the ship that comes from the sea and continues upstream.

It is useless to try to predict all the ways you might get hurt, but it is not useless to try to understand how you already were. What is a mother if not a home in the world? I once read that opiate addiction satisfies the need for mother-love—whatever receptors are bound up in the relationship between mother and child are satisfied in a similar way by junk. I feel sad that my mother didn't get what she needed, and I'm still angry that her lack became mine. But the wonderful thing about adulthood is realizing that we all are deficient, and after a certain point no one is accountable for that but ourselves.

My husband once asked me what I wanted to do in my writing. I said I was good at predicting what will happen. He asked me if that's all I wanted or thought was important, to be a fortune-teller. I don't. I don't know how it will all work now. Though my mother is still alive, though she still struggles, something has changed. The spell has been broken. And I'm trying to figure out what I'm supposed to do when I'm not on watch.

POISON PENS
Gayle Brandeis

A word after a word
after a word is power.
—From "Spelling" by Margaret Atwood

My mom wields a mighty pen. If she is upset about something—a moth in a sealed bag of pre-washed lettuce, say, or an evil president—she'll write a letter to complain. She has been doing this for as long as I can remember. She calls her missives "poison pen letters." And she often gets results.

A couple of decades before Michael Moore was able to get guns out of Kmart in his movie *Bowling for Columbine,* my mom did the same thing at our local Kmart in Evanston, Illinois. She was utterly appalled to discover on a visit to the new store that had opened in our town, that guns and ammunition were available to the general buying public. As soon as we got home, she whipped off letters to both the local Kmart store and the corporate offices. She also rallied the PTA troops at my elementary school. As chair of the safety council there, she had spearheaded a letter-writing campaign that inspired the city to install a No Turn On Red sign at a busy intersection used by students walking to and from school. She was able to summon up enough outrage among moms that Kmart had to listen. The manager invited the group to the store to discuss their concerns, and they ended up pulling weapons from their shelves.

When I was a girl, I would watch her sit down with her slender gold pen and an ivory piece of stationery, or a Bic pen and a legal pad, a look of sheer determination on her face. Sometimes she sent her letters directly from home; other times, she sent them to work with my dad so his secretary could type them up to make them look more professional. I just knew that when she sat down to write, she was angry and she was trying to do something about it.

I watched her write letters to doctors, to manufacturers, to senators and principals and relatives. Once, she wrote to a fancy French restaurant in Chicago to say that she was shocked when a cockroach ran across the table during an important business luncheon. It was an outrage, she wrote—one of the best, not to mention most expensive, restaurants in town, infested like that! The restaurant was deeply apologetic and offered her a free dinner for two, which she happily accepted. She was always glad to benefit from her poison pen. The power of words—they can even get you onion soup and *boeuf bourguignonne* and crepes Suzette!

My mom never took me by the hand and told me, "Gayle, writing can change things. Writing can right wrongs." She didn't have to. She modeled it beautifully. And from a young age, I tried to follow her lead. I wrote to Jimmy Carter to ask how I could stop pollution. A box came in the mail a couple of weeks later, filled with trash bags printed with Woodsy Owl—Give a Hoot! Don't Pollute!—along with pamphlets telling me how I could clean up my community. I hated cleaning my room, but I spent hours on the beach across the street from my apartment building, picking up cans and cigarette butts and strange flotsam that washed up on the Lake Michigan shore. I was excited knowing that my letter had been heard, that I could make a difference with both my words and my deeds. And I could get boxes in the mail if I wrote letters!

When I found a thumbnail-size pad of paper printed with green bubbles in my Cracker Jack box, I wrote "Thanks for the stationery" on one of the tiny sheets and put it in an envelope to send to the Cracker Jack headquarters. I wasn't expecting to receive anything in return, so it was a surprise when a big box arrived, filled with at least twenty boxes of Cracker Jack. I didn't know how they had found me—I hadn't put my name on the note—until my mom told me she put my name and return address on the envelope before she mailed it off.

My mom would sometimes send letters on my behalf. When I was about ten, she bundled up some of my poems and sent them to Golden Books, thinking they might publish them as picture books. Golden Books wrote a very lovely letter back, saying that my work wasn't quite right for them, but they admired my talent and encouraged me to keep writing. This was a huge affirmation for me as a young writer.

My mom actually continues to write letters on my behalf, to act as my unofficial publicist. I'll admit, there are times when this is embarrassing. I've balked when she's told me her plans to contact media outlets. I have a real publicist, I've told my mom. It would look unprofessional for newspapers and radio stations to receive glowing promotional letters from an author's mother. She is always stung by my rebukes. (And often ends up sending letters anyway. Her local paper printed a small item in the local gossip column that said something like "Proud mother Arlene Brandeis let us know that her daughter Gayle's second novel just came out from Ballantine, as part of a two-book deal!") Even with the occasional cringe factor, I am grateful for her support—and her letters have actually led to a few reviews and bookings!

My mom also continues to wield her pen in the name of justice. She helped legislate divorce reform after contacting Illinois Senator Carol Moseley Braun, and is currently on a mission to protect women travelers after a scary encounter in an Egyptian hotel. I am glad to have had her example throughout my life as proof that words can have true power in the world.

This is something I try to pass along to my daughter, as well. She sees me write novels and essays and poems and weekly action alerts for CODEPINK: Women for Peace, and I hope it helps show her that our voices are important, that our ideas and imaginations and passions and angers are worth recording, worth sharing with the world.

When Hannah was younger, she seemed to know this intuitively. She sang wherever we went, spontaneous—sometimes surreal—lyrics that trilled from her mouth like birdsong. She was happy to be heard, happy to trust her voice and where it wanted to take her. And I was happy to encourage her. She was a natural—at a singing camp, she hogged the microphone so much during the "Willie, the Whistling Giraffe" group number, they had to turn the mic off. She was bold and fearless, and people who weren't just her awed-and-biased mother called her gifted (and stubborn and strong-willed). When she was about six, she drew a poster at home with markers on a huge piece of cardboard for a concert she wanted to put on in our backyard. "Come See Hannah When She's Still Young!" the poster urged.

It breaks my heart to think we didn't have a video camera back then, that we couldn't have captured those unfettered, unselfconscious moments of self-expression. Hannah is thirteen now, and I'd love to be able to show her the freedom she felt, the pride she took, in her young voice. "Come see Hannah when she's still young," I'd tell her. She's still inside you.

When I used to hear about girls losing self-esteem, self-confidence, around the age of twelve, I was sure it didn't apply to Hannah. She was a force of nature. She wrote an eighty-page play when she was nine years old, and received an honorable mention for it in a national playwriting competition. Anything she set her mind to, I knew she could do. Her boldness was so refreshing, so inspiring to me. In sixth grade, though, I started to notice a difference in Hannah. She became more reserved, more shy. More concerned about what other people thought. Less likely to burst into song. I didn't think it would happen, but there it was.

I tried to draw out those old Hannah sparks when I saw them flare. And the sparks were definitely still there. Hannah is vegetarian, and was upset that there weren't more meatless options in her school lunchroom. She put together a petition that she circulated around the school during lunch and recess to ask for fresher, healthier cafeteria choices. I showed her where she could find some articles to bolster her position and she added them to her clipboard. I was so thrilled to see her drive and determination, her reignited belief that her voice could make a difference. She received over thirty signatures, including some from teachers and staff, before her own sixth-grade teacher found out about it and took her clipboard away. I told her I'd be happy to help her take her fight to the principal, to the school board even, but she didn't want to push it. She felt she had done what she could. I didn't want to push her, but I also wanted to make sure she knew she had the power to stand up and speak out, that that power would always be there, even when the sixth-grade teachers of the world try to take her clipboard away.

I had a difficult time when I was Hannah's age. We moved when I was thirteen, and I had trouble making friends, I was so painfully shy. I was ill for a year with what at the time was diagnosed as Crohn's disease, and then pretended to be ill for another year because I wasn't ready to be a real teenager in the world. My mom wrote lots of poison pen letters to my doctors because she didn't believe their claim that there was an emotional component to my illness. I could see how much passion she was pouring into those letters, and was strangely glad to give her a sense of purpose. In a perverse way, I may have extended my illness ruse because I wanted to honor her crusade.

I picked up my own pen during that time, as well. I wrote a column for the local chapter of the National Foundation for Ileitis and Colitis, and I created my own newsletter, *The Gastro-Intestinal Gazette,* filled with information and inspiration for coping with inflammatory bowel disease. Of course, there was something twisted about the whole enterprise, since I wasn't truly ill at that point. But I received letters from readers thanking me for my work, and even with all the weirdness, even with all the lying, I knew that my words could make a difference.

Though she would be mortified to know the role her poison pen letters played in extending my illness, my mom is happy to know how much her poison pen letters have inspired me to use my voice as a writer and activist over the years. I know Hannah has at times felt pressure from me when I've encouraged her to use her voice, when I've reminded her of her boldness as a young girl. She sometimes thinks that I'm putting too many expectations on her, that I'm wanting her to be something she's not anymore. I have been trying not to do this to her, trying to honor where she is, trying to encourage without expecting, trying to not let my own passion determine her path—it can be a tricky balance to walk, the line thin as ink.

Her confidence has ebbed and flowed, in quite dramatic arcs, in the year since the petition. To my delight, it seems the old Hannah has been breaking through more and more lately, like sunshine. I continue to be inspired by her singing, by her wild sense of humor, her subversive streak.

I still have a lot of shyness in me. My mom has taught me

to push through that shyness by using the written word. She's taught me that from the comfort of my own home, I can write letters and op-eds and stories that can change minds and hearts, even change policy. At the same time, my daughter has taught me to not push too hard, to remember my own limits and boundaries, to give her and myself space to grow and find our own way. To use my pen to try to make a difference, but also not to use it to inject the poison of my expectations into the people I care about the most.

And really, I don't like to think of my pen filled with poison. I like to think of it filled with something sweeter. A balm that has the potential to heal myself, as well as others. I want to wield it with honesty and compassion, with the determination I learned from my mother, the boldness I learned from my daughter. I want it to sing freely.

NOT THE DAUGHTER SHE HAD IN MIND
Ann Hood

Women know
The way to rear up children (to be just)
They know a simple, merry, tender knack
Of tying sashes, fitting baby shoes,
And stringing pretty words that make no sense,
And kissing full sense into empty words.
        —From *Aurora Leigh* by Elizabeth Barrett Browning

The daughter of my mother's dreams was a cheerleader. She jumped higher than anyone else. Her splits were perfect scissors. She cartwheeled straight into the arms of the handsomest football player around.

Instead, my mother got me.

As a small child, I fell all the time—up the stairs, down the stairs, over my own feet. When a pair of strong glasses stopped my falls, I suffered the humiliation of lenses as thick as Coke bottles and cat glasses in varying shades of gray and brown. I was clumsy, nerdy, bookish.

My mother had been the social committee chairman in high school, a popular girl with gaggles of friends. When she read my dark haikus about the ocean, and death and loneliness, she must have seen that our paths were different. But somehow she still had hope that I would become the daughter she'd imagined for herself.

When cheerleader tryouts were announced in ninth grade, I waited my turn in line behind girls doing backflips across the gym floor even though I'd been banned from ballet, thrown out of tap, embarrassed off the CYO girl's basketball team. To calm myself, I recited the words to "The Sounds of Silence," finding comfort in its poetry.

Even now, thirty years later, I blush when I remember my cloddish jumps, my off-key chanting, the way I kept one hand on my glasses to keep them from falling off. Yet I still raced to the list of new cheerleaders the next morning, as if my mother's desire could put my name there. My disappointment was only made worse by having to tell my mother that night, over what should have been a celebratory dinner, that I had let her down.

Although she did not make me feel her own disappointment, I knew it had to be there. Somehow, the daughter she'd ordered—the funny, popular one who could hit a softball out of a school-yard and cheer a team to victory—went to some other family, and I landed in ours. She could not feel my pride in reading all one hundred Nancy Drew books in a summer, or writing my own novel, thirty-two carefully handwritten pages.

"Go outside!" she'd admonish me, as I sat in my room reading or writing or listening to Simon and Garfunkel records. "They're playing kickball!" How could I explain that the ball's ferocious speed scared me? That I hated to run in front of a crowd of neigh-borhood kids? In front of anyone at all? Then my mother would do the most amazing thing—*she'd* go outside and join the game. She could ride a bike, kick a ball and pitch better than anyone I knew. My pride in her abilities only made my lack of them seem bigger.

After my cheerleading tryout debacle, I gave myself over to my own strengths. "How can you sit inside and read all the time?" my mother would ask, more puzzled than sad. I could only shrug. Reading and writing and staring into space, thinking, were my favorite activities. I was not the daughter of her dreams. I was the misfit daughter who preferred English to math while she actually liked doing math problems for fun; who eschewed matching outfits from bargain basement stores to vintage clothes that, as my mother said, "A stranger wore and threw away!"; who chose a life in New York City with an actor boyfriend, over "settling down" in our small hometown with a brand-new house full of coordinated furniture. "Aren't you ever going to settle down?" she'd ask me when I changed apartments or restlessly traveled around Europe. Even after I had published my first novel, she worried about me, wondering if I was going to ever get a real job.

This isn't to say my mother and I did not get along. She was the only mother I knew who would drive past a boy's house who had broken my heart, just to see the light on in his bedroom. She liked Simon and Garfunkel, too, and let me play their tapes constantly and loud. If I couldn't sleep, she'd get up and the two of us would sit in Dunkin' Donuts, sipping coffee and eating glazed donuts in the middle of the night.

Sadly, our small family of four suffered its share of loss, until it was just my mother and me left. Time had not diminished her hopes for a daughter who decorated her house with holiday knickknacks, or owned a sofa and chair that actually were made of the same fabric. But it had allowed her to watch how this daughter, the one she ended up with, saw the world as a lopsided, mismatched place filled with books and folk art and clothes that smelled vaguely of mothballs.

This is not to say that my mother understands me or my choices, nor that I understand hers. When my husband and I bought a two-hundred-year-old house, she shook her head in disbelief; she dreamed of shiny floors, a kitchen island, sliding glass doors. How did she end up with a daughter who loved old things? My mother likes to spend a day at the mall shopping, or playing the slot machines at the nearby casino; I like to stay inside knitting or reading, away from crowds and noise.

Long ago, perhaps in that junior high gym, I stopped trying to be that other daughter and simply became me. I'm not sure when—or even *if*—my mother let that other daughter go, but somehow we have found what is alike in us, to forge an unlikely friendship. I am stubborn and determined and opinionated and independent, just like my mother. If I wasn't, I would have tried to be what she wanted rather than who I was. I would be living unhappily in a suburb somewhere, a former cheerleader, with a colonial dining room and a closet full of matching handbags and shoes. But the traits I got from her allowed me to leave her dream behind and follow my own.

The other day, my mother called me. "I had the strangest dream," she said. "I dreamed *I* was married to Paul Simon." I couldn't believe what I was hearing. My mother did not know that for years, I had had dreams in which I was married to Paul Simon. "Wait a minute," I interrupted. "I've had the same dream." My mother wasn't at all surprised. "Like mother like daughter," she said.

She told me something else too. "I am so proud of you," she said. "Of your work, of your parenting skills, of the way you are living your life." I wonder if she saw in that moment how I jumped higher than anyone and cartwheeled across the floor, out of joy that I'd made her proud. Maybe she got the daughter she'd dreamed of after all.

FORGIVE ME
Elise Miller

A-tisket, a-tasket
A brown and yellow basket
I sent a letter to my mommy
On the way I dropped it

I dropped it, I dropped it
Yes on the way I dropped it
A little girlie picked it up
And put it in her pocket
   —Ella Fitzgerald

My mom and I stand at the railing, feeling the mist on our faces from Niagara Falls. It is the worst day of my life, the day I have had an abortion, in the year I am to graduate from college. I am pretty sure the father was a campus bartender I hooked up with in a hot tub one cold, rainy night, but it could have been the running back on the football team in his red race-car bed. The fact that I don't know for sure, the fact that I barely knew either of these guys, coupled with the cramp-inducing scraping of my insides, leaves me breathless with accountability a few days later. This is my rock bottom. I can see my responsibility in this pro-miscuous pregnancy through my years and tears of victimhood. Finally. It's like I've been hiding in a darkened closet all these years from a crazed killer, when all the time the killer was me. The first baby I conceived gave his or her life for me, for my enlighten-ment. I stand at the railing, dosed with Motrin, mortified.

As the falls roar below, the seed of a new awareness is planted in me as surely as that other seed has been uprooted. My mother loves me. She is there for me in my darkest hour, no matter what horrible names I have called her, no matter that she moved us halfway across the country when I begged her not to, no matter that she never gave me anything resembling a birds-and-bees lecture. In another ten years I'll realize I never would have listened anyway.

Just last night on the phone with my mom, she warned me, "Don't talk to any strangers," when I told her I was on my way to the subway. I'm thirty-seven years old. When I was little she preferred me to play inside, lest a homicidal psychopath be waiting among the old oaks in our yard in the tony Philadelphia suburb where I spent my prepubescent years. And so I stayed indoors where my mother snored peacefully, a Stephen King novel fanned across her bosom, while my father chased me around the house with his belt, screaming, "The more you run, the harder it's going to hurt!"

The afternoon we found my mom sobbing in the family room closet was my first clue that divorce was coming, like a long-awaited houseguest. I was nine. One of my older sisters, from my mom's first marriage, had been in a car accident. She had a concussion and was in a coma. When my parents visited her in the hospital, my dad yelled at my mom for asking the doctor what he thought was a stupid question. With my mom a wreck and my dad worried about appearances, it was the wake-up call we'd all been waiting for. Finally, says my mom, she knew without a doubt or a justification that she had to leave my dad. She took to the closet, in preparation, maybe. My sister sacrificed her skull, in a way, for my mom's salvation.

As a teenager, my mother was still afraid of my demise. She would drive me to every rock concert I asked her to buy tickets for, because God forbid I take public transportation and wind up crushed under a pile of crumpled steel or dismembered in a

Dumpster by a knife-wielding stranger, which led, in a way, to my first orgasm at fifteen with the lead singer of a British new wave band. When I told her on the pay phone in the concert hall that I'd be heading with the band back to their hotel, my mom said, "Elise, are you sure it's really them?" As if my safety depended on this peroxided bunch of leather-clad twentysomethings being the genuine article, as if that would make them safe, familiar friends of the family. (They really were the band, by the way.)

And when it came to drugs, she shared her boyfriend's pot with me, because God forbid I buy it from an outside source who would undoubtedly cut it with strychnine. "I'd rather you smoked Jim's marijuana than get it from some stranger. At least this way you know it's safe." But Jim didn't have acid or cocaine, and so I got those from an outside source. And meanwhile, it turns out, my mom didn't really know where Jim got his stash. I asked.

My friends told me in high school, "Your mom is so cool," while I hurled I-hate-yous at her like they were frozen pudding pops and she caught them all without a fight.

"How can you let me talk to you that way?" I'd ask her after I told her to go fuck herself.

"Honey, if my ego depended on you, I'd be dead by now," she'd say, and I'd marvel at her stamina while I raged that nothing I said to her seemed to make a difference. When I lost my virginity at thirteen, I couldn't wait to share the news with her and gauge her reaction. I remember it still. "Oh, honey," she said, slumping her shoulders, as if I'd confessed to getting a D in algebra. She was disappointed, not devastated.

Now that I'm a mom myself, I see some strength in her ability to separate her ego from my bad behavior, which is not to say that I will allow my kids to get away with disrespecting themselves or others. But when my son acts out (he's three) I look back and don't know how my mom didn't take it personally just *once*. And when I was fourteen, having sex and smoking pot, I yearned for consequences like my friends got, like the Cosby kids got when they broke the rules. I knew, even if I couldn't articulate it, that discipline equaled love, and I felt like I was the only teenager who begged her mother to ground her. *Pass me that doobie, woman, and oh, by the way, would you mind disciplining me?*

When I was young, my mom was the angel and my dad was the devil. The angel kissed my toes and sat with me on her lap for long stretches while we wept through "Lady Sings the Blues" or "Imitation of Life" into the wee hours on the wood-paneled Zenith in the red-painted family room where that closet beckoned her. And when she finally wised up to the devil's furious ways after nine years of marriage, she went and sat on the floor in the dark, remembering to close the door behind her.

How did my mom marry a man who hit his children? I tell myself that things were different then. I tell myself that she was hurting, that she made mistakes and was doing the best she could. I tell myself that self-help sections in bookstores didn't yet exist. That you became a teacher, a secretary, a nurse or dental hygienist and you married a Jewish doctor or lawyer and you didn't question any of it. And I reach a point where I forgive her. And I do the whole thing over with my father. I tell myself that my father never got the love he craved from his own parents and he became a doctor for his mother but not for himself and that made him miserable and take it out on us because he didn't know any other way. And I forgive him, too. How could they have acted any differently? They used the tools they were given. Sometimes I believe my forgiveness, and sometimes I think I'm full of shit, because forgiveness isn't finite. I can be forgiving one day, have a bad night's sleep and unforgive the next morning.

I was the only kid I knew who jumped for joy when I got the news that my parents were divorcing. I skipped into her bedroom one sunny afternoon, light on my feet for not having to look over my shoulder every time I so much as sneezed, and found my mom lying across her bed, crying.

"What's wrong?" I asked, wondering if my dad had returned with his belt.

"I miss him," she sobbed, tears and spit ruining her good looks.

"Why? He's a jerk," I said, because this was as obvious a fact as the dirty white shag carpet under my cowboy boots. Why would my mom miss a jerk?

But she did. She missed the jerk so much that she replaced him with a newer model. Soon after my parents split, my mom fell in lust with a younger man, and drove us in her silver Nova from the Main Line to inner-city Chicago on the cusp of my puberty. With the Sold sign staked in our front yard, I gripped her ankles while she dragged me around the kitchen, begging her not to move us and telling her that Jim was no good. She said, "The more you say that, Elise, the longer it's going to take me to find out for myself," and lit another cigarette on the stove.

So we moved to Chicago and I morphed from a Chinese jack playing, chino-wearing suburbanite into a chronically furious, slutty teenager trailing a cloud of my mom's boyfriend's pot smoke behind me like a ragged wedding train. This new guy, Jim, while he didn't chase me around the apartment with his belt, was no better than my dad. He drank all the time, and fancied himself the fifth Beatle, endlessly pounding "When I'm Sixty-four" on our out-of-tune baby grand piano that had fit so nicely back in our big house on the Main Line. And he made fun of me. Of my *hips*.

Even though I thought my mom was crazy for being attracted to my dad and Jim, I still learned all the wrong lessons and followed suit with jerks of my own. I didn't need car wrecks or killer strangers to ruin me. I did it all by myself. The shittier a guy treated me, the harder I fell. And guys who treated me like shit filled my adolescence like a baby grand piano in a two-bedroom apartment. I lost my virginity as if it were a standard requirement for teenagers everywhere. I was in such a hurry. There was no pleasure, only the feeling of relief when it was over, as if I'd accomplished something mandatory, like a PSAT.

So after my abortion and my Niagara Falls revelation of personal responsibility, I entered therapy, healed some and met my loving husband, a "keeper," as my mother likes to call him.

But I still loathed my mom.

And then I had kids.

My son was born in 2004, and two short years later, my daughter. Now I talk to my mom weekly without wanting to strangle her more than twice during our conversations, and I even ask her for advice. Just the other day I called her and asked her what she taught me, because I thought maybe she'd remember something I hadn't. After a sigh, she offered this: "To get up every morning and go to work. Or school. To be responsible for your homework. To make your bed, which you never did then but you do now. Oh, honey, your apartment is adorable."

"Thanks, Mom."

"But I think kids learn more by example than by lecture or anything else." This time I sighed, and then she said, "I taught you to marry a keeper by not doing it myself!" And she laughed. And I did, too.

So my mom taught me to marry a keeper. And to laugh at

myself. And if I couldn't laugh as a stay-at-home mom of two kids still in diapers, I'd be in the coat closet sobbing just like she was all those years ago.

Mostly what my mother tells me is that I'm wasting valuable time and energy worrying my motherly worries because I'm there for my children emotionally and physically. I provide a safe, loving environment, I have a supportive, loving, involved husband, and it will all turn out okay in the end. It already is okay. I already have it all.

All those years I raged at her for not worrying about me more have folded inside out, finding me seeking her wisdom on how to worry less. If my son has cereal for breakfast, lunch and dinner, for example, as long as it's not an everyday occurrence, no harm will be done.

Maybe ironically, she admonishes me to make sure I'm paying attention to my marriage, that it's okay to not want sex for a stretch, but that I should try to at least hold my husband's hand on a regular basis. She knows she screwed up regarding men, but she knows a good thing when she sees it. And I listen to her.

My daughter is ten months old and for now, she clearly worships me. Still, I am already starting to feel the force of her female powers in betrayed looks and lusty wails that make her older brother's cries seem tepid by comparison. As I look into the depths of my little girl's big brown eyes, I wonder how my mother survived my metal-mouthed onslaught of hostility. She says she was my doormat, because she felt guilty for marrying a man who treated me badly. I had enough to deal with, so she willingly became my punching bag. But if my kids are to be anything like me and I am anything like my mom, how will I ever bear my children's inevitable disdain? But then my good husband reassures me that I am not my mother. (Or my father.) And then he swears that he never hated his mom, not even when he was fourteen. This is what I tell myself during insomniac moments. Because our kids have his genes, too. Like a Buddhist chant I repeat this to myself.

But since I walked the slutty walk, I am hell-bent on imparting my experiential wisdom to my daughter. There are some things worth worrying about. I guess I am not my mother after all.

I want to teach my daughter that she is worth spending time with, whether it's sitting together in the living room playing Boggle or traveling the world, so that she doesn't ever feel desperate for attention and validation. I want to teach her that self-respect is more valuable than any friend or any boy, and that she'll survive standing alone if respecting herself means saying no at the risk of losing jerks who would pretend to be her friends. I want her to take responsibility for her actions and for her happiness, and to never hold anyone else accountable for her choices, since doing so would make her a victim like I used to be. But I also want to teach her to forgive herself when she screws up, which she will. And then I will work to forgive myself, because I very well may feel that her mistakes are all my fault. I want her to question the monsters in her head, but to know that it's okay to hide out for a little while when life feels overwhelming, but hopefully not on the floor of a darkened closet.

What my mother did not teach me lays the foundation for what I want to teach my daughter, and I hope and pray that I can be a living demonstration for her. Of course as a mother of two, I can tell you that being a shining example of anything worthy of emulation is sometimes impossible. I'm more like a greasy example of dirty-haired, irritable exhaustion. But my good husband and I, we've been together for sixteen years. I feel safe and loved and free to be myself.

And he loves my hips.

VINNIE AND INKY AND MARGARET AND ME
Ayun Halliday

"But Vinnie! How will these folks know it's my period?"
"Good question—and as usual, I've got an answer:
send 'em a It's My Period Postcard on the next page!"
—*Vinnie's Giant Roller Coaster Period Chart & Journal
Sticker Book*

The big, red-themed, women-only party I'm planning to throw upon my daughter's entry into the wonderful world of menstruation is feeling less and less abstract with every passing day. Better lay in some balloons. The whole puberty thing appears to be barreling toward us much faster than I'd anticipated. The operatic mood swings, the unmistakable curve of her budding rack…whether attributable to the antiseizure meds she's been on for the last five years or some gnarly hormone in her public school's low-budget milk, I can't say. Once upon a time, it seemed safe to assume she was biologically programmed to follow the same schedule I'd been on, and when I was her age, I was a no-nothing little pancake, anxiously paging through *Are You There God? It's Me, Margaret,* whenever the clandestine copy that circulated around my fifth-grade classroom found its way into my hands. Actually, I think I was in sixth grade, but there's no forgetting the furious, panicky shame that I, too, would be subject to the messy, bloody, between-the-legs situation that allegedly happened to all girls sooner or later.

It wasn't that I feared growing up. My fantasy life seethed with boys, antiperspirant and sex. I observed my teenage neighbor, sitting at her feet as she filled out the scorecard she used to chart the peaks and valleys of the Top 40. I loved my dollhouse and the teddy bears I'd had since infancy, but I understood that I'd be leaving them for something better. I might have even been open to the idea of getting my period, if I could have been assured that my mother would never, ever get wind of it. The mothers in Margaret's world seemed less reserved than my own. They kept pace with their menstrual-obsessed daughters, pelting them with questions, informational pamphlets and the universally popular but implausibly named Teenage Softies. From a supply-side stand-point, I could see the necessity of the maternal purse and car, but I would have rolled my own sanitary napkins out of paper towels and dead leaves before I'd have brought the subject up. Anytime a program Mom and I were watching together was interrupted by a commercial for Kotex or Modess, I quietly took leave of my body. It's sort of funny that I never ran into her out there on the astral plane. The evidence seems to indicate that she, too, was unwilling to stand and be counted when the conversation unexpectedly headed south. I got a queasy feeling when I imagined what life would be like should my mother take a mind to start behaving like the mothers in *Are You There God? It's Me, Margaret*. Fortunately, she seemed more likely to put her hairdo underwater, change her own oil or wrestle alligators before she'd barge into any bathroom where I, her only child, might be trapped on the toilet, a prisoner to bloodstained undies.

Everything I knew about menstruation, I owed to Judy Blume, a *Redbook* article I found by accident, and friends with better lines of communication than the ones available to me. I'll never forget the shock I experienced as a passenger in a crowded station wagon in which menstruation was being loudly and casually discussed. I barely knew these people! Susan was my classmate, but it wasn't like we were friends. Her mom was dropping me off after our one and only playdate, before continuing to the mall with Susan and her teenage sisters. The candid way those older girls discussed their periods. It was like they'd forgotten their mother was sitting right there at the wheel. Mrs. Wolf didn't bat an eye. In fact, she joined right in, to double-check that Susan and I understood that getting your period meant you were also capable of getting pregnant.

"Really?" Susan asked, wide-eyed and unabashed. It was totally bizarre. Also informative and thrilling. Then we pulled up in front of my home planet and I got out.

There are many areas where my upbringing lacked for nothing. My mother cooked wonderful meals I failed to appreciate, laundered clothes I could have laundered myself and provided round-trip chauffer service to all sorts of lessons, rehearsals and social engagements. In hindsight, I'd trade the laundry and the rides for a box of sanitary napkins discreetly added to the footlocker I took to camp the summer I was fourteen. I dreaded the pamphlets that had started showing up on all my friends' pillows, but my mother must have marked our door, because the pamphlet fairy knew to give our address a miss. With no pamphlet, there was no conversational opening, not that I would have been the first to speak. At the time, it was a relief. I thought I was getting away with something. I was too green to realize that my mother was bagging out by allowing her embarrassment to trump mine.

When I finally got around to doing what Margaret and all her friends had been so excited to do, I was resourceful enough to hack it on my own, sort of. I mean, when you come right down to it, commercial feminine hygiene is really nothing more than a souped-up version of paper towels and toilet paper wound many times around. I've heard of cultures where the ladies make do with moss. Sounds kind of comfy, actually. So does any tribal initiation that doesn't involve cutting. Ululating, for instance. Special big-girl necklaces. That kind of thing.

It's this kind of wishful thinking that caused me to snap up a copy of *Vinnie the Tampon King's Giant Rollercoaster Period Chart and Journal Sticker Book* a few years back. It's not for me. It's for Inky. She was only six-and-a-half at the time, but I didn't want to take the chance that this heartwarming volume might go out of print before her uterus can start shedding its lining on a monthly basis. We've got all sorts of changing bodies/where do babies come from type literature lying around where anybody, including the children's friends, can get hold of it, but this one I stashed. It was purchased as a special present, the one Mommy plans to give her at that big, red party. (I already have the perfect dress.) I had to hide it good, as Inky was going through a sticker-freak phase and had a very keen nose for pressure-sensitive, adhesive-backing. Not that it wouldn't have filled me with pleasure to see my little girl's bunk bed plastered with tiny caricatures of a man who dedicated his book to "all those menstruators out there—past, present and future." I just want to save them until they can be applied toward their intended purpose, as place markers on the numbered roller-coaster tracks Vinnie has thoughtfully provided for readers to keep track of their cycles. Can you tell how much I love this book? It comes with a bright red, zippered Tampon Case, labeled as such, with a prominently placed box in which the owner can write her name. Plus, it's got cramp-comforting recipes, a resource page, and pullout postcards ("Greetings from the PMS Ranch"). It's not mine to keep, but you bet I'll be giving myself something by giving my daughter an exuberant, self-loving alternative to the unhelpful attitudes of those who would have her treat this normal function of her healthy female body as something unspeakable, a reality best kept under wraps.

Ever since acquiring this wonderful present, I've been pre-occupied about what will happen if I go down in a plane or get hit by a taxi before I get the chance to give it to her. I've given her father explicit instructions as to where he can locate it in the event of an emergency. Just to be on the safe side, I've also drilled these coordinates into his best friend, Sean, should Greg be too grief-stricken, skeeved out or absent-minded to remember. Maybe I should also tell a few of my women friends. It's on top of the wooden cabinet above the metal filing cabinets, right under the ceiling, between the bins labeled Taxes and Family Videos, on top of the *Femmenstruation Rites Rag,* a Xeroxed zine covering a whole host of related topics, from Sex While Bleeding and Anne Frank's Blood Diary to Mood Lodges and homey monthly rituals. If memory serves, the *Rites Rag* is where I got the idea for the multigenerational, red-themed, first-period party, an event I've been contemplating since Bill Clinton was president.

Speaking of things showing their age, with less than a week until my forty-third birthday, I'm wondering how many tattered eggs I've got hanging around the old nest. It's possible Inky's skinny, young bod will hold its fire until mine has run its course. I believe the technical designation for a woman past the age of menstruation is "crone," a term I find difficult to embrace, even if it does signal an end to birth control and hopefully, monthly break-outs. I wonder if there's a way a last-period party could be combined with a first-period party without it seeming too much like a coffin at a christening. Emily Post isn't going out of her way to offer much in the way of assistance here. Party-wise, I don't need to be on the receiving end of one so much as I need to throw one.

I wish there had been proselytizing, self-crowned Tampon Kings when I was growing up, that *Are You There God? It's Me, Margaret* wasn't something I read crouched in the narrow space between the wall and my bed. If I could do it over again, I'd be less furtive, less inhibited and more like Inky. Not only is she compassionate, affectionate, beautiful and smart, she's got waist-length hair and a built-in distaste for traditional gender roles enforced too strictly. Which is not the same as saying she'd want boys at her Period Party. All due respect to Vinnie, but give Mama credit for having *some* sense. My sweet, funny daughter is all the excuse I need to finish knocking down some walls I once willingly reinforced, unaware that hemming things in is a high price to pay for keeping things at bay. I hope one day in the near future Inky will consider honoring me with one of the *Period Chart's* wallet-size Official Co-Rider cards. They were designed to be handed out to sympathetic friends and family members, folks a girl can count on to have her back and be nice to her when she's having her period, possibly even because she's having her period. I would keep it with me at all times, tucked between her school picture and my driver's license. I would carry it discreetly. I would carry it with pride.

A WELL-EARNED SOAK
Catherine Crawford

I'm in the tub, for God's sake, Mother.
I'll just be a minute, for goodness' sake.
Pull the shower curtain.
—From *Franny and Zooey* by J. D. Salinger

I have a tiny scar on my left foot. Until recently, when I've looked at this one-inch streak I've thought about how it got there and would focus mostly on my brother Timmy. Specifically, I'd think about my father's wrath when Timmy failed to report the broken window.

Here's what happened: I had been innocently dancing and singing in the shower, playing ring-around-the-rosey over a big blue bucket with my mother, my older sister, Margie, and my little brother, Billy, when suddenly my foot split open on something sharp. The clear shower water suddenly shaded pink.

It was a summer evening during the infamous California drought of the late seventies, and we had to bathe using a bucket of water. Timmy had been playing baseball in the backyard earlier in the day and accidentally misfired his ball toward the shower window. Poor Timmy was in deep because not only did he shatter the window without 'fessing up, but he did a shoddy job of clearing the broken glass. Timmy, like the rest of us, was pretty small and he was terrible at baseball. Neither of these attributes could have been very easy for a twelve-year-old boy in the suburbs to take.

Now that I have two daughters, I am vigorously reanalyzing all of my childhood memories. When I'm putting on my socks in the morning, my mind often begins to reel. I begin to see my mother in the shower with her own two daughters (ages eight and ten) and another little baby boy, Billy, my only younger sibling. She didn't shower with us very often, but on certain warm summer nights she made exceptions. Did she enjoy herself, splashing and singing with us, watching us dunk limbs in the bucket of water that was supposed to be saved for the lawn, or was this the only way that she could actually get clean without an interruption from us? Or both?

These days, I'd be tempted to trade a kidney for a long, hot bath. However, if I can convince my nine-month-old daughter, Daphne, to hang out with her dad and chew on toys, I have no choice but to leave the door open for my more mobile, three-year-old, Oona. She's a "big help," insisting on washing my hair for me, and pleading with me not to cry if I get water in my eyes—something I've found impossible to avoid when a little kid takes a soaking towel and tags you in the face with it. It's never relaxing and the bathroom is always trashed, but I do get clean.

I come from a family of thirteen children. There are nine boys and four girls. My father, out of necessity I guess, ruled like a dictator, an Irish Catholic Mussolini with a hidden heart. Although he tried to keep emotions to a minimum around the house (as do most old-school, Irish Catholic fathers, dictatorial or not), he couldn't control my mother's outspoken glee that she had daughters. "I love all of my children, of course, but I am just so thankful to have my girls"—we must have heard that once a week. It was such a familiar mantra that sometimes I'd feel sorry for my brothers. Then they'd do something like hold me down and let the dog slobber all over my face and all sympathy disappeared. All things considered, Dad did a good job. We all felt loved, but never really felt the need to express it.

Still, one of the perks to being a cherished daughter was open access to our mother in the bathroom. Of the sixteen wakeful hours of her day, my mother spent fifteen and a quarter of them working hard, but almost every night after dinner she took a well-earned, forty-five-minute bath. And every night after dinner, Margie and I (sisters Patsy and Tina were already grown and out of the house) would congregate around her in the tub. We wouldn't get in, but we'd sprawl out on the bathroom floor and chat. If the conversation ever veered in an uncomfortable direction, usually dangerously close to exposing one of my many lies ("No, Mom. I think it *would be* fun to jump off the roof." "I didn't do it. Did Mrs. Sibley say she saw me?" "No. Phone's ringing. I'll go get it.") or my own saucy slip of the tongue, I could simply run out—Mom was submerged and immobile. This rarely happened though, because we cherished and protected this time. I was, admittedly, a sassy kid ("the only one that ever gave me any trouble" is another of my mother's familiar sayings), but somehow, usually, I managed to behave during Mom's baths, instinctively knowing these moments were special. If I had any talent with a pencil and could draw, I am confident I could do exact renderings of my mother's body from 1976 to 1984.

Now, I'm in the tub and Oona can't resist keeping me company. Thankfully, she has recognized that her oft-proclaimed love of a cold bath does not jive with my *need* of a hot one; she wants no part of my preferred temperature and stays out of my bath. It took a little back and forth: "Your mother lives in mortal fear of a cold bath." "Mommy, what's mortal fear?" Nonetheless, we got there. Oona is still a bit young to control most of her impulses, but I can already see that she treasures our bath time. Just like my mother was, I am immobile in the tub; there's no escape. She wants to wash me, and although she doesn't know it, if she's anything like me, her impressions of my arms, breasts, tummy, knees, will play in an endless, Proustian loop in her memory.

I can still see my mother perfectly, lying in the tub with one washcloth under her head and the other spread out over her nether-regions. She was willing to share anything with us, yet still she maintained decorum (one of the few things that hasn't made it into my new role). Her eyes are closed and she's laughing. I like to think that her laughter is the result of one of my quips, but now that I've experienced things from her point of view, this well-remembered bathtub demeanor may have had simply been Mom assessing the wonderful absurdity of her situation.

We are in the "big bathroom." Though it was smaller in square footage than the "orange" bathroom that I shared with about eight siblings, I was told the "big" referred to Mom and Dad. And actually, it *was* quite big, California big—especially compared to my current Brooklyn bathroom's cramped quarters. There is a bang on the door: "Dorothy! Hurry up. The water is getting cold." I know my parents made many sacrifices raising thirteen kids, but the thought that they shared even their bathwater seems a little excessive, and I had to verify this memory with my sister Margie. *True*. Maybe it was all in honor of the drought, or maybe they knew that the poor, battered water heater had at least six more customers that evening, or maybe it was just to save money on the heating bill. Money was always tight. (It was a lack of funds to pay for a proper chimney sweep that prompted one of the oldest brothers to put Margie on a specially constructed wooden swing and lower her down the chimney: "And I got paid a buck," Margie reminded me when I asked for verification.)

Lately during our tub time, unbeknownst to Oona, I've been giving a few pop quizzes. With Daphne in the mix now, I feel like I'm missing many of the little milestones I used to obsess over. Not long ago, when Oona "read" *Harold and the Purple Crayon* to me (almost verbatim) I began to cry and had to hide my tears. I hadn't realized she'd ever seen the book. I've discovered that while she's deeply intent on "really, really cleaning my toes," I can grill her about what she does all day at preschool. I am reminded of my mom propping a couple of dry sponges on her belly as a safe place to rest my spelling list while she waited for me to formulate my answer. Perhaps she did work a full sixteen hours a day— if your definition of work includes preparing us for spelling tests, listening to book reports or going over the multiplication (and later periodic) tables.

There were those times when Mom was allowed to be alone in the bath. She usually read. Of course, when she came out, Margie and I (and maybe another sibling) were often in her bed. It was the only one with an electric blanket, after all. Also, the sheets always smelled *so good.* Anyway, I'll never forget when she emerged after having read Judy Blume's *Are You There God? It's Me, Margaret* (to our utter amazement, *in one soak*). About a week earlier, my mother had come across the book in a bookstore. God! An eleven-year-old narrator named Margaret! *Her Margaret* was eleven. Perfect! My sister Margie devoured the book and promised I could read it next. Since Margie seemed to love the book so much, Mom just wanted to have a quick look first. Coming from the bathroom that night she was clad, as usual, in one of her impossibly comfortable-looking thick cotton nightgowns, the Jergens cold cream still slick on her face. She was emanating, however, not the usual after-bath calm we were used to. My poor mother was still processing the fact that she'd just introduced *her Margaret* to sex. In our house, this wasn't supposed to happen for another ten years. Minimum. After that, she had no choice but to have *the talk*. Margie's recollection of the talk is almost funnier than the events leading up to it: "So, if you want to imagine sex, just imagine a big thing that kind of comes into you. It doesn't feel that good." I'm sure this was just a strategy to keep Margie chaste for as long as possible. Oh, and very soon after this event I got the book from the library.

On my last visit to my parents in Portland, Oregon, where they retired when I was a freshman in college, I made the sad realization that my mother's bathroom door is no longer open to me. A combination of bad knees, a newfangled bathtub that's "too deep," and a shift in Mom's time management (with no kids in the house, she'd rather be tinkering on eBay than wasting time in the tub) has brought about a preference for showers. I haven't seen my mother naked in over a decade. I always assumed that I knew what she looks like, but if I really think about it, I see the body of a forty-year-old, not a septuagenarian. Is it Mom's feelings about me, her attitude toward her own body, or just our new "woman to woman" relationship that has brought about her modesty? Examining these questions, I realize that even my mom (my mom?) has body image issues.

As a kid, it seemed that my parents operated in an orbit outside everyone else I knew. We ate stew (about once a week), we never, ever, ever were allowed sugar substitutes—"goddamned phoney balonies have no idea what they are ingesting!"—and on every special occasion we had bacon and eggs for breakfast (still do). When, at the age of ten, I asked if I could go on a diet, I got a "what the hell for?" and an extra large helping of dessert that night. My parents were naturally slim, not skinny. They were robust. They ate asparagus with dinner and ice cream after.

Now, as a thirty-five-year-old, I think about my mother at that age and new memories emerge. I remember going shopping for bathing suits before our annual summer trip to Los Angeles to stay with my mom's only brother, Uncle Jerry. (By the way, Uncle Jerry's place served as a shrine to the dominant culture my father disdained—cola, a swimming pool, hulking bags of popcorn, medicine.) It's really the only time I can remember Mom spending any time in front of the mirror (except the ten minutes she stole to "put her face on" before work or church). She would ask us, over and over, what we thought of her "big bottom" and point out how veiny her legs were. Margie and I were so comfortable with her body that we never saw a flaw. "It looks great!" her little judges always said.

It's possible that the day I saw Oona walk for the first time was the same day I saw her primp in front of the mirror, looking over her shoulder for the back view, then turning to the side. An eleven-month-old can't possibly know if her Huggies look good or not, so I can only blame myself (and my husband, thank you very much) for Oona's habit of rigorous self-examination. It makes me shudder to think how easy these habits are instilled. I fear that soon she'll add self-criticism to her routine, and I try to keep myself in check.

Right now, Oona seems to love me so completely and un-conditionally that I'm never self-conscious in her presence, but I do wonder how she'll see things later in life. Will she turn to her memories of me for understanding her own bodily imperfections? I have a large scar right below the bikini line from a couple of C-sections. After the second operation, one of the sutures opened and I developed an infection, giving me a "flourish" of extra scar tissue on the left side. Oona loves to point at my "boo-boo" and discuss the nurses that used to come each day to put a bandage on it. (That was after they thoroughly flushed out the open wound, but, thankfully, she doesn't talk about that. It still makes me cringe.) I'm not yet comfortable exposing this scar to my husband, but I'll let Oona inspect it to her heart's content. She'll even rub her stubby little fingers on its raised surface and ask me if it hurts. She hasn't inquired how I got the "boo-boo" yet, but I think I'd better compose an answer soon, as not much goes without interrogation lately. I'm conflicted: is the concept of scars, childbirth and daily visits from a nurse such a good topic for a precocious little girl?

Maybe my mother's openness during her bath was her own method of easing us into womanhood. As I mentioned, we were a large, Catholic family, and with that came a sizable, daily serving of repression. There was little talk of such unsavory things as needs, feelings and, above all, sex. I can remember when Stanley Kubrick's film *The Shining* aired on television; it was only during a scene with a naked woman that all children were forced to leave the room. Images of blood-filled corridors and hacked up seven-year-olds were fine, but nudity was verboten.

Although we never talked about it, Mom's body was on prominent display while she bathed, so we knew what lay in store for us. Right now, I can't comfortably keep Oona out of the room while I take a bath—having a three-year-old beat on the door while lying in the tub takes all of the magic out of a good soak. But even when I can reason with her, I hope I'll keep my door unlocked.

THIS IS WHAT MATTERS
Ellen Sussman

*You sing in my mind like wine. What you
did not dare in your life you dare in mine.*
 —From "My Mother's Body" by Marge Piercy

"You don't need to speak Yiddish. You're a Yankee," my mother told me, then turned to her brother, and said something in rapid-fire Yiddish that sent him into gales of laughter. My father shook his head and shouted more Yiddish words and everyone roared. I sat in my seat at the dish-cluttered Formica table, amidst my boisterous relatives, caught in a whirlwind of words, none of which I could understand.

Every Sunday, all of my mother's relatives would drive down from the Bronx to our house in Trenton, bringing carloads of food from Aunt Selma's store (Aunt Selma was a butcher who once appeared on *What's My Line?* to the delight of all of us), and we'd sit around the too-small table in our too-small kitchen to feast and gab. We ate blintzes and smoked sturgeon, bagels and lox and herring and whitefish salad. All of my relatives spoke Yiddish, and though I suspected that most of them could switch to English— the heavily accented, grammatically convoluted version—they told their stories in the language of their homeland. I feasted, I listened, I yearned to understand. But my mother would remind me, again and again, *"You're a Yankee. You don't need to speak Yiddish."*

My mother was officially a Yankee, too, having been born in the United States, only months after her parents and five brothers and sisters journeyed from Russia to New York. (I never learned

the whole story of their journey—it, like the language they spoke, was not meant for me. *"It's the past, it's over,"* my mother would say. I know my family fled the terrible pogroms near Kiev, but once, when Aunt Rose tried to tell me what she saw from her hiding place in a barn, my mother shushed her. *"It's over, Rosie. We're here now."*) When the family first arrived in New York, they moved into a Jewish ghetto in the Bronx, and my mother didn't learn English until she started school at age five. English wasn't needed in her immigrant neighborhood; all the store owners were from the Old Country, the family friends were landsmen, and the children she played with spoke the language of their parents.

Why couldn't I speak the language of *my* parents? Maybe it's because my mother wanted a different life for me than she'd had. My mother wanted me to have everything she didn't have. It's a common immigrant story—and my parents played out the rags-to-riches scenario well. Neither of them went to college; neither had the money for such a luxury. My father used to say, with great pride, that he went to the School of Hard Knocks. He started a successful bus company, and as I grew up, I remember the arrival one day of a brand-new sky-blue Cadillac, and later a mink coat for Mom. Then came the announcement that we had joined the Jewish country club.

There were no books in my house. I don't remember my parents ever reading. The TV was always on—my mother didn't like quiet. For family outings we went to sporting events in Philly. I don't remember ever going to a museum or to the symphony. Once a year, we got on a bus or train and went into New York City to see a Broadway show, usually a musical. For our family vacations we either went to the Catskills or to Miami. I remember the year we finally took a plane to Florida, instead of setting out for the three-day drive to get there.

Until I was twelve, all of my friends were Jewish. In those days, in Trenton, the Jews primarily lived in one of two modest neighborhoods, and we lived in the one called Hilltonia. We kids—there were dozens of kids in the neighborhood, all of whom seemed to be the same ages as my brother and me—walked to school together and carpooled to Sunday school and Hebrew school together. We played sports together on weekends— baseball, basketball, touch football, sledding in Cadwalder Park in winter. But after the 1968 racial riots in Trenton, most of our friends left the battered Trenton public school system. My brother and I headed to Princeton Day School, our first venture to a foreign land.

I remember my first dinner at a friend's house. The father was a well-known editor at a publishing company in New York. They ate dinner in the dining room, something we only did for the seder at Passover. They rang a bell for the maid to bring the meal, to clear the dishes. And most astonishingly, they discussed books, politics, world events, while eating their roast lamb and baked potatoes. Later that night, I sneaked into their library and gazed at walls of bookshelves, miles of books, and I remember feeling my first stirrings of anger at my parents, a sentiment so unfair, so cruel, given all that they had done for me. But they hadn't done this!

And so I vowed to have a cultured life, a sophisticated life. And yet, while creating that life for my daughters, a world of books and museums and world travel, I would often wonder along the way, what am I giving them that my mother never gave me? What did my mother give me that I'm failing to give them?

"What languages do they speak, Mommy?" my daughter would ask before guests arrived for dinner. I was married now, and my international businessman husband and I had moved to Paris with

our one-year-old daughter. Five months later, our second daughter was born in a French hospital. For five years, we raised them bilingually, multiculturally, with weekend trips to museums and dinner parties with friends from all over the world. My daughters were certainly no Yankees. They were international children. They spent mornings in the children's art atelier at the Centre Pompidou, they went to French school, their friends were Irish and Iranian and German and Kenyan. They learned to choose their favorite Camembert from the *fromagerie,* they cheered for the puppets at the theater in the Luxembourg Gardens.

When we moved back to the States we chose Northern California as our new home. There are no Jewish neighborhoods here, and even the typical California girl has morphed into an "Asian, Indian, Middle Eastern, European" hybrid. My daughters attended a French school in Palo Alto and by the time they were in sixth grade they began to study Spanish. My younger daughter, at nineteen, is now comfortably trilingual.

Our house is filled with books. My second husband has built wall-to-wall shelves throughout the house. Still, books spill over, filling benches and end tables and creating towers on the floor near our bed. In the evenings, we sit and read by the fire in our book-blessed living room. There's a TV in a small back room of the house but none in the bedrooms or living room. We've traveled with the girls to Costa Rica and Mexico, France and Italy. With their dad, they've gone to Australia, Switzerland, England, and jetted from ski slope to private beach to country ranch.

It is a long way from the shtetl to this.

I want my girls to be global citizens of this world—with all the advantages and gifts they've been given—yet I want them to have a firm sense of where they've come from. Technically, they came from that four-bedroom apartment in Paris—but I'd like them to know that they historically come from *good Russian peasant stock,* as my mother would say. I'd like their understanding of the world to go beyond the rarified playground of Parc Monceau. And yet, if I barely know the stories of my aunts, uncles and grandparents, how can my daughters know their stories? What can I give my daughters to keep them rooted in family history?

When my younger daughter was born in Paris, my husband and I named her Sophie. It's a common French name, but at that point, nineteen years ago, American classrooms were not yet filled with Sophies. When I told my mother her name, Mom complained. "How can you give a baby the name of an old Jewish grandmother?" We like the name, I told her. It's new and it's old. It's French and it's from the Old Country. My mother died a few years later, much too young and much too soon. A week or so before she died, she told me how much she loved her *Yiddisha maydela,* her little Yiddish girl, Sophie.

Sophie went to a small school in Mountain View that prides itself on admitting half of the student body on full scholarship. Many of Sophie's friends lived in East Palo Alto, a subcontinent away from our own Palo Alto though it's only across Highway 101. For a year or two, I would urge her to invite her friends over for dinner or a sleepover. She'd head to their houses often and I wanted to reciprocate. Finally, after a couple of years, she agreed to bring some girls home with her. "I'm embarrassed," she told me. "Our house is so nice. Won't that make them feel bad?"

Somehow my own teenage experience had gotten turned inside out. I wouldn't invite my Princeton friends over because my house was so small, so unsophisticated, so insufferably middle class. My daughter was ashamed to have so much more than her friends. "Invite them for game night," I told her. It's a family tradition—we share a meal and then bring out the board games. My daughters love game night and it's now their way of bringing someone new into the family. The laughter at the table has nothing to do with the number of cars in the garage or the cost of the new marble kitchen counters.

Last summer, Sophie went to Mexico with American Friends Service Committee, to work with the poorest of villagers, building fireplaces for healthier cooking conditions, setting up vegetable gardens for sustainable living. The community would work together, sharing tools and skills and taking turns when the work was too hard. At the end of the day, the families would invite all of the kids into their dirt-floor one-room homes and they would celebrate their accomplishments, feasting on chicken with mole and tortillas and rice. When Sophie came home she asked me why, in this country, everyone has so much and yet families are so splintered and people complain that they want more.

I have a hard time explaining the American dream. I am that dream, the poor immigrant's child who had all the opportunities that her parents never imagined. I'm proud of my daughters because they don't take their affluence or their privileges for granted. They know the world looks different on the other side of Highway 101. They want to give other kids a shot at the American dream.

And maybe their generation's greatest contribution could be to change the nature of the dream. To make the dream about more than the acquisition of wealth and material goods. To make it also about the opportunity for an education and good health and joy. I remember those family feasts on Sunday morning at my house in Trenton. Though I didn't understand the words my family spoke at the table, maybe my genetic code was right there, on the platter with the lox and bagels. This is what matters, I realize now. Not the size of the kitchen or the number of books on the shelves, but the laughter at the table. No matter what language is spoken.

OTHER PEOPLE'S MOTHERS
Katrina Onstad

All that is new is telling the truth.
I'm here, that somebody else,
An old tree in the background.
—From "Little Girl, My String Bean, My Lovely Woman"
by Anne Sexton

I am not the only mother my daughter is going to know. Other people's mothers will move through her, change her when she is not looking, come to her when she is grown, shadowy and pulling. They will show her that what she got—me—wasn't so bad, maybe, or that what she missed was something huge, maybe unforgivably so. She will resent me for not being these moms, and maybe one afternoon, cling to me a little tighter, having seen someone else's mother behave in a way so foreign, so fearful, that she will not tell me about it.

These other mothers will highlight my uncoolness. She is two and they're doing it already, with their twelve-hundred-dollar strollers, their yoga-perfect bodies and me, slightly crusty and exhausted, always working and quick to yell.

But then I watch her, spinning naked in the living room, running to me to collapse, laughing; our safest place, in each other's arms. I think about what I learned from these other mothers, and I think of all the new ones out there waiting for my daughter, legion and unmet; her studies in contrast, her possible worlds.

My daughter will meet the mean mom.

In 1978, in Vancouver where I grew up, this mom was large, like the middle ball of a snowman, rolled into an electric-yellow housecoat. I only knew the word *housecoat* because my friend Ana said it in a murmur, head down, when I asked why her mom was wearing a nightgown at four o'clock. Mrs. K was wearing it because she did not work, but my mother did, and *that must be very hard on a young girl, coming home to an empty house?* Every sentence a question: *Hard to be a latchkey kid, isn't it?* I was too busy eating cookies (cookies! We never had cookies in our house) in the Ajax-scented kitchen to ask what "latchkey" meant.

Ana was large and freckled with wrists like wedges of wood. She had a tiny toddler sister who stuck to Mrs. K's legs in their shiny orange stockings. Love was limited for Ana, as was everything in her house: only two cookies, only a half hour of television. I remember the change in her mother's voice when she squealed at the sister: *My precious surprise! My little gift!* The slight thwack on Ana's bottom when we were watching TV: *Why don't you go outside? God knows you could stand to run around a little, don't you think?*

For years, none of this seemed strange to me, age seven, eight. It was the way of this other house, it was Ana's mother's way. But I remember distinctly when it revealed itself as ugliness. I was wearing a polyester button-down shirt covered with pictures of cowboy hats and cacti. The shirt had been my brother's and it was the first fashion love affair of my life.

I sat on Ana's bedroom floor, stacks of rainbow stickers at our feet, and her mother came in with the little sister behind her, *squinty sidekick.* Ana kept her eyes on the stickers.

"You really like that shirt, don't you?" said Mrs. K. "You like it so much you wear it every day, don't you? It must be hard for your mother to do laundry when she works?"

I felt a heat rising in my cheeks. My mother, dragged in front of me as something useless. But this woman was wrong. I didn't feel unwashed, unwanted. I did not recognize her version of me, or my mother. I knew that in my house, there were no plates of cookies at four o'clock, but there was Sunday night dinner, with Yorkshire pudding and opera. And weeknights, after supper, my parents drinking too much wine, talking politics, rattling the newspaper in the living room, watching *I Love Lucy* reruns. Even my brother would come, his legs covered in mud from playing soccer in the rain. We would sprawl across our purple corduroy furniture, ashtrays overflowing on the coffee table, and it was something like love.

I stood up and went to the front hall, leaving the stickers and Ana's shame brewing behind me. I put my jacket over my shirt and didn't look back. I walked past the even, green lawns of our quiet neighborhood on that Saturday afternoon, picturing my mother on her bed, feet under a mohair blanket, reading glasses on her nose. Just by being there, she would invite me to curl up against her, safe from the cold front of judgment that I knew, for the first time, lay in wait up ahead.

My daughter will meet the foreign mom, and learn that some children are required to love their mothers more deeply, and sooner.

Henry was the cutest boy in fifth grade. I remember him as honey-dipped and tiny, sprinting through the school hallways in an endless supply of striped rugby shirts. Above his nose, a small cosmos of freckles. He was something I watched, the way a farmer might stand back and watch a favorite horse run, and the horse runs, indifferent.

I was the tallest girl in the class, nearly as tall as our teacher, a redheaded woman with a guitar. This height difference alone made Henry and I utterly unknowable to one another. I think he avoided standing next to me as much as I did him.

Henry was smart, too; he understood things first in the room, nodding first, looking bored first, waiting to be taken away to the afternoon advanced classes where the science boys built models of compounds with Styrofoam balls.

He wasn't a crush, really, but a mystery. How did he navigate the social tunnels so easily? Friendly to everyone, funny but not obnoxious, never grating against people the way I did. I was just realizing my strangeness; how I provoked a slight cringe from the teacher at my fifteenth question, or the exhausted way the librarian looked when I showed up for school a half hour early, ready to talk books. But Henry floated; he displayed no exertion. I was in awe.

We had an assignment: Go door-to-door selling address labels to raise money for the school. Our maps were handed to us—blocks, addresses, little squares indicating the houses on our route—and sealed in plastic bags to keep the rain out.

A Sunday in the fall. I put my rain boots on, the hood of a yellow raincoat. Where was my mother? My father? It would never have occurred to them to come with me, and I would never have asked. We weren't scared yet. In a few months, children would start disappearing from the streets, and then a man named Clifford Olson would confess to murdering eleven kids in and around the city. After that, we got locks and keys and traveled in packs.

I approached a large, green house with a perfectly trimmed topiary hedge, my cold hands stiff in the rain. I prepared my speech: *Hello, I'm from Queen Mary Elementary...* The door opened and a small woman stood there. She was Chinese. She looked puzzled.

"Hello—" I began, and she shook her head, eyebrows furrowed. She was small enough to be a child; how old was she?

"No English," she said thickly. I hesitated, and considered turning around, walking away, but she opened the door wider and called behind her in Chinese. Then Henry appeared, as if he had been inches away all the time. This moment was as surprising as any of the daily shocks that marked my life then: His mother is Chinese. *Why didn't I know that? What else don't I know?*

"Hey," he said. I knew some Chinese kids, and two black families, but I had never met anyone who looked white but wasn't. Henry moved toward his mother, put a protective hand on her arm, spoke to her in a language I didn't understand. His features meant something different suddenly: that tanned skin, those sleepy eyes.

She nodded and walked away.

"She's getting money," he said, and we stood there with nothing to say to one another.

In that moment, Henry became something more than the long, impressive list he already was; he was also a conduit, a decoder. His mother needed him in a way I could not fathom. My own mother had taken to lecturing me about the importance of independence, autonomy. "We want you to fly, fly. See the world! Don't look back!" she would say, and I would nod, secretly terrified, wanting only to be safe in the chaos of our home, forever.

Henry's mother returned with a check. As Henry filled out the form, it occurred to me that surely he would have sold his mother address labels himself. She didn't need these. His mother was helping me, handing over the check with a large smile. Henry locked my eyes with a chin-out pride, and put his hand in hers.

Holding his mother's hand in front of another child! This

was an age when I had begun to cross streets if I happened to see my mother before she saw me. This was the edge of years of battle and shame over my sullenness and her too-loud laugh; my absence and her overpowering presence. I did not know yet what Henry knew then: that my mother and I would switch places over and over again in the years to come, that we would be called upon to translate the foreign world to our confused and rusty ears.

My daughter will fall in love with the single mom.

Emma's mom came before Emma. A hot day near the end of summer. My mother was in the kitchen, emptying the pottery plates from the dishwasher. "There's a girl your age moving to the block," she said. "She's at her dad's in Oregon, but her mom came by. She'd seen you biking on the street."

What did she want? To reserve me as her daughter's friend? This seemed both pathetic and thrilling. I filled in the blanks: some nervous mom making a phone call to her daughter in Oregon, assuring her that the move would be successful, luring her with the information that there was even a girl her age on the block, and she would be in her class, and it was all going to work out.

From this, I pictured Emma's mom as protective, more Brady than my own mother. My mother, who had lived in London and traveled Europe and who'd had boyfriends before my father, was always a little older than other kids' mothers, but younger, too, in her silver jewelry and ponchos.

Soon, Emma roller-skated up the street, and I roller-skated back down with her. The house was something entirely different from what I knew, and the mother different still. It was one of only a few rental houses on our block, and there were many, many people living in it. An ex-stepdad, a current boyfriend (a well-known local actor), a half sister, a family friend who was a DJ. I had never heard the word *DJ* before. Blues music blared from the stereo. Stacks and stacks of records covered every surface. Dirty dishes were piled in the sink. I looked around for a dishwasher, but there wasn't one. Emma's mom sat on a lawn chair in the overgrown backyard with the female DJ, glasses of white wine with ice in their hands. She looked like a teenager: long, full hair, a mole by her nose, thin legs in a short skirt. In two years, Madonna would emerge, and we would tell everyone that Emma's mom looked exactly like her.

But all I knew then was that she looked nothing like my mom, short-haired, efficient, trim.

"I've heard about you," she said, smiling that gap-toothed smile. "I'm Rebecca."

I'm certain I blushed.

Over the coming year, as Emma and I became best friends— or imitated some version of best friends I had learned about in novels—Rebecca was in flux. She worked as a waitress at an upscale bistro where we could go after school and drink hot chocolates at the bar. Then she took a job in a clothing store, and she gave us wide plastic belts that were being thrown out. Once, she found a long-sleeve, button-down silk shirt with a small lipstick mark on the collar. "Here, give this to your mother," she said. "She's straighter than I am."

My mother—straight? My mother, who smoked and drank and swore like a sailor? But after that moment, our house started to look straight to me: it was so clean, so ordered. We had bedtimes and a list of chores stuck to the fridge. We were as conventional as the suburbanites my parents scoffed at on drives out of the city.

Rebecca watched the same TV shows we did, and asked us questions about boys. She had a pencil-line leather skirt and dresser drawers filled with makeup and perfume. I had grown up hearing so much about equality that I had never seen how powerful it was to be feminine. Watching her walk out the door with her bright red lipstick and fishnet stockings, she looked beautiful and strong, and I hadn't known yet that those two things could be knit together.

One night I slept over in the half sister's empty bed. The house was filled or empty according to a series of custody arrangements; kids and half siblings and stepsiblings moving back and forth across the continent like mail.

I woke in the middle of the night to find Emma missing. I got up, pulling my nightgown below my knees, and walked down the dark hall. The door to her mom's room was ajar, Emma asleep next to her. I hadn't slept against my mother in years. Rebecca, with glasses on her nose, was reading a fat paperback with embossed writing on the front.

She smiled kindly at me. "You okay, hon?" she whispered. I almost wept with jealousy: the simplicity of it! The ease!

And then another night, I woke up in that bed to the sound of Rebecca and the actor boyfriend screaming in the hallway, shadows storming a sliver of light under the door. "You fucking bitch!" "You fucking asshole!" And objects thumping against the wall; a glass shattering. Emma's back was turned to me, rigid in the air, and I knew that this was something we, who never stopped talking, would not speak of.

Over the years, Rebecca and Emma moved from rental to rental in the city to accommodate the shape-shifting family, which sometimes included men, sometimes just a mother and daughter alone. Emma and I got good at putting together her brass bed, screwing the knobs on, smoothing the sheets. At Christmas, Emma would line up the presents from the boyfriends on that bed: a Sony Walkman, a cashmere sweater. I would finger these items jealously, lash out with cruelty at her glamorous life, and miss her terribly when she went to Oregon in the summers. She got tanned and slim, larger breasted and wiser, while I sat on that same lawn reading, seething with boredom, day after day.

But I remember, too, how often she stayed at my house overnight, showing up on the doorstep, dashing in as if being chased. My mother bought a large piece of foam and sewed fitted sheets for it. This makeshift bed stayed on my floor most weeks. On weekends, Emma would lie a few feet below me, the two of us talking in the dark. I remember going upstairs one morning, and coming down to find my mother in her familiar place at the round white table in the kitchen. Emma was weeping, keening. I stopped. My mother hunched over my friend, listening, her hand circling her back.

"They fight all the time," said Emma. "I hate it!" My mother murmured and took her in, held her in her arms, rocked her back and forth. I stepped back into the hallway, as if I had walked in on two lovers.

Rebecca got rich, marrying a financial planner. It was during this time, when we were finally in high school, that Emma and I began to drift apart. I think we came to feel that in looking at each other, we could only see who we had been so recently, and those were people to be forgotten.

We fit in to the new world of high school differently. My bossiness and eccentricity had a small currency; I found a few allies who liked foreign movies and college rock. Emma became a little dangerous. She began smoking and disappearing with the pretty girls. Her mother called our house one night, searching for her. I glanced up from the television as my mother talked to Rebecca on the phone, assuring her that no, no, she hadn't seen her daughter, not in ages. My mother's eyes staying on me for a long, long time as she spoke.

My daughter will know the dead mother.

Ben was a great love, a midtwenties obsession. On our first drunken evening, he said: "My mother died. She was very beautiful. She looked like an Ivory girl." When I saw pictures shortly after, I learned something new about him: He had no propensity for exaggeration.

This mother had died young and beautiful, leaving behind three equally beautiful children. She was so beautiful that there was a movie about her, and a novel by a famous writer. I wanted to know everything, thinking I could get to befriend her somehow, trying to imagine what she would think of me. She began to fill up the spaces in our relationship, casting a speculative shadow.

"My mother would have liked this film.""Do you think your mother would want you to go back to school?"

I had a feeling, deep down, that she might have liked me less than her son did: she who had lived off the land, who was often atop mountains in photographs. I was drinking a lot then, religiously devoted to black T-shirts and late nights. I had no romance for the sixties.

Early on in our affair, I woke up in the dark and Ben was crying for her. She had been dead fifteen years. "Do you think she would be proud of me?" he asked, weeping. I held him in my arms and meant it when I said yes. These nights were occasional, and then more frequent. I saw his depression shadowing him, along with all the other things his mother's death had wrought: an unstable father, a toxic closeness amongst the siblings, Ben's certainty that he was only ever alone in the world.

His father remarried several times. He was living in a small town in Manitoba, earning money cleaning the local hospital and painting oversize canvases with trees. One Easter, the siblings gathered at the house, everyone arriving by bus. Ben's dad was jovial as he drove to the bus station three separate times, proud of all these scruffy, artfully impoverished kids and their boyfriends and girl-friends. Most had half dropped out of college and counted themselves creative geniuses, all wearing their wounds like badges of honor.

Ben's dad found the documentary that had been made about the mother's death. While his new wife did dishes in the kitchen, he plugged it in to the VCR, and everyone lay on the floor in the living room watching the dead mother, blond and laughing, talking about how she was going to die soon. Ben was a child in the video, and the interviewer asked him questions that made him sound wise about her illness, resolved. He used words that a child's mouth should never have formed. I don't remember exactly, but something foolishly insightful like: "I'll miss her, but she won't be in pain anymore."

It was silent in the room.

I had never loved him as much as in that moment, young Ben on the television, my boyfriend next to me on the cat-hair covered couch—and I knew this love was not the cure, either. His loss had been his life for too many years. I couldn't pull him back.

Things change. "Stop mothering me," he said many times, irritated. But how could I not? How could anyone not mother him, this tall, broken boy?

We broke up eventually, a mess of infidelity and depression tarnishing a golden ride that had lasted several years. I think of that mother the most, the dead one. I feel for her now in a way I never understood, as I watch my own children and imagine the unimaginable end to all of this.

It is this dead mother I never met who tells me what I need to know about parenting. She tells me never to stop, and warns me away from absence. In this way, she makes me a better mother, as does Rebecca, whose floating home of her own design reminds me that family is fluid and alive, and we are here to revel in it. And in my laziest, worst moments, I recall Mrs. K's small cruelties. I catch myself snapping and snarling and think: *This will stay with them. This matters.*

From these mothers, I learned that I want scale and breadth for my daughter; I want her to know a multitude of ways of being. I want her to move through other people's rooms, to witness kindness and difference and the intimacy of lives that are nothing like her own. And when her friends begin to pass through our door, witnessing her home, I will be self-conscious, I think, hoping to count to them, and waiting for them to change me in return.

All these mothers lead me to my daughter, reminding me that she is mine temporarily, and only by chance, the greatest, random double-sided gift.

SAY YOU, SAY ME
Emily Franklin

That night is only the background of our selves,
Supremely true to its separate self,
In the pale light that each upon the other throws.
    —From "Re-statement of Romance" by Wallace Stevens

At the playground my three-year-old daughter, Ellie, is busy climbing the ladder to the top of the curvy slide. I wrestle with the wood chips that invade my flip-flops and wave to her. Ellie returns the gesture, her wave all arm as though she's flagging down a ship. Around me, other parents, caregivers, grandparents, do the playground dance of half-noticing someone else's child.

"She's so adorable," an older woman says. I smile a thank-you. Ellie positions herself at the top of the curvy slide and swooshes down. I meet her at the bottom. Another mother appears to help her toddler on the swings. She studies Ellie for a moment and then starts with playground chatter.

"You're brave."

I assume she means letting Ellie climb to the top of a rope ladder unassisted. "She'll be fine. She's a great climber."

The mother offers a bag of crackers to her boy. "Not the rope. I mean…" She points to Ellie, who is now running the length of the wooden bridge, her untamed curls bobbing in the fall wind. "I mean—she's so colorful!"

Up until now I have hardly noticed what Ellie is wearing. Upon closer inspection, the tally is this: orange pants her dad and I picked up in Iceland for one of our sons, purple socks, hand-me-down sandals, and a velour light blue-and-navy striped shirt. And her wire-rimmed glasses—without which she would hardly be able to see—they make her eyes appear giant, Mr. Magoo-large, overtly innocent and sweet. An as-yet-uncreated Muppet.

"She dressed herself," I say and shrug.

"Timmy, don't throw sand," the mom says and pulls her son away from the box. She leans in conspiratorially. "He has no interest in dressing himself—and the few times he has, he throws together the weirdest combinations." She says this and then blushes, thinking she might have insulted me, broken the playground rules of casual chatter. "Not that there's anything wrong with…"

"It's fine," I assure her, and I mean it. Of all the emotional issues of parenting, I am not invested in how my kids look. "Ellie's got her own sense of color. Doesn't bother me."

"Well, you're brave," the mom reiterates.

Bravery? Is such a word applicable to kid fashion? My own mother would disagree with the word choice, and yet growing up, she never would have allowed me out in public in Ellie's chosen style.

Case in point: the day before fourth grade at my new, fancy private school. All the girls are invited to Melinda's house to play and to meet me, the only new kid.

"Ready to go?" my mother shouted up the stairs at our new house. We'd moved that summer and I was still getting used to the echoes, the stairs that squeaked, the wide-board wood floors that proved to be excellent skating material in socks or tights. Clad in typical end-of-summer attire (collared shirt, khaki shorts, sneakers), I presented myself at the bottom of the stairs.

"Go change," my mother instructed. She looked immaculate, as usual, in a linen top and fitted trousers.

I was shocked. What was wrong with my shorts? "We're just playing outside, Mom. Everyone's going to be wearing this."

157

She made me change and I arrived at Melinda's in my seer-sucker pink-and-white dress with Peter Pan collar and sandals that buckled on the ankle only to be greeted by a swarm of dirt-caked girls in torn T-shirts, ragged cutoffs and sneakers. I was humiliated. Not only did I stand out, I stood out in a voice that wasn't mine. It was my mother's. I shot her a look that could wilt cacti.

One of the other mothers stepped in. "Don't you look adorable!" Nods all around.

"Come on, Emily, we're climbing trees!" The girls urged me to join them. I wanted to go but couldn't. I would ruin the dress my mother bought me. The problem was solved eventually when Melinda brought me into her room, lent me shorts and a shirt and I sucked up the blisters that came from my bare feet rubbing into the sandals.

This scene was not a one-off. More often than not, appearance played a large part in my relationship with my mother. So much, in fact, that it's all but disappeared in my relationship with Ellie. It's not that I want to exclude how she looks from the equation of how she fits in the world, but rather I want it to take second (or fifth or sixth or twelfth) seat.

I never want to put pressure on her to look a certain way, and I often address what she does rather than how she looks doing it. For better or worse, I am married to a pediatrician, and I read his insider magazines. Many a pediatric article has been written on the effects of focusing on girls' looks rather than their achievements. I notice how people say to my boys, "You've got quite a pitching arm there." Or "I heard you playing the piano, wow!" And then to Ellie, "Don't you look adorable in your dress!"

I climb up the rope ladder and meet Ellie at the top of the climbing structure, taking in her outfit again as I hug her. She likes the velour top because it's "the softest" and she dresses herself each morning in whatever suits her; sometimes dresses and tights, other times hand-me-down jeans from her brothers or a rainbow striped shirt passed on from her cousins in California. Granted, she is three years old and my mother and I have survived thirty-five years of being image-conscious together, but I'd like to think I won't impose on Ellie so much of what was ordered on me.

My husband and I make sure she's tidy for family holidays, or dressed up a bit for her great-grandmother's ninety-second birthday, but we don't attach a sense of importance to it. *What are you going to wear?* isn't an emotionally loaded proposition. I often felt that meeting my mother's expectations with my appearance was so important, so crucial, that there was no way I could succeed.

"You look wonderful," my mother says as I meet her for lunch in London where we were then living. "Where did you get those shoes?"

"You don't like them?" I looked down at my feet. I'd splurged on the shoes—they were wingtips, brown and maroon, and later I would come to loathe them, but right then, in Kensington, I wanted her to approve.

"I didn't say that."

"But you did." And she had, but not with words. With the unspoken nuances that only the mother and daughter can feel and see.

"They're just a bit…" She paused, trying not to hurt my feelings but still be honest.

"Just say it."

"Manly."

The lunch dissolved into a discussion of feelings versus accessories, my simultaneous desire to dress and to speak for myself and yet at the same time, gain her blessing over my chosen outfit.

She manages to look elegant in just about anything—jeans, suits, even the dreaded culottes. Outfits that work and speak out about the person she is.

I, in fact, have never been an "outfit" person. There are two kinds of shoppers—those who buy outfits and those who do not. I am in the later camp and now, at thirty-five, I understand I will never change. I grab a top that I like, a pair of shoes, pants that go with nothing I presently own. My mother shops in outfits—this shirt with these pants, this dress with these tights. It's not that I have no fashion sense, only that I buy and wear whatever appeals; at this point, with four kids under eight, my "wardrobe" is primarily of the jeans and T-shirts variety.

I am not one of the mothers that show up at afternoon pick-up in full makeup, tweed jacket, skirt and boots. I'm the mom hiking footballs and chucking a baseball in the yard with the same polar fleece I've had since grad school. I mix it up sometimes, with sweaters and every now and then a skirt, but by and large I wear what my life dictates. My mother doesn't mind as much now, but the fear of dressing wrong, of somehow making a fashion faux pas, still lurks in the background not only for me, but for my kids, her grandchildren.

Case in point: Thanksgiving a few years back at her house. She and her new husband had the combined modern family (seven kids, sixteen grandchildren) coming over for turkey and football. "Make sure you dress the kids," she's instructed. Hidden in that request was one for me and my husband. "I will," I assured her. I understood the pressure of throwing a big meal, of bringing together people who are suddenly related. "No jeans" was her final dictum. Despite our annoyance (we were thinking nice jeans and a clean, pressed button-down or sweater), we avoided denim entirely, only to be greeted by our entire stepfamily who were all…wearing jeans.

I used to think that I could change my mother's opinion about clothing, about appearance. Since having a daughter, however, I've come to realize that like many issues in parenting, dressing our kids is all about having a voice. More than just the typical parental need to control through what our kids eat and what they wear, I think my mother was trying to make sure I fit in. That she would have, in my shoes.

I do not blame her for her desire to have me look a certain way. Perhaps she thought of me arriving at the pre-fourth-grade party in shorts and thought I'd be miserable if all the other girls were in dresses. Perhaps if we'd shown up wearing jeans to Thanksgiving, we might be disrespecting our new family.

"I'm going to pick out my clothing for tomorrow," Ellie says when we're back from the playground, bathed and getting ready for bed. She opens her drawers and yanks out underwear. The rest of the clothing she gives real consideration: Leggings? Pants? She settles on a white skirt and tie-dyed blue shirt, polka-dot socks and sneakers. As long as she is dressed weather-appropriate, I don't care what combination of items she dons. My mother is picking Ellie up at school tomorrow. Will she notice the outrageous shirt? Wonder at her choice of pairing it with a skirt? Maybe. But she will no doubt recognize Ellie's voice in her outfit, see her determination, her love of color, and appreciate her reasons for the skirt ("it's flowy on my legs").

"Good job," I commend her for putting all the clothing out herself.

My husband once came home from the playground and said someone had asked if we were Swedish. When he'd asked why, the woman had mentioned Ellie's clothing, the mismatching colors, the patterns blending. "Swedish?" he'd asked.

"Like Oilily," I'd explained. "Or Marimekko. You know, intentionally odd and eclectic."

But Ellie doesn't know yet that her clothing is different. And the few times she does notice that she stands out, she doesn't change her mind. My hope is that she'll be able to continue this, especially in the precarious teen years when having a single voice is challenging.

My mother drops a nearly asleep but very happy Ellie off the next afternoon and tells me about their day. "We went for a walk in the park. We picked up leaves and we read books. Her skirt is stained. Did she use paints?" I look at the skirt.

"No," I tell her. "I washed it with a blue tablecloth and it ran." I am about to justify myself, my letting Ellie go to school with the stain, my inability to sort clothing for a wash (in my defense, I do know how, I just sometimes chuck everything in at once and hope for the best). But I don't. "It's okay, Mom."

My mother smiles and gives me a kiss on the cheek before she leaves. She takes in my T-shirt (it started the day clean and now has spit-up on not one but both shoulders), my jeans (rice cereal on the thigh), my socks (ripped from a nail in the wide-board wood floors I came to appreciate in my own childhood and sought out in my own home). Mainly, she takes in my smile as I hug Ellie hello.

"I'm a mess," I tell my mother before she can say it to me. My clothing is the billboard for everything my days consist of now. But they don't tell the whole story. My mother wrestled with piecing together her own life and making sure that her exterior— and mine—were always pristine even when things were rocky. Now, with Ellie, maybe I don't have to do that.

"You look happy," she grins. "You look like a mom."

Ellie wants my attention, wants me to pick her up after her

long day. "Can you take the baby?" I ask and hand my four-month-old over to my mother. She coos over him and he grants her a toothless smile and then promptly spits up on her. She laughs. "Oh, no. Right on the sweater." My mom goes to mop herself up.

I wrap my arms around Ellie, shifting her weight from my chest to my hip the way I did when she was a baby. I wonder if she will continue to make bold fashion choices, if she will want to stand out or to blend in. I hope I am giving her the voice to do either, to do what feels best to her. "Well, needless to say, I'm going to have to change," my mother says, the baby still in her arms, her sweater darkened with water from the attempt to clean it.

"Look at what I made," Ellie says with my mother back in the room. She slides on the floor and goes to her schoolbag. She unfurls a crinkled painting done in splashes of magenta, green, bright blue.

"Was it fun?" I ask. Ellie nods. "You sure like to paint. The blue and green remind me of an ocean."

"A big ocean," she agrees.

"And that shirt you have," my mother says. "The one with the design on the front."

Ellie nods. "I know that one. Can I wear it tomorrow?"

"Sure," I tell her. "If you want to."

How she looks—adorable, stained, sweet, sloppy, hair brushed or not, does not mean for me what it meant for my mother. It's not that I eschew all pretense and let Ellie show up for her great-grandmother's party in jeans, but that I want to teach her a balance—sometimes you shove on sweats and other times you need to dress up. But more than all that, I want her to know that my happiness has very little to do with how I look. That my self-worth isn't based on exteriors. That I hope hers isn't, either.

That said, if Ellie grows up and wants to have everything

match or decides she's happiest in twin sets and pearls or doesn't leave the house without an "outfit," then I will support that.

I remember showing up at the party in my seersucker dress and, right now, rather than the embarrassment of being singled out—I remember something else. The feel of my mother's hand around mine as we stood in the driveway surrounded by other women and their daughters. How she admitted her mistake and let me leave and change. I squeeze my mother's hand now while Ellie's legs are still wrapped around my waist.

"My Grammie is your mom!" Ellie says, as though no matter how many times she's said or heard the fact, she cannot quite believe it to be true.

"Yup, that's right."

The three of us, all dressed how we like, are together. My mother and I are marked with the mess of motherhood, the love, the kisses, the paint splotches, the marks and dings of trying to be heard, of being brave enough to let go.

NOTHING ELSE SEEMS AS TRUE AS THIS
Calla Devlin

For Mary Rongerude

But when I had a daughter
I named her for you, as if pulling you back
through a crack between the bricks.
—From *"Best Friends"* by Sharon Olds

I knew I wanted to be a mother before I knew I was a lesbian. When I was nineteen, an undergraduate at a small private liberal arts university, I met Jane. She was a freshman, eighteen years old, fresh from Catholic girl's school in the Pacific Northwest. She looked like a sunflower, long-limbed and blond with bright eyes. When we first spoke, I never could have imagined she would be the person I would raise a family with, eighteen years later.

I don't remember meeting her, but she remembers me. She visited our college campus as a perspective student, and recalled sitting in the lobby of the dorm with me and a few other world-weary freshmen. Despite the ceiling fan and open windows, the old building held California's high desert heat. I remember the lobby, the arid air, but I don't remember telling Jane the university's attributes, about why she should leave the Northwest for a small college town sixty miles east of L.A., which was the equivalent of six hundred miles if you didn't have a car like me. She came and said hello the following August, only I didn't remember her. Most of the incoming freshmen resembled each other, slim blondes with sunflower faces, wearing expensive clothes meant to look vintage. I couldn't pick her out of the crowd. I doubt I could have picked her out of a lineup.

Jane says we were at the same party during her first week at the school. Usually I'm the one good with details, but she can describe the suite of rooms on the third floor, the hippie décor, the tapestries tacked to the walls, the stoner music spinning on the turntable. I was drunk and engaged in a passionate conversation with someone else equally as drunk and passionate, someone besides Jane. I would never characterize Jane as forgettable, and when I finally had a conversation with her, which took place a day or so after the party and after my burdensome hangover wore off, she claimed a place in my head and then my heart.

When we were in our mid-twenties, we discussed starting a family. We both wanted children, but it took us another ten years before we started. I struggled with the idea of motherhood, with re-imagining what it would mean to be a parent, of shaking off my own experience as a child growing up in an unstable and precarious family. Jane, however, came from still-married parents who loved her unconditionally. When I met them back when I was nineteen, I remember being both skittish and mesmerized. A nineteen-year-old college sophomore, I was still trying to hide the fact that I was raised by a mentally ill mother and ditched by a drunken father. I was orphaned by circumstance rather than death. Jane's family was not only intact; they were affectionate, affluent and athletic. They resembled each other in all the right ways.

My mother tried her best, but her best was dreadful. While I didn't fare well as a minor, I have as an adult, largely thanks to Jane's family. I was absorbed into their fold long before they could say the word *lesbian* without stuttering.

Jane's parents, Dave and Mary, were conservative Catholic republicans, and at first, they didn't know what to do with me, this girl their daughter brought home. Over the years, they incorporated me into the family like another daughter. I helped cook meals and polished the silver for holiday dinner parties. Eventually, the awkwardness of how to refer to me (friend? lover? girlfriend? mate? partner? or wife?) was replaced by the comfort of family. Mary, with her remarkable generosity, became the mother I always wished I had.

Jane and I had been together for twelve years when we first began to start a family. Jane would carry the baby. My health eliminated me as the birth mother. But there was more to it. Yes, Jane had beautiful, long legs and she had better skin, but she had the family, the blood relations, the good genes. I had the fingerprints of my mother's mental illness and my own health issues. So Jane carried our daughter, and I am not biologically related to my daughter nor to the woman who taught me what it means to be a mother.

When we committed to starting a family, Jane and I agreed we needed to be as comfortable as possible about being same-sex parents. There was never a doubt that our child would be welcomed and loved, but there was the need to assess comfort levels. By having a two-mom family, it required us—and our greater family—to come out instantly. That was easier for those living in San Francisco, Seattle and Los Angeles. It proved harder for those in North Carolina and rural Oregon.

Despite the warm and open relationship I had with them, I was most concerned about Jane's parents, specifically her father. Conservative Catholic, country club republicans, it was painful to visit them during an election year. Oregon was plagued by years of anti-gay ballot measures, and Dave and Mary's neighborhood was littered with homophobic lawn signs. Hateful ads ran on the radio, television and in the newspaper. Their city welcomed anti-gay legislation and their county was a stronghold for right-wing organizers. I didn't know how they would feel introducing our family to their neighborhood acquaintances. I feared these encounters, and after driving past the campaign lawn signs, arrived at their home restless and tense.

We coped by talking. We mused over baby names, new holiday traditions and future baby-proofing requirements. When alone, we asked Jane's mom and sisters to broach the issue with her father. We launched our own campaign within the confines of our family, the get-ready-for-the-lesbian-moms initiative. Our grassroots efforts proved effective and, after a couple of years, it was as common to discuss our family planning as much as it was discussing Jane's married sister's baby plans.

We spent a year trying to get pregnant, a year of waiting where our months were bisected: half-filled with eager anticipation and half with disappointment. I spent the time getting organized: I made lists, created files, ordered books and evaluated queer parenting organizations. I devoted one file to domestic partnership forms, another to legal referrals. Jane called our friends with children and performed market research on everything from breast pumps to strollers. We argued over cloth versus disposable diapers. We wondered if it was too early to get on preschool waiting lists.

A friend of mine, a mother, told me it was important to know who you are before becoming a mother. Parenting was all consuming, and in the early years, personal time disappeared. At her suggestion, I examined what I knew about my life, about myself, before I crossed the threshold of motherhood. I came up with more questions than answers, almost all pertaining to who I would be as a nonbiological mother.

I learned I was scared. I harbored the normal fears of becoming a parent, but I unearthed a deeper set of fears. I was going to be a mother without giving birth. I was going to be mother number two, a vice-president mother to the president mother. I didn't know how to reconcile my insecurities, my feeling of in-adequacies because I couldn't be the birth mother.

I spent that summer allowing myself to feel fully, to admit that I wanted our child to look like me: my uneven complexion and my family's overbite. I wanted to see myself in our child, even just the flaws. I wanted the stranger passing us on the street to comment on our resemblance, on the obvious fact that we were related. I wanted irrefutable parenthood. But this went beyond resemblance. I wanted our family to introduce me—without pause, hesitation, clarification or qualification—as the other mother.

While I was confident in their love for me, I worried about Jane's family. Their approval was paramount and I needed to feel like they saw me as much as a parent as they would see Jane. It was difficult separating them from their neighborhood, from the election-year bigotry. While they remained registered Republic-ans and they went to church on Sundays, I also knew they adored Jane and they cared about me.

After our year of trying to conceive a child, we went to Oregon for Christmas. Dave and Mary built their dream house overlooking the eighteenth hole of their country club's golf course, and when we walked into their home, there were not one but two Christmas trees. Jane's parents greeted us with warm embraces. Holiday decorations graced every room, and Mary beamed as she always did when her daughters came home.

The room glowed from the Christmas lights, and we all shared a relaxed comfort. We settled into the couch and looked outside. The wall facing the golf course consisted of enormous windows and rain collected in puddles on the grass. Bare trees peppered the course, with a backdrop of evergreens. It was Christmas Eve, and the following morning, we learned Jane was pregnant. Her parents were joyous and I knew then what would become my foundation as a parent: don't operate from a place of fear, but from one of generosity.

Jane and I had remarkably different experiences welcoming our daughter into our lives. She was the one with child: She had her stomach patted and evaluated by strangers, she had her legs in stirrups, she had the epidural. I was in the ambiguous role of the other mother, the mom *without* child.

As we prepared for the birth of our daughter, I found myself vacillating between hesitation and elation. I saw my binary existence as a product of the two guiding, yet conflicting, images of motherhood: my mother versus Mary. As my mother had succumbed to mental illness, Jane's mother, Mary, came to occupy that maternal role. My memories of my mother embodied all of the fear I had that I would fail my daughter, that I wouldn't teach her how to be in the world, that I wouldn't provide that fundamental nurturing. Then I had Mary, the very embodiment of generosity. Fortunately, Mary was engaged as possible as we awaited the birth of our child. Her presence was profound, simply because she was there. When not visiting, she was on the phone and busy mailing us care packages. She was a steady guide in the world of expectancy and uncertainty. Yes, she was a seasoned mother ready to become a grandmother, but she was also a constant reassurance that I could be a good mother.

The images of my own mother receded the more I opened up myself to Mary. I had lived with a residual anxiety for my entire adult life, a by-product of my mother's erratic behavior and the endless instability in my childhood home. While Jane's parents took me in as their own, I didn't fully embrace my in-laws until the pregnancy. It wasn't a conscious test or decision. It was as though I had spent years learning a new language only to finally feel fluent. The fluency was in parenthood and Mary was my teacher. When Jane gave birth, Mary stood at Jane's right and I stood at her left. We welcomed our child together. Upon reflection, I see that moment as one of my greatest gifts.

My daughter was named Lucia Mary after her grandmother. She didn't resemble me in the least, with the exception of her red hair, a color completely absent on Jane's side of the family, but present in mine. The rest of her physical characteristics belonged to Jane. But when it came to Lucia's actual mothering, it could not have been more equal. I fed her from a bottle and, for her first year, she slept for hours on my chest. As I rested with my baby asleep on me, in the moments between reading *The New Yorker* or a new novel, I wondered how my mother must have felt when she was in the same position.

I doubted she sat for hours rocking me, much less feeling the full heart one feels as a parent. It's not that I thought of my mother as heartless, but I know now that she wasn't capable of parenting. She was young when she had me, and then had my following sisters within two years after my birth. I know she wouldn't have chosen motherhood, given a full range of choices. She wouldn't have chosen my father, she wouldn't have chosen her friends, she wouldn't have chosen me. As I sat with my own daughter asleep on my body, I tried to remind myself that my mother was ill, that her rejection was of everything—her entire life—not just her children.

Yet, how could anyone *not* feel fulfilled by her own child? I didn't birth Lucia, but I could not have wanted or loved her more if I had. I conceived her with Jane, from the very first doctor's appointment to fertility treatment to the birth classes, to cutting the cord after she was born. My daughter is a part of me in a way that is the most sacred and profound. I know Mary regards her own daughter, Jane, in the same way. I don't know if I will ever reconcile that my mother missed that experience, that she was unable to attach to me in the most fundamental way a mother attaches to her child.

Fortunately, I had Mary as a teacher and surrogate mother. Lucia was very bonded to her grandmother, who visited every month of the first year. That first year was precious, one I wish we could have documented more thoroughly than with even the hundreds of photos taken. After Lucia's first birthday, Mary visited again. She woke up Saturday morning, and as we ate breakfast, she complained of a backache. That was in September. In November, she was diagnosed with late-stage pancreatic cancer, and she died the following May on Memorial Day. Her last lucid day was Mother's Day.

In those last months, we did our best to cram what should have been two decades into weeks. It was a family immersion program, and we traveled to Oregon for a week per month to spend as much time together as possible. The more it became clear that chemotherapy was not working, that the cancer was far too advanced and aggressive, the more we tried to make every moment meaningful. We embraced, we told each other we loved each other, we detailed the meaning we had in our lives and in our family. It was an extraordinary time, but it wasn't that much of a change in the way Mary led her family. The generosity was more pronounced and urgent, but it was the same way she lived her life.

Not that grief can be simple, but mine felt so complex it was difficult to navigate. Mary was the only mother I had known my entire adult life—nineteen years—equally as long as my own mother had been in my life. I grieved them both simultaneously and, ultimately, what I learned about being a mother was from the two of them. I defined my own parenting style in opposition to my own mother's mistakes, a careful process of elimination: don't leave the kids alone for hours or days, listen to them when they speak, make sure they are fed, make sure they are touched, make sure they know they are wanted. And Mary taught me to be a mother unconditionally, to have unwavering confidence in who you are as a mother and who your daughter is to you. To love.

Lucia and I took regular walks to the playground, stopping at a café on the way. The coffee shop was just a few blocks down from where Mary, Jane and I bought Lucia's first birthday cake. I am unsure which my daughter enjoyed more—our regular strolls, the café treat or the playground. She was old enough now to place her own order, a small hot chocolate, but not too hot. She chose a table near the espresso machine and eyed the counter as we waited for our drinks. We engaged in conversation initiated by my articulate three-year-old:

"I love hot chocolate, Mommy."

"Yes, honey, I know you do."

"After this, we're going to the playground."

"We are—you're right."

"Mommy, when we're not together, I miss you. And you miss me. We miss each other."

I paused and met her eyes. She smiled and nodded, emphasizing her point.

"I miss you so much when I'm not with you," I said. "All I want is to be with you, all of the time."

"That's because you are my mommy," she said.

"Yes, I sure am." And, as we sit in the café, nothing else seems as true as this.

A GIRL GROWS IN BROOKLYN
Sara Woster

From that time on, the world was hers for the reading.
She would never be lonely again.
—From *A Tree Grows in Brooklyn* by Betty Smith

My baby is taking after her father. She is freakishly strong and at eight months old, August is almost walking. She did not get this physical vitality from me. So disconnected are my own skeletal, nervous and muscular systems that the idea that I might parent some sort of child athlete has never once occurred to me. But I went and married a natural-born athlete and now I am worried I will be forced to spend my weekends at ballparks with round buttons of August's face pinned onto a three-season anorak. And as bad as that sounds, that would not be the worst part of having an athletic daughter.

The worst part is that she may have none of the sedentary nature that is required for somebody to curl up with a good book. To be a lifetime reader you must be part invalid, like me. You have to be able to lie on your back on a couch or a bed with a book in your grip for hours at a time without bedsores appearing or hands cramping. A good reader generally looks consumptive even in the peak of summer. So this burgeoning tanned athleticism of my daughter must be stopped right now. If we have any hope of having a close relationship, I need August to stop bustling around and start reading; it is my plan to take a page from my mother's book of parenting and use books to communicate.

My entire family is made up of avid readers. At Thanksgiving and Christmas, family members would disappear from the table only to be found hours later on beds and couches squinting down at open books. Growing up, we happily received B. Dalton gift certificates and bookmarks as birthday presents.

Our love of books was no accident: my mother is an English teacher turned librarian and the way that mothers preen and tan their daughters into pageant winners, we were given magnetic letters, board books and library cards and were built into readers.

My mother was always holding out some book and asking if I had read it, so it seemed very normal the day that she handed me her own hardbound copy of *A Tree Grows in Brooklyn*.

"I think you'd like this," she said. "It's one of my favorite books."

It seemed a normal enough selection at first, the protagonist, Francie Nolan, was a girl my age, but twenty pages into the book, my world was thrown upside down. This book was a dirty, filthy book. At ten years old I was not even allowed to watch the sexual innuendos and busty ladies of *Three's Company,* yet my mother handed me a story where Katie, the mother of the protagonist, shoots a pedophile in the penis as he attempts to rape her daughter.

Good Lord.

The book was terrifying. The women in the neighborhood stone Joanna, an unmarried seventeen-year-old, just for bringing her baby out in public, a man tries to starve his pregnant daughter to death, and don't even get me started on the violin teacher with a foot fetish. The pages were filled with sexual innuendos, violence, exposed breasts, endless illegitimate pregnancies and a very slutty aunt. My mother had a difficult time talking to us about shaving our armpits and she gave me this? Maybe this book was another example of her getting somebody else to explain sex to me. She and I were rescued from a sit-down sex talk by a progressive school in a liberal public school system that offered sex education to any student who could get their permission slip signed by a parent. And like most parents, my mother happily signed the task away.

And here was that same modest mother giving me a book where Aunt Sissy worked in a condom factory, had three "husbands" that she called John and allowed a man to drink from a bottle of whiskey tucked in her massive bosom.

Not willing to concede that my mom was a pervert, I had to search for other things in the book that might have interested her.

I was certain that she was using it to point out how lazy I was. She had no problem verbalizing that daily, but she drove home her point with the book. Through page after page, these Brooklyn kids mopped saloon floors, collected tin and ran around arguing with butchers for better cuts of cheap meat. And here I was moaning about drying the dishes or hanging up the clothes on the clothesline. I should be grateful, the book told me, for my mother; at least I wasn't waiting in line all day on a Saturday just to buy stale bread.

There were plenty of behaviors in the book for my mother to admire: saving coins in a tin can, reading Shakespeare every night, cleaning wooden banisters, scrubbing things and being cheap. But there was also a lot of behavior that I knew she would think was bad because she is rigid about morality.

This fact made one of my favorite scenes in the book the most confusing in terms of the book being a recommendation of my mother. In the scene, Francie and her dad are on a walk and they pass a prostitute.

After the prostitute propositions Johnny, Francie asks her father the obvious.

"Was that a bad lady, Papa?" she asked eagerly.

"No."

"But she looked bad."

"There are very few bad people. There are just a lot of people that are unlucky."

My mom couldn't possibly think that was true. This is the same woman who made snorting sounds at the stories on the evening news of politicians or evangelists who got caught cheating on their wives. But here she was handing me a book with such a generous take on human frailty.

And she had to have known that I would not be able to read the book without falling in love with Aunt Sissy, the warmest character in the book—she was also the sluttiest. Even at that age, I think it was clear to my entire family that people like Sissy were the ones I would grow up wanting to hang around. At ten, I loved our next-door neighbor, nicknamed Cricket, who was a biker chick with cornrows in her hair and silver stilettos on her feet. Cricket and Sissy were not that dissimilar and my mother hated Cricket. If I had been brave enough to ask her what she thought of Sissy, my mother probably would have skirted the whole promiscuous issue and instead focused on the fact that Sissy had a full-time job and she was nice to her sister.

And the core tale, of the tree that wouldn't die and the people who wouldn't give up, is most likely the one that my mother liked best. These people were nailed over and over again with huge problems to the point that I was scared to turn the page to see what other bad news they would have. But these wretched people kept trying, page after page.

And as a fan of risk-taking and big dreams, my mother probably loved the scene as much as I did where Francie and her little brother Nelly participated in the yearly Christmas toss, when you would win a free tree if you were not first knocked over by the blow. The vendor wishes he could give them the tree instead of throwing it at them, but knows that he is doing them no favors not to prepare them for life.

That lesson was probably the one that she most hated to give me, but is actually the most important one. It is a goddamned, rotten, lousy world, and she was realistic enough not to hide that fact from me.

By the very fact that she chose to give me this book, when I finished reading it, I had a brand-new mother. This woman that I thought had the world's most narrow idea of what is proper behavior actually had a wide expanse of what she could handle reading about in books. I'm not saying that she liked the sex parts of it—that was probably something she suffered through to get to the meat of the story—but I did know that she would never have told us we could not read something, even if the content was salacious or sexual. If asked, my mother would probably place people who don't let their kids read certain books somewhere in between the people who don't believe in evolution and the people who drink a lot of beer during the day. The only thing that was ever banned in my house was a *Glamour* magazine that my eleven-year-old sister brought home with the yellow text on the cover proclaiming "How to Give the Best Oral Sex Of Your Life."

I think that the only reason people withhold books from their kids is that they are frightened by the power of books. Books can open a kid's mind, they can cause them to consider an out-of-state college and can make them be magnanimous toward other people. Books make the world more human and human behavior more palatable. Maybe through the empathy that comes from reading literature, my mother thought I could learn how to be empathetic towards people in real life, as well.

Books offer the ability to walk in another's shoes. As an adult, I have friends with drug problems, drinking problems, gossiping problems, shopping problems and sexual extremes that involve the Internet. I have friends that are cheaters, liars and shoplifters, and not one of them do I want August judging. Don't get me wrong, I'm all for judging. I judge a lot of my friends for being superficial, greedy or evil. But I am not going to judge somebody for being a whore or seeking comfort in a glass of anything alcoholic. And since I don't want my daughter to do that, either, the best way I can influence her is to give her books with lots of wonderful and messed-up people living in them.

Not only will I use books to teach August how to be empathetic towards others, I will give her books to teach her about everything. Before she starts middle school, I will give her *Go Ask Alice,* in the hope that the scene where Alice is high on acid and clawing at her own skin will keep her as scared of drugs as it did me. I can't wait for August to have a run-in with some idiot at school and I can give her *Catcher in the Rye* with the line, "All morons hate it when you call them a moron." I will give her *To Kill a Mockingbird* to learn about racism. When she starts hurtling toward womanhood, I'll give her the Judy Blume box set.

And I will give *A Tree Grows in Brooklyn* to August when she seems like she is prepared for a lot of human frailty, a ton of human strength and some really graphic scenes. And that moment will only happen if I can wrangle her out of her tracksuit and shin guards and into a reclining chair.

But when she reads it, she will be seeing the world with more savvy eyes since she is a Brooklyn baby herself. The exotica of this world that I saw when I read it will be missing. Betty Smith's version of New York was magical to me. The Sioux Falls, South Dakota, of my childhood was a restrained place where people didn't hug; instead they gave the silent one-finger wave from the steering wheel of a truck. Nobody honked their car horn in anger or made out in public. But Francie's neighborhood is a loud and wild place where women wear nightgowns in the middle of the afternoon and scream out their windows, calling people lousy bastards. People are allowed to sleep when the sun is out? They can yell swear words out of windows? *Where is this fantastic place?* I wondered. There couldn't be many Lutherans living there.

And maybe the gesture of handing August that book, one of the few inheritances I have to offer, will show her that I have faith in her ability to view the world with compassion. Maybe giving August that book will make her more compassionate toward me, as it made me toward my mother.

Reading is one of the greatest gifts my parents gave me and I get excited when I think of giving books to August. I cannot wait to give her *My Antonia, The Heart is a Lonely Hunter* and *The Grapes of Wrath*. Will she love words the way I do? Will the sight of full bookshelves make her feel at home? Will she get hooked on the serendipity of books and love how one leads to the next to the next to the next and love how they all seem to come into your life right when you need the lessons or comfort they offer? If I can get her to read, I will be giving her the most affordable luxury of life. Even if poverty keeps her pinned into one place, she can always escape into books. Between what has been given to her and handed down and desperately purchased by her tired parents at the airport, August already has many books. They topple out everywhere and I spend half my life returning them to their shelves.

August should already be accustomed to all these books, because she spent plenty of time around them as a newborn. I was not a very good first-time mother. That first year my husband worked a lot, traveled even more and, transplants in Brooklyn, we were far from helpful grandparents and too poor for child care. I suffered from a real loneliness and a sense of having no idea who I was anymore. Being a mother made me feel trapped and pinned down, and in response, I spent most of my days out in the world just trying to connect to somebody.

And I went where I have always found comfort in the past: to rooms full of books.

August accompanied me on my all-day circuit: coffee shop, bookstore, library, coffee shop, bookstore. I hope that in those early days, maybe the smells of the books entered her psychic space where childhood smells and sights stay until they rise up later in life and lead us somewhere. Because I need to invade her psychic space, if I'm going to fight all of those active impulses that she is being given by her father.

Why is it so important to me that she read? What do I think reading can give her?

Solace. Humanity. The sense that we are not actually completely alone in this world. It gave me the idea that my life could possibly exist outside of Sioux Falls. As a New York kid, she may not need that. And maybe one book will change her life. I love the idea that she will stumble across a line in a book and the clouds will part, the sun will appear and the bright rays will illuminate what it was she was put on the earth to do. I'm hoping her bright rays shine down on investment banking, but that's between her and her illuminating moment.

Reading is sometimes a burden, as well. You become a loner with weak eyes and a weird frame of reference. You become easily annoyed by ignorance. You risk becoming a smarty-pants. And a reader can never feel sated. Will August, like me, practically have a panic attack from thinking, *All those books! All those books I have to read!*

My reasons for wanting her to read are selfish, as well. Maybe if I can make her read, then we will find a way to communicate, even in those quiet years between when she grows breasts and when she picks a college, when it is hard to say anything to one another that doesn't sound exasperated.

So I will grab her early, take the soccer ball from her hands and make her become a reader. Because once you are a reading addict, there is no amount of animosity toward your mother that will prevent you from accepting a good book and all of its hidden lessons.

WHAT MUST HAVE SEEMED LIKE GRACE
Ann Fisher-Wirth

She had always known a thousand ways to circle them
all around with what must have seemed like grace.
—From *Housekeeping* by Marilynne Robinson

On my office desk, I keep a black-and-white snapshot that my father took of my mother sixty years ago. She stands in front of a heavily mortared stone wall, or perhaps the side of a house, in Wetzlar, Germany. She wears a black coat, underneath which I see the neckline of a white sweater, and silver-and-cloisonné earrings that intrigued me all through childhood. She is freckled, with full lips, a Roman nose, beautiful arching brows, fluffy forties hair, and large round eyes; once, seeing this picture, a student whistled. "Wow, what a movie star." She holds me, one-year-old. I'm grabbing my bonnet string, looking down sideways, and as she wrote on the back of the photograph, talking as always. When I miss her—which is often—I look at this picture and remember how lucky I was in her love.

My mother was the goddess of my childhood. But much about her life will always remain mysterious, for though I knew her intimately, with every fiber of my being—knew her touch, her voice, her scent, the gurgling of her stomach as I rested my head in her lap—I did not know many things about her. She grew up in a reticent age and was a private person, a lady, a Nebraskan.

Bits about her...
One day my mother and her sister, Irma and Virginia, both children, ducked into a church to escape a sudden rain. Someone was reading

the Lesson. What they heard made them convert to Christian Science, putting behind them their own mother's warnings about galoshes and pneumonia. My mother's father worked in the stockyards in Omaha, doing something important, riding Rex, his palomino. My mother's father was in business, and his partner absconded with the funds. He made good the losses, so that, all one winter, my mother had only one dress to wear to school. My mother's mother wanted to be an actress, but her father wouldn't let her. My mother's sister died—but how and why she died, a year after her marriage—well, my sisters and I heard different stories. Or no stories. By the time my mother was thirty, she'd been married and divorced and had her daughter Joan, and lost her whole birth family.

At the start of World War II, my mother moved from Omaha to New York City with Joan. Divorced and newly orphaned, she realized that if my father, her fiancé, did not survive the war, she would need to make a life for herself and support Joan as a single parent. She began a rapid rise in the fashion industry as a reporter for one of the trade journals—work she adored. But when my father returned from Manila just after Christmas in 1945, with a typewriter that smelled of jungle rot and skin dyed orange from the anti-malarial drug called atabrine, she promptly gave up her life and career in New York to become an Army wife and bear my father two children.

My mother was that perhaps-rare phenomenon: a genuinely happy, fulfilled, creative, traditional housewife. She followed my father to Wetzlar, where he was stationed for three years during the Occupation. There, my little sister Jennifer was born, and I learned German along with English.

The house we lived in belonged to a Nazi major, who left razor blades in the yard and I would play with them. There was little in the stores. My mother couldn't buy floor wax, so she invented it out of shoe polish, melted candles and gasoline. Sometimes, at the PX, she had to buy cans that had lost their labels, so it was anyone's guess what they'd have for dinner. People would come to the door, wanting to sell their heirlooms for bread and bacon—once, a Lutheran minister with ten Nazi-shattered fingers. She taught local women English. She cut up her living room curtains to make diapers for orphaned babies.

We came back to Pennsylvania in 1950, and lived there for five years—probably the happiest years of my parents' lives. There, we got a dog and planted flowers. We ate three meals a day, using our very best table manners. *Mabel, Mabel, sweet and able / Keep your elbows off the table,* my mother would often remind us. Sometimes she told us stories about her life in New York in fashion, when she worked for a woman called Toby. All during childhood, we played a fashion-based game called Let's Describe; it involved, simply, describing glamorous imaginary clothes and the houses to host the parties to wear those clothes in. We passed the kinds of days that people long for when their lives have been torn by grief and war. But then my father was sent to Korea. Then we met him in Japan. Two years later, he retired and we moved to Berkeley. These were to be my parents' golden years; they would joke about buying a little red sports car after we girls grew up, and driving around the country together, a beret on his balding head, a scarf in her auburn hair. But then my father collapsed one night. He was operated on a few days later, for brain cancer. Though he recovered for nearly a year, he collapsed again on Labor Day, 1962, and three months later he died.

I asked my mother once why she and my father never fought. She said they had lost so much, and lived through World War II, and their lives were filled with so much separation that they knew how to treasure the time they had. They were deeply in love; the union between them was absolute and palpable. Though my mother married again and lived until 2003, my father's death was the loss of her life.

From 1955 to 1957, my father was stationed in Japan, where we joined him after he finished a tour of duty in Korea. During our years in Japan, my mother took up painting—just as a hobby, while we girls were at school. She had majored in art at college, but had to give that up because of the Depression: she needed a dependable source of income. Over the years, as we grew up and she had time, her painting continued to blossom. She was a very talented painter, especially of abstract landscapes, but though her teachers invited her to exhibit professionally, she always preferred to keep her painting private. Yet—and here is the thing about her—she also wanted to be known. When she moved away from Berkeley at age eighty-six, she held the garage sale of all garage sales, clearing out not only her things but also my stepfather's things, layer upon layer of possessions accrued for decades all over the world. Among her offerings were the portraits she'd made in painting class: all of strangers, and not nearly as good as her luminous landscapes. She was crushed that no one bought them. And though Jennifer, Joan and I treasured her landscapes and hung them proudly in our living rooms and bedrooms, Jennifer heard her mutter that day that no one had ever valued her art.

Although it's true my mother was the goddess of my childhood, I realize now that I was hurt in some ways by her absolutely unswerving insistence on good behavior, good manners, privacy, self-sacrifice. As an adolescent, I split—as did many young women of my generation—into two selves: public and private, aboveground and subterranean. I became the black sheep of my family, my nonconformity culminating in an unwed pregnancy and the stillbirth of my first daughter when I was eighteen. This was a matter of secrecy and shame—though if the truth be known, I didn't feel shame and my mother loved babies so much that at some level, beneath her conventional response, she didn't feel it either. Mostly, it was a matter of incredible grief. When I first showed my mother a group of my poems, years later, her reaction was, "These are beautiful, Annie. You must never try to publish them."

And yet, as my father had done, my mother absolutely supported the importance of their daughters' education. After my father's death, she became a high school English teacher, and one day when I was complaining about having nothing to read, she told me I was old enough to appreciate her favorite novel, Virginia Woolf's *To the Lighthouse.* I date my fate as an English major from that day. I sat cross-legged in my room high in the Berkeley hills, reading and falling in love with *To the Lighthouse* as the sun went down over the Bay—and no literary character has ever reminded me as much of my mother as Mrs. Ramsay, with her beauty, her maternal tenderness, but also her "wedge-shaped core of darkness."

When, in a fit of adolescent boredom, I decided that I wouldn't go to college, she put me in the car and drove me up and down the state of California, patiently stopping at one campus after another until I agreed to apply somewhere. She drove from Berkeley to Claremont to attend every single play I ever acted in, even the production of Ugo Betti's *The Queen and the Rebels,* which attracted an audience of eleven, on a Sunday of pouring rain.

She was behind me every step of the way as I went through graduate school—which took a decade, because my then-husband was also a graduate student and during those years I gave birth to three children. She flew down to Claremont to take care of the kids while I typed his dissertation. She slipped us checks when things got bad, as when my three-year-old Jessica told her over the phone, "Grandma, we're just like Hansel and Gretel—we have *only one penny.*" And, when my dissertation was finally done—and later became my book on William Carlos Williams—she read it over and over, every word.

My mother left me a legacy that for years I couldn't live up to. My daughters and oldest son, the children of my first marriage, had a far rockier childhood than I did. They are the children of a bitter divorce. This is a tragic history I still find difficult to talk about. But eventually the five children in our family—mine, my husband's, and ours—have come to love each other, and to know and believe in our enormous love for them. Knock on wood, to me our family feels wonderful and firm now.

But this is an essay not about families, but just about mothers and daughters. So, what have I given my daughters? Besides an interest in gardening and cooking, a passion for dogs and children, and a lack of talent for sewing? Besides heartfelt admiration and a love for them so deep that I could never come to the end of it? I'm not sure what they would say, but I can think of several things.

First, I've created a path in my own life, which, I think, has shown them that women can accomplish a great deal in the public arena. I earned my Ph.D. at thirty-five; I'm now a professor of English at the University of Mississippi, where I teach American literature, poetry seminars and workshops, and a wide range of courses in environmental literature. For years, after my first foray into poetry, I didn't write a poem. In my mid-forties, I started writing poetry again—and as far as writing, that's my passion now. I've been supremely fortunate in my career path: I have a job I love, a job that allows me to keep redefining myself and that constantly challenges my creativity. Second, I tried far less than my mother tried with me, to keep my daughters docile, keep them quiet. I believe I let them be what they wanted to be—and frankly, I always found their adventures fascinating and moving. They are powerful women; I am as proud as I could be of their fierce dedication to truth and social justice. I admire the leaps they make; I think certain kinds of self-confidence are easier for women of their generation than they were for women of mine. I admire how beautifully they do things. I admire their gregariousness, their toughness and their courage.

And what have they given me? That is easy to answer. When my first child died, I thought I would die. My living children—sons and daughters both—pulled me back into the world. I wanted to be a mother ever since I was a kid. They gave me my life.

THE POSSIBILITY OF YOU
Amanda Coyne

> I am not the mare
> buffeted, days now, in the pasture
> below me, head down, rump to the sea,
> worn so out from standing she won't
> graze. Child at the window, a voice
> says, Heart, come to the table for tea.
> —From "As Memory" by Linda McCarriston

Whenever I travel from Alaska to the Lower 48, I stare at the girls holding and strolling their babies. They look so young to me, barely old enough to drive. Their legs are foal-like. Their skin lightly sun-soaked, calling to mind butters and caramels and lightly toasted marshmallows.

They should be in front of a fire, I think, at some clearing at the end of a country road, chugging bad wine, with nothing more profound on their minds than if they look fat in those jeans, the idea of having a baby as foreign to them as, well, as their lives seem to me.

And then I think, scratch that. No way. They're perfect the way they are. I've spent some time on some country roads in my life, drinking wine, standing in front of that fire. And it didn't do me a whole lot of good. In fact, it landed me in Alaska, writing a letter to a child that I don't yet have, and can't quite decide if I should be allowed to have, if nothing else (and there is a lot else) because of where I've decided to live.

Being trapped in one's house for eight months, nearly every errand fraught with danger, the lack of certain civil amenities to take the edge off—a robust snowplowing operation, a culture of shoveling one's sidewalks and of community gatherings, a little warm glowing wine bar down the street—has worked out to be dandy for a certain type of people, but it plays hell on new mothers. Sled dog mushers do really well up here. So do inventors and, well, convicts. Multifaceted personalities abound. I have a pretty good story, but it means little in Alaska. I don't jump out of airplanes. I haven't been rescued by the Coast Guard. I don't spend some weekends quilting and others slithering through the thicket, my rifle's eye poised at a big grizzly who's pissed and who's heading my way. I haven't had a frostbitten digit amputated. I don't live in a cabin without running water. I don't even ski.

But I'm not put in a box here. I'm not categorized. For good and for bad, there's a limitlessness in Alaska. For all its physical heaviness, there's a lightness of being, a lack of the weight of history. You can be what you want to be up here. Whenever I leave and come back, the first thing I do when I get off the airplane is to take a deep breath. It's big here like no other place. It's big enough for all the deep breaths in the world.

You see a lot of me in Alaska. But you don't see those others: girls whose days are a series of to-do lists and by-the-hour date-book appointments, whose husbands get up early for Rotary and who spend the rest of their days in offices working to ensure that our country runs with robotic efficiency.

There's a version of that girl here, but she tends to be a bit older, and has had some experience somewhere that has made her decide to do something good for the world, and she usually has a petition in hand to show for it. Usually, I can't be bothered to stop and add my signature to the long list of my fellow citizens who worry about the gold being mined, the oil being drilled. I'm living smack-dab on the front lines of global warming, and I understand that if things are going the way that scientists are predicting, you'll be living in a world of droughts and floods, famine and thirst. People will be shooting each other over depleted resources, and the market for sunblock will be sky high.

Why don't I care about this?

I could go on about the promise of technology. But honestly, I've just got too much on my mind lately to be too concerned about what might happen, someday, far away. Here's just a little taste: Your uncle John, my brother, is on some kind of heroin binge again. Tony, your father-to-be, struggles with depression; and although it's something that he's winning, it takes a tremendous amount of energy on both of our parts. Then there's your grandmother (my mother), who emerged recently from some sort of government imposed half-death to plunk herself down about a mile away from me. She just finished up a twelve-year prison sentence, and she chose Alaska as the place of her reemergence, she says, because she needed to breathe, too.

And then, of course, there's the possibility of you, which at this point, if there is going to be a you, might require more than a certain amount of assistance.

When Tony's feeling good, he thinks we should go for it. Get all those cycle-schedule things, those ovulation packages, those thermometers, turn my body into a biological project. He likes projects. Projects involve fixing, joining things, turning chaos into matter. I tend to think that there's no use forcing the matter. That if you really want to be here, you'll come, and all the pills and the thermometers and the raised legs won't change that.

If you do end up coming to us, Tony will build you the best crib that a child could ever have. He'll think about it endlessly, spend his evenings making drawings, talking woods and slats. He'll check it constantly. Oil it, test its sturdiness, do the things that men do to things that they build.

I'll hover over it, watching you sleep, trying to enter your dreams. He'll be the one to make sure you make it to your doctor's appointments. I'll be the one who will tramp through your world of forests and fairies and fight the scary monsters for you.

He likes arguments settled, long early-morning talks where feelings are laid bare, where secret longings and pinings and those tiny resentments are given air and wilt in the sunlight. I've always insisted on the mystery of the inchoate, the magic in the unseen and the unspoken.

But now you (I mean, the possibility of you) have me wondering if I haven't insisted a little *too* much. It seems to me that as we age, it's the things we keep insisting about ourselves, the aspects of our personalities that we claim unalterable, which become less and less becoming, more and more perpetuated out of weakness. Those things can take us over, turn us into caricatures.

Caricatures shouldn't be allowed to have babies. Real babies demand real people, like those girls I see strolling their babies in Denver and Houston. Like the person I might be, or come close to being, if I get something right, finally, after all these years.

There are feelings that I've allowed to remain unspoken and unimagined for too long. I fear that if I continue to ignore it, I'll be the woman who, when you get a few glasses of wine in her, won't stop talking about that *thing* that happened to her when she was young. I'll be the woman who laughs too loudly at bad jokes at parties, my eyes flitting about, never focusing on anything. I'll be the woman whose mouth and opinions are too firmly set, who starts her sentences with "I'm the kind of person who…" The kind of person who never knows what kind of person she really is.

And how can I expect you to be formed when I am still so half-formed?

This may hurt you, but with or without you, your father is a real person. I grow weary of his demons, his lack of religiosity and transcendental feeling. But the core of him is fully formed, his center always center. He has *values*. And I'm lucky enough to be madly in love with him, a fact that continues to astound me.

On the face of it, he and I have little in common. His parents grew up in the same speck of a town in Wisconsin, a place where the wives still wear beehives, where the husbands' thumbs are mangled from farm equipment, where they convene for games of cards on Friday night *up*town at the local pub.

They began dating in junior high and haven't wavered in their commitment to each other since. When they made *good* for themselves, they moved the family to Lake Forest, Illinois—announcing their entry into the upper class with a bang—when Tony was a boy and hadn't left. His mother gave up a nursing career to raise her children, volunteer for Hospice and collect German porcelain figurines. After work, his father would come home and supervise the building of a model train set, which needed its own house in the backyard. The newspaper gets thrown away everyday at 9:00 a.m. and the coffee is decaffeinated. You might have a hard time finding a dusty nook to sit in and quietly read a book, but you'll never trip over a stray shoe left on the floor or be in want for any kind of pain relief. If you emptied all the medicine cabinets in the house, there'd be enough aspirin and ibuprofen to keep a small town numb for a week. They put their faith in science, in pills, in instructions and directions, and in each other. I've never met people who were so loyal to each other, and now they are loyal to me. They take care of me, and they will you, too.

In the various houses that I was raised in all across the country, constant hangovers ensured that we were always out of aspirin. It wouldn't be hard to find a newspaper dated from months before, smelling vaguely of cat urine and stuffed in the corner of an oversize chair. My father was a writer (and sometimes a successful one), whose hands were only made to punch at keyboards. If something broke in our house, he'd kick it, and there it would remain, broken and kicked. My mother's taste in art tended towards the *grotteschi*. Once, she commissioned an artist to paint tiny goblins peaking from behind the oranges and apples in a perfectly nice still life. Our family asked for directions instead of using maps. Or we just drove around, aimlessly. And in a way, I'm still driving.

You'll never want for dolls in number or variety. Tony's mother has a whole room of them, all so content with their apple cheeks and rosebud lips, holding their little bottles, sitting on their little rockers. My mother spent much of her time in prison making *dolls* out of contraband material. They looked so real that the Haitian women took them for voodoo dolls and caused a ruckus over them, resulting in her doll-making privileges being taken away for a while. (There is some truth in the claim that I didn't do enough for her in prison. I didn't write weekly. I didn't organize any protests over her long sentence or have bake sales in order to get her a better lawyer. I didn't send her picture to any of the numerous groups formed to protest long federal sentences like hers. I did, however, visit at least once a year, and I did call my U.S. senator when the prison told her she couldn't make her dolls. I argued first amendment rights to an aide. "Dolls?" he said. I never heard back.)

You'll never want for dolls, or stories, either, many of which will revolve around your grandmother. When you complain about a too-small Christmas tree, say, an overcooked turkey, an Easter basket filled with books instead of chocolate eggs, I'll no doubt not resist talking to you about the Christmases and Easters and Thanksgivings I spent visiting my mother in prison (conveniently forgetting that I was an adult during these visits). And as you get older, the stories will get more complicated. You might hear me talk about what it was like to have my government on one side of me and my mother on the other. Sometimes, I might cry about it, as I do sometimes. Or, I might do that funny "ha, ha" thing that I do also, and belt out, unexpectedly, "I was drunk the day my mother got out of prison."

And I'm sure, at least once, the following scene will transpire: I'll be visiting in the Midwest, where my two sisters live. And after we have put all the kids to bed, we'll sit around someone's kitchen table and we'll talk. One of them will ask me how she is.

And I will say, "She's good. Great, in fact," and then I'll talk in an overly chirpy voice about how absolutely great she is.

And then they'll glance at each other out of the corners of their eyes.

They have things called "boundaries" now. They have children who depend on them, and fulfilling careers and houses and mortgages that they pay (on time!) and one of them, at least, a husband, an Iowa boy if there ever was one, whose feet could not be more firmly planted on the ground, whose view, when he looks out of himself and his family at all, is only of the straight line on the Iowa horizon and not beyond.

You will have snuck out of your bed, because a part of me will be in you, and when I was a child, I burned for adult conversation. There was a mystery in that talk, far more enticing than Barbie-gossip with little Susie. Indeed, the clanking of silverware, the sound of the wine being poured into the glass, the smell of cigarettes, the conversation that I just knew someday I would be able to decode, could almost put me in a swoon. (Perhaps the hardest thing that I've had to come to as an adult is the knowledge that the trappings will all be there. But that conversation will still, and always, be a version of what one Barbie said about another, and that although I've been around the world, the most exotic place I've ever been is the brief time I spent in childhood.)

So there you will be, at the top of the stairs, hidden in shadow, and your aunts and I will be talking about *her.* And by our tones, you'll no doubt guess who *her* is.

I will continue in my overly chirpy voice, talking about how much she's changed, how much she's following the rules, how much people like her and, for good measure, how nice it is to have her cook for me again: thinking that this might cinch the deal. That if I can leave them with an image of her in the kitchen, where she was at her best, instead of, say, in her "sewing" room, separating piles of white powder into plastic bags, her sitting unrepentantly in the sad plastic chair in some prison visiting room, then maybe, just maybe, I can bring us all back again, home again.

They know this about me, understand my motives, and they won't be fooled. They think that there's something unhealthy with this obsession of mine with home and forgiveness.

One of them will want to say, "How can you? After all she's put *you,* particularly you, through?"

And I will want to say, "She's part of us. How can you two just give up on us?"

But none of us will say any of this. We'll talk about exercise and diets. We'll talk politics and local news. We'll talk about child rearing and relationships, and you, the girl on the top of the stairs, will hear that thing that isn't said, in the way that children do. You'll hear the static beyond the words, and something in you will know that there's more to be known here. That there's more to the story than simply a grandmother who spent twelve years in prison, a mother who was or wasn't drunk when her own mother was released. You'll know there's more than bad holiday visits and a woman at odds with her mother and her government.

When I was a girl, I once hid in the shadows as my mother told her own sister how bad she was at ironing and how much my father yelled at her for it. She said something like, "I just can't get the collars right," and she was sobbing. Even then I knew that she wasn't crying over collars, and I filed the scene away to be translated later.

Here, now, it's later, and here's the translation: my mother was in her thirties then, she had four children, an overbearing, snappish husband. She couldn't keep a house clean, she had no interest in keeping a house clean. She wanted to be a writer, like her husband. But he wouldn't let her, because he knew that if she wrote, she'd sail away from him and wouldn't take care of his children or cook his meals and iron his shirts. She was crying because she hated her life, a life that was wrapped around us, her children.

I'm not particularly envious of those girls I see in the Lower 48, whose bodies are ripe, and who, unlike me, now need to take pills and use various plastic barriers to keep something like you from usurping their bodies.

I, unlike so many women my age right now, am not decrying the cruelty of biology, how our emotional and psychological readiness does not at all correspond to our physical capabilities. In some ways, I think, it serves us right for being so gullible as to listen to our tenured professors, in whose classrooms Sylvia Plath's fate loomed so large. It serves us right, maybe, for not noticing how many of those professors had children at the appropriate time, and how they weren't going around sticking their heads into ovens.

To be envious would involve a certain insertion of a self at about that age, and the two just won't mix. I spent my early twenties reeling, hopping from one idea to the next, one philosophy to the next, one plan to the next, one relationship to the next. And there is no way that I could ever have settled for the men that these girls at the airport have. It would take years and a move to Alaska for me to appreciate how it can be, settling with one man, and now I know there is nothing in the world like it. Domestic peace is the most glorious peace I've ever known, and I have no doubt that it would only get better with you around.

Don't you want to share it? As I just wrote these words, I knew that there was trickery going on. This, of course, is not a letter to you. I'm sorry for this. I realize that even before you've had the chance to be born, I'm turning you into a means for my own creative expression, using the possibility of you as an opportunity to make something right.

You'll no doubt be raised with stories. I'm a writer, and that's what I do. I tell stories. I use parts of my own life to tell these stories. So much of me won't be hidden from you. And when you get old enough, if you're interested, you'll be able to read more stories: you'll read about past relationships, about struggles with drugs and booze and ideas. You'll read some stories about your grandmother's time in prison, about your uncle and his heroin obsession, about your father's depression.

Those I've told and retold. But here's one you'll only find here: one that, until now, I've never had the courage to tell. Come fly with me and let me show you something. Let me take your little hand, and come with me through the thicket of memory, to a place where a part of me has been trapped, frozen, where all of this trouble began.

In this place, I'm sixteen years old and I'm walking up the

steps to board a Greyhound bus, heading for Marietta, Georgia. There's a man there, waiting for me. The man there is not a monster, but he's weak. And when he gets me, it won't be pretty. My mother knows this. A part of her knows that she should stop me because of it. But there's her own man with her and I'm too young and too irresistible. She's running out of options and maybe, just maybe, if I'm gone, there will be peace.

I think of that moment all the time. I thought of it when she stood shackled in front of the judge. I thought of it every time I saw her sitting in one of those hard plastic prison chairs. I thought of it when, just recently, she walked down the airport terminal, after twelve years spent behind bars, coming to a harsh place, to be next to her daughter who judges her so.

I don't know a lot about truth or about justice, about right or wrong. I can't pick a political party, a stance on things like abortion or the death penalty. But I do know what festering resentments do to somebody. I know how powerful and righteous they can make you feel. I know how you can hold on to them, turn them into a part of your personality that you feel you have the *right* to have.

Whoever you are or who you might become, if you remember nothing else about what I might teach you, remember this: we like to hold on to pain and justify it by creating false narratives for ourselves, and in those narratives we always come out looking more noble than we have a right to.

So let's go back to that place, together, and look at that scene again. The bus pulls up, she looks at me, and isn't there something in her eyes that I can't, or won't see? Isn't there a well of shame there that will eventually take her to places that no woman should ever go? Isn't this the start of the thing that drove her to deal drugs and then to prison? After she broke that one taboo, what was left for her? Why not just sink all the way down, as far as you can go? Why haven't I allowed myself to see that other part of her? Why have I kept both of us so trapped for so long?

What I'll tell you is this: She's living right up the road from me, and she's waiting patiently. So let's just go, you and me. Our first mother and daughter outing. Come to me, and let's tell it to her together. Let's say, "Come out of prison. We've both been there too long."

And then, let's get on with life. Let's get on with having you.

PHONE BUDDIES
Laurie Gwen Shapiro

"Good-bye!" she whispered. Then she summoned all her strength and waved one of her front legs.
   —From *Charlotte's Web* by E. B. White

"Tell her Grandma is asking for her," my mother says adamantly, like all she needs to do is tie a raffia bow around the problem to fix it.

The fact that my daughter, three-and-a-half, refuses to talk on the phone would be frustrating to any grandmother, I suppose. Except the grandmother in question had to wait until her late seventies for a first grandchild. Also, being a retired fund-raiser, she loves, above all, enthusiasm. Conversely, she is annoyed the most by unresponsiveness.

"She had a really bad day. I'm going to leave her alone."

"Three-year-olds only have a bad five minutes. She's probably fine now. Enough of this crap, Laurie, please call my grandkid to the phone."

Corked, I don't tell her that Violet had a full-throttle meltdown after being teased at school that day. Back home, I finally calmed her down. Now I cringe as I survey the current landscape: a calm kid, oh so calm, popping plastic Zoob construction pieces (her current favorite grandmother-sent overpriced toy) into their sockets.

"Would you like to talk to Grandma?" I say, defeated.

Her eyes glance over at me, a desperate plea followed by a look of betrayal. "No!" Violet dives under her Dora the Explorer quilt bought by Grandma Jean to celebrate her move out of our family bed. She pretends to snore.

I drag her by the hand to the phone. "Please be nice. Grandma Jean loves you."

"Yes?" Violet says harshly, as my clamped hand prevents her from fleeing.

She listens, then says, "I told you last time I'll talk to you in April, when I see you."

"That was pleasant," I say, back on the phone.

My mother, the ex-fund-raiser, will not capitulate. She was so eager to greet this little girl into the universe that she joined my apprehensive husband in the delivery room to help hold down my thighs. She was the first to talc this kid's bottom, first to dare trim her fingernails with a clipper.

The picture of Violet flayed out deliriously in the snow in her violet snowsuit? My mother sent the snowsuit.

Violet's violet tricycle? Violet's play kitchen? Both from Grandma, too. (Grandpa "signed" the cards, too, in Grandma's handwriting.) No, Grandma will not wait until she comes to New York in April, two months from now, to talk to her only grand-child.

"She is getting into brat territory."

"Who's the brat here?" I protest. "She loves you, she just hates the phone. And you're forcing the phone on a shy kid."

"What little girl hates the phone? I saw her chattering away on the toy cell phone I gave her."

"She was having imaginary conversations with imaginary friends she can control."

"We are going to be phone friends," my mother says the next morning, "Don't try to stop us."

She is highly motivated.

There are people persons, and then there is my mother, who in 2005 is still friends with the woman from Rome whose wallet she found in Herald Square in 1979—a wallet stuffed with thousands of dollars—and the woman still sends a poinsettia to Mom's house every Christmas, in gratitude.

She is e-mail buddies with the Chinese-American woman she consoled on a Jet Blue flight, the one with the denigrating dissertation on the history of chop suey.

She is friends with the Jamaican woman who washes her hair at the salon; she's been to her house for a jerk chicken lunch after lamenting she never tried jerk chicken. She is friends with the chief of the Seminoles to whom she has given fund-raising advice after inviting him to a Friends of the Library luncheon to talk about Florida's First People. She is friends with a very flamboyant film publicist she met in a South Beach café, and gets a "plus one" invite to every art house film premiere in Miami, where he parades her around the after-parties like she's the Queen Mother on leave from Buckingham Palace.

Speaking of queens, she was sort of friends with Leona Helmsley up until just before the Queen of Mean died—they met through a fund-raising luncheon Mom threw in her honor—and after months of working together the so-called Dragon Lady pronounced my mother, "Absolutely delightful."

As a child, I lived to please. I dutifully complied when sent over to cutely ask for Telly Savalas's signature in a Los Angeles hotel lobby, and when we went to Amish Pennsylvania I donned an Amish sunbonnet and dress. My brother mocked my submissiveness relentlessly. But he, too, was quickly taught to at least greet people the way my mother deemed The Right Way. In Violet, also her own flesh and blood, Mom has met her biggest challenge. It's not all bad. Violet truly loves Grandma, but only when she can see her face. The most successful interaction to date was on Mom's big rocking chair during our last visit to Florida. Grandma captivated her one grandchild with the tragic story of her cat Franco who one day ate too many SpaghettiOs and kept jumping and jumping and jumping until he died. Violet was mortified but completely engaged, especially when she heard that Franco sired many orange kittens in the neighborhood who occasionally popped into Violet's great-grandfather's candy store for a hello. That day was kind of magical—they were interacting so miraculously well that my husband and I went out vintage clothing shopping in untapped Broward County Goodwills with nary a worry. When we returned they had just finished Old Maid and had moved on to pick-up sticks. That night Violet tried on costume jewelry, which Mom called pirate booty. She spritzed her grandmother's atomizers, and fell asleep on my parents' bed, exhausted. When I moved her off the bed into the guestroom she stank of Chanel No. 5.

Yet a week later, back in New York, she still wouldn't come to the phone when summoned.

My daughter has nothing approaching my genetic enthusiasm. When participation is required, she takes after her father. Paul's so laid-back that during father-daughter games of hide-and-seek, he never bends his knees when ducking around corners, and almost always brings along his coffee to keep sipping.

My father who never cries is crying on the phone. "He thinks, that's all he said." *He* is the "cancer" doctor my mother went to on her internist's advice when the bloating in her stomach looked suspicious. They hadn't wanted to alarm us before.

The tickets are booked in minutes, so we may be there for the official diagnosis. My father, the absentminded scientist type, usually has my mother to keep him steady.

When we touch ground in Fort Lauderdale, my brother calls my father's cell. Mom is weak enough to be checked in at her local medical center, awaiting the formal diagnosis. David and I drop my husband and daughter off at the retirement community, so Paul can shield Violet from Bad Hospital Conversations. My brother and I remain mute until the crunch of hospital grounds gravel against our tires.

My brother takes a breath and opens his door: "Here we go."

Dad is there when we open the door. "He's about to come in," he says from the corner, just as there is a door knock.

"He" has "Bad News." The extra water weight was, as per his suspicions, due to ovarian cancer—not fat. She could try the operation, but at her age, eighty-one, he suggests she probably should just go for quality of life. She has about six weeks.

"I'm sorry," he says, as he shuts the door.

What would anyone else say in this situation?

My mother says, "Thank you, Dr. Doom and Gloom. Anyone want a tissue?"

"Mom, Mom," I'm still not sure it is not a mistake. No one dies of cancer in our family. I let loose a wail.

My father and brother have yet to speak. In fact, my father looks like he may never speak again.

"Laurie, stop crying, I need to focus," Mom says. "He said there was an operation. David, schedule me."

"But he said it was very dangerous!" I protest—I'm even more of a train wreck now.

She eyeballs me with wet eyes. "I'll take that risk, that's my glimmer of hope. I want to live longer than a month." She even winks and references our private battle. "Long enough to get my grandkid to talk to me on the phone."

"There will be two grandkids to live for," my brother says,

voice wobbly. It hits me: my kid at least knows her grandmother. David's wife is pregnant. Will their child ever meet his grandma? And also: what is it about the phone that is so damn important to her? Where is this inappropriate thought coming from?

"I want them both calling me on the phone," she says in that chatty voice she used to distract me from ouchy falls. How is she even keeping it together?

Now my father who never cries is sobbing.

My mother will be under the knife within forty-eight hours.

When she survives the operation, which ran three hours longer than expected, even the doctor is amazed.

A week after the operation, my brother offers to stay with Grandma in the hospital a full day, so Violet will get some full-on mommy time. She will then visit the hospital for the first time.

A Florida DJ's voice floats out of the black convertible in front of us as Paul drives us to Flamingo Gardens, a local wildlife sanctuary. Two giant tortoises are mating, and an unthinkable noise is coming out from one of them. Paul rushes his innocent over to the flamingoes with: "Flamingo feathers are turned pink by carotenoids."

"How do you even know that?" I demand.

"Guess which parent of yours knows a lot about flamingoes?"

He reminds me that my nondriving mother has talked him into taking her to Flamingo Gardens six times over the many years we've been visiting her, three more times than she has convinced me to go.

"Can we see the vultures?" Violet asks a few seconds past admissions.

She remembers? Violet was twenty months the first time she came, all caught up with feeding a heron, and I could see her yawning—time to go back to my folks' house—but Mom insisted her barely talking granddaughter absolutely needed to see the vultures and the bobcats. "Vultures! Can you say vultures?" Mom said determinedly as I fumed by the bobcat cage.

My brother calls me on the cell.

"Mom wants you to buy Violet a gift before you visit the hospital with her. And she wants you to tell her she's buying it for her."

After we park at a strip mall near University Hospital, I grab Violet's hand to head her over to the Petco Store next door to Toys "R" Us. "Where are you going? You buy the toys, I don't do that."

"I need time with kittens today."

It's true: Paul has never had to buy a toy with two enthusiastic gift givers in the family, wife and mother-in-law. He emerges, weirdly, with a Chinese New Year Barbie in a silky red dress, and a Taco Bell food set.

The hospital is a few minutes away, and shortly after we emerge on the cancer ward, Mom weakly waves to Violet from her bed.

Violet looks confused, but, thank Heavens, gives her an un-prompted kiss. "Thank you for the gifts." Something of a silver lining: better behavior just when we needed that to happen the most.

"I'm glad you bought that for her," Mom says to Paul. "What did I get her?"

"I'll show you," Violet answers herself.

My mother helps her open the packages, tells Paul that a Chinese New Year Barbie and a Taco Bell food set is exactly what she would have bought. Paul smirks at me, and kisses his mother-in-law on the forehead. Soon, Violet is deep in fantasy play, oblivi-ous to grown-up conversation.

When a nurse arrives to check on the patient, I enlist Paul's help again. "I actually want to stay for this, can you take her out just for a bit?" He sighs, knows what's coming from a kid bad with transitions, and literally drags Violet away from feeding plastic fajitas to Barbie at the base of her grandmother's bed.

"Shh, shh, you'll get your bean burrito later," he silences her outside the hall. "Mommy needs you to be good."

My mother is in fine spirits when she calls New York on Saturday. Two months have passed since the operation, and her doctor is now "cautiously optimistic." Maybe the first chemo drug was a dud, but the new one has produced downward numbers. "Tell me a Violet."

I tell her how she likes saying the word *igloo* now, and that I helped her build an igloo out of ice cubes.

A few days later, Violet gets a picture book featuring an Inuit child eating blubber. Also a tiny baleen whale carved from a walrus's jawbone. A note enclosed explains that it is from my mother's Inuit *tchotchke* collection. My lapsed Catholic husband, always eager to use a new Yiddish word, says *tchotchke* out loud after a sip of Coke.

"Did you know she said the word *Inuit?*" her pre-K teacher says at pickup. "And *baleen?* How did she learn that word?"

For spring break, we head to Florida. On a day with an unhappy mix of high humidity and heat, even for southern Florida, we decide to go to the Muvico Paradise 24 movie theater in Davie, built like an Egyptian temple. My weakened mother shivers from the extreme air-conditioning, but when Violet gambols about the lobby with four-year-old energy, occasionally stopping to finger the fake hieroglyphics, my mother decides this four-year-old obviously has Big Interest in Ancient Egypt.

That night at the Chinese buffet restaurant in Pembroke, we sit on a bench in front of the restaurant with men whose bellies you see before you see them, and women walking by with shopping bags, condo blondes, rows and rows of condo blondes with identical hairstyles.

My mother intertwines her frail fingers with Violet's little rosy pink fingers and asks if she would like to learn more about Egypt.

Violet says, sure, like she's been offered a grape lollipop, and my mother nods at me, pleased with herself.

"You were forcing an answer," I say.

Two weeks later, long after I have forgotten about the Egyptian discussion, a cartouche with "Violet" in hieroglyphics arrives in the mail.

"Did you like your package?" my Mom asks, after she forces me to put Violet on the phone.

"Yes," Violet says, a one-word honest answer.

"Say thank you," I whisper.

"Thank you," Violet says miserably, and runs off to my bed again.

"We're making progress," Mom decides.

More books about Egypt arrive, and I have to hand it to my mother, soon enough Violet asks my husband to scan her favorite drawing of Cleopatra and help her e-mail it to her grandmother. She requests that I read the Egyptian books all the time, and she goes to school talking sarcophaguses and Ibis and Ra. And *feluccas,* the word for Egyptian boats I never knew until my daughter taught me.

"Tell your mother to curb it with the knowledge," my husband cracks. "If I were in school with Violet I'd peashoot her about now."

Another visit to coincide with the newest chemo, after the last one has started resisting. One clear blue-skied morning my mother decides it's time for Butterfly World in Coconut Creek, founded by a man keen on observing animal behavior.

She is the frailest I have ever seen her, but tells Violet cheerfully, "If we sit here, the butterflies will land on us."

Violet eagerly sits snugly close to her with fingers out, and sure enough, within seconds a bright yellow butterfly lands on her finger. She is rapt. My mother smiles at me.

In the gift shop she insists we visit, she really needs a chair. But she limps around, eager to drop a hundred dollars on butterfly paraphernalia for my kid. Dress-up time butterfly wings, a butterfly tote, two different pairs of butterfly post earrings.

"Mom, let's go, it's all too much, and her ears are not even pierced."

"For when they are. Even if I'm not alive you can tell her I bought them for her."

My parents arrive four days early for the big fifth birthday in New York. Mom tells me as she unpacks that she came despite the considerable hassle, because this joyous occasion is her major motivation to keep alive. But the day before the big party Mom admits she's in a really bad way.

It's 8:30 a.m. rush hour, we try to get a cab to the office of a famous cancer doctor a friend of mine knows through her father.

A livery cab driver is picking up my neighbor and daughter to take them to the kid's school. I explain. At the word *hospital* the door pops open.

The famous doctor does not like what he sees.

He clears for an immediate CAT scan. He clears for an immediate admission to Mount Sinai.

She has eight weeks.

She is not going home.

When Aunt Etta arrives at the hospice, my mother immediately begs her to tell me the tale of the day she and my mother saw the Hindenburg flying over New Jersey to Teterboro Airport. Although I have never believed her, Mom swears the whole school came out to wave to the Zeppelin, ten minutes before it crashed. (Her absurd story hinges on my aunt's corroboration.)

"Yes," my aunt says, as she smoothes her younger sister's sheets to cover exposed feet. "They were waving to us. Bunch of Nazis."

When Etta is in the bathroom, my mother asks me to buy a specific book at Barnes & Noble she wants me to read to Violet: *Charlotte's Web*.

I remember the year she read that to me I didn't want to sleep in my own bed, just in case my mother or father would die.

I have sidestepped the word *death* many times. I'm the one who quickly discards withered helium birthday balloons found behind the sofa, the one who fires off small talk when eyeing a stilled goldfish that needs to disappear until a new one can be bought.

But the day after my mother dies, my cousin Jackie, a kindergarten teacher, calls me to insist a five-year-old needs somewhere for a loved one "to go." Even if we decide not to take her to the funeral.

An agnostic-bordering-on-atheist, I reluctantly use the word *Heaven,* hoping she'll take it.

Boy, does she.

But according to Paul, who cares for her while I care for my father, the newly enlightened offspring wants the full inventory of Heaven. Is there an escalator in Heaven? Are there malls in Heaven? Is the dead pigeon we saw on Columbia Street in Heaven? Is the squashed rat we saw on the F train track in Heaven?

I dutifully try a month later, to fulfill one of my mother's last wishes. We're up to the dreaded passage in *Charlotte's Web* when Charlotte announces she is dying.

And then a page or two later, she is dead.

"Why did she have to die, Mommy?" my daughter asks in tears, almost as if on cue, and I am not sure who she is talking about, or exactly how to answer her when I am still so angry at my mother leaving me, and making me the matriarch of our family, at forty. The fact that Charlotte's three daughters are new friends with Wilbur the Pig is barely comforting to her, or even to me. I break a sleeping rule, and she climbs into bed with me from the get-go and holds on to my hand for dear life before she will fall asleep. Stronger memories of the night the dreaded passage was read unfold in my head: Mom read the same book to me after a family funeral my parents mistakenly thought I was old enough for at seven. I kept demanding her to promise she would never die. But Mom said the answer was in this book. The answer was in life, not death. I had no idea what she meant. I simply had nightmares for months.

My disabled father, who now lives with us, seems waxed in the same position, hunched over his computer playing chess with a virtual opponent, but one glance at the window—dark closing in—tells me that time has elapsed.

Still, I know where he is, and I would be more worried if I could not see him. He would like to try Florida again in the winter, with an assistant.

My daughter's vocabulary is increasing again with my father in residence—in strange ways. She knows the word *special* means big frank. Her favorite ice cream is now pistachio. Her favorite cookie is a Mallomar, which, she says, sounding very much like an eighty-seven-year-old born-in-New York cookie expert, is only available in the winter because the chocolate melts.

From a man whose temporary bookshelf reads: *Winning Chess Openings, 10 Most Common Mistakes in Chess, The Chess*

Doctor, Easy Endgame Strategies, Samurai Chess, she has learned the names of the chess pieces, if not exactly taking to the game the way he hoped.

"I'm sorry your wife died," I overhear one day after he lost his temper when all the white pawns were missing from his set, and she told him they were in her dollhouse, again. "Is that why you are so angry?"

"Do you remember her?" he asks with a careful voice.

I continue to eavesdrop.

"Of course I do."

"What do you remember?"

"Grandma had *a lot* of energy."

"Do you remember what Grandma liked to do?"

"Was there anything she did not like?" she says without irony.

My father laughs as he grinds pepper on his eggs from an olive wood peppermill Mom bought in an Israeli gift shop, a peppermill that caused one of their biggest foreign tour bus wars ever.

It is good to hear him laugh. I miss that laugh.

"She didn't like it when you wouldn't talk to her on the phone."

My daughter clutches her cartouche.

"Can we call Grandma on the phone now? I want to ask her what Heaven is like."

"I bet if there is a Heaven gift shop, she's in it," Dad says, still not spotting me.

She reaches for the receiver. "Can I hit the numbers?"

The irony is lost on Violet of course. But still, we talk way past her bedtime, and not just about why she cannot now or ever dial Heaven. We make a pact to honor my mother by thinking of each person one meets as a person who is better off treated with kindness from the get-go.

"You don't have to be kind the way Grandma was, but you have to find your own way to be kind."

My brother's son, Kal, who did get to meet his grandmother for thirteen months, will soon enter rooms smiling, and his sunshiny nature will remind everyone of my mother's. Violet will soon become, much to her parents' surprise, a hot ticket for play-dates.

And much to my family's surprise, I'm not such a reluctant matriarch after all.

MOTHER HUNTING
Kaui Hart Hemmings

A mother's happiness is like a beacon, lighting up the future
but reflected also on the past in the guise of fond memories.
—Honoré de Balzac

I feel something on my leg, the back of my upper thigh. It must be swollen. I think of what I have done to make it swollen and remember the other day at a coffee shop when I was trying to open the door and push the stroller through while holding a cup of coffee. When I finally shuffled through I let go, but the stroller is not one of those Hummerlike strollers, so it got lodged in a crack and the door came flying against my leg. A man stood behind me watching, not helping, just watching me struggle, and it made me feel so ugly because if I was pretty he would have opened the goddamn door. *Fucker,* I mouth to myself then remember I'm on a preschool tour and shouldn't mouth or even think about fuckers. I rub the back of my leg, and I'm surprised by the softness, the lack of sensation and then the bump slides a little lower down my leg and I realize what's happening. What's happening is I have to get my daughter into a preschool in San Francisco, which is like trying to get a smile at the DMV, and having dirty underwear balled up into the leg of my jeans isn't a good start. Because that's what the bump is—dirty underwear. I took my jeans and underwear off last night, together in one neat movement, threw them on the floor, woke up this morning and put on the same pair of jeans, underwear firmly planted in the knee regions, and now I could feel this ball of panty creeping toward my ankle.

"What's wrong?" Georgia asks.

"Nothing," I say.

She's my hippie friend. When you have children you become friends with people you wouldn't normally consider. Our toddlers are at my apartment with a babysitter. I pull on her shirt, which I'm sure is organic cotton. She reminds me of people in my yoga class who all try to out-*om* each other.

"Isn't this place great?" she says.

I don't tell her about my balled-up briefs.

"This is the climbing wall," the director says. "Volunteers worked all weekend to put it up and the kids are just crazy about it."

I pray my panties won't make it down to my ankle, especially since I'm wearing those damn cropped jeans that are supposedly so cool now.

We are led through the craft room and then the tour comes to a halt outside and I look around for dogs, worried that one will come up and sniff the back of my knee. The tour director smiles at me and I try to look as goony-eyed as the rest of the mothers here.

"I've been talking a lot," the director says. "Do you have any questions?"

"Yes!" Georgia says. It's like I'm a teenager and she's my mother. I cringe and pretend I'm not with her.

"What do you do about the child's emotions?" she asks. Georgia has gray hair, which is sort of rude, to me. I mean, why can't she dye it? I'm very short and so I always wear heels as an act of courtesy.

"What are you talking about?" I whisper.

Apparently the director knows exactly what old Georgia means because she nods and immediately says, "We respect them. We respect all emotions. Even anger. If someone is angry, we'll say, "Hey, when I'm angry, I like to throw a ball in an area where other children can't be harmed. I just want to pick up a ball and throw it as far as I can, after first checking my space."

Georgia nods and seems very satisfied, as do all the mothers around me. All of them are wearing sneakers or flats. I'm wearing kitten heels.

"Let's go," I say to Georgia.

"We haven't even learned anything yet," she says.

I shake the pamphlet. "It's right here. They're going to reiterate everything on here. It's like the first day of school. The teacher just reads the syllabus."

"Well," she says.

That's her answer to everything. The director continues on. I am so ready to go. I don't care about the school's philosophy. *We're play-based,* they all say. They value imagination and a child's uniqueness. Some value economic diversity, which to me means that they value extremely wealthy people so that they can let in a few poor kids and then write in their brochures, "We value economic diversity." They all purport that the children will thrive and grow, as opposed to rotting and receding like in other preschools.

After the tour we walk back to my car.

"That place smelled," I say. I crush the flyer in my hand and then I reach up my jeans for my underwear. It's like I'm back at college again, doing the walk of shame with my underwear in my pocket, tearing up a phone number, vowing *never again.*

"What's that?" Georgia asks.

"Panties," I say. "I carry backup."

Georgia, ever eager to document, takes out her camera and takes a picture of me with the school in the background. I hook my panties on my thumb.

218

"I want that picture," I say. "I'll tell E about this one day. *Her silly mother. Trying to get her only child into school without showing her panties.*"

And I will tell her about this day if she finds the picture and asks. I'll be happy to elaborate on anything she may find, but that's the catch: she needs to find the objects. Until then, stories will remain stashed. That's how I discovered my own mother—by rummaging through her drawers, unearthing relics, souvenirs, pictures, objects with stories and histories behind them.

I won't tell my daughter that I won, lost, cried, lied, felt elated, but maybe one day she will find one of my old cassette tapes and I'll be forced to explain that I used to make up dance routines to *Cold Hearted Snake* then reward my exertion with a tube of frozen cookie dough. I can see her reaction now in my head—the same reaction I had when my mother happened to cough up an old tale: a mixture of pride, delight, disbelief and humiliation.

In my daughter's lifetime, I'm certain she'll feel loved, humiliated, lonely, proud and afraid. She will feel superior, poor, fascinating, smart, dumb, beautiful, ugly and fat. She will feel like staying home with me. She will feel like going out and getting smashed. She will feel horny. But I won't tell her any of this. I also won't tell her that I once felt these things, too.

When I was around ten years old, I was looking through photo albums and I came across my mother's old high school yearbook. There were captions under the senior's photos meant to mark that moment in their lives. I looked up my mother's picture and her caption said, "I've got a book of matches." I didn't get it until I looked up my dad's picture. His caption read, "Come on baby light my fire."

Now, that's a find. That's a lesson.

Discovering your mother as a person, as a girl, is like discovering a fortune you never thought you wanted or needed, and I plan on keeping this tradition of seeking and finding, of gradual discovery. I don't have a lot of great advice for her, but I do have tangible items that reveal the life I led with and without her. I remember piecing together my mother's life, object by object, and realizing that if I was in high school at the same time as she was, we would have been terrific friends. This has always comforted me.

I put the picture of my tour with other photos. Just a normal day in San Francisco. *This was when I was touring preschools. See that on my thumb?*

There will be no lesson, just an object, an impression, a glimpse of me at this time and at this place, and then, as I did with my mother, she can create her own stories, piecing together the strange evidence collected over time into a kind of hieroglyphic, a touchable proof of us.

KNOWING WHAT TO LISTEN FOR
Ashley Warlick

> Talent is like electricity. We don't understand electricity. We use it.
> You can plug into it and light up a lamp, keep a heart pump going, light
> a cathedral, or you can electrocute a person with it. Electricity can do
> all that.
> —Maya Angelou

My friend Esther has just delivered her firstborn, Luke, at twenty-five weeks. Miraculously, she is still carrying his sister, Tessa, and with surgery and medication, she hopes to carry her to term; one baby in, one baby out, both fighting for the same chances, the same progress, the same mother. When I get this news, it's night and I am driving downtown to meet friends for a drink, the winks of Christmas lights strung through the trees overhead. I feel overwhelmed with that transposing sort of dread and gratitude, the realization of all that can go wrong and how lucky I have been, the divided heart of parenthood. I pull the car to the side of Main Street, and because I am crying, because I am scared for Esther, I call my mom. She knows what to say in these situations.

My mother is a nurse. She was a nurse before I was born, and she worked in the neonatal unit of a pediatric hospital, caring for babies with birth defects. This was in the 1960s, when what could go wrong with a baby seemed somehow blunter than it does today, without the advantages of folic acid and prenatal screening and microscopic surgery. Her patients were the ones born with hearts or spines outside their bodies, club feet, cleft palates, water on their brains, the ones who were unlikely to survive.

Before I was born, when she and my father were newly married, my mother fell in love with a baby in her nursery. This baby was beautiful and sick and originally released for adoption, an arrangement that fell through when her prospective parents learned the extent of her heart problems. She became a ward of the state, Baby Jane Doe, and she spent the first months of her life in intensive care. My mother, who still has a picture of this baby, named her Camille, and before long, her doctors began to refer to her as Camille Warlick.

Camille would be three years old before she could begin to undergo the surgeries to correct her heart, and her medical care would always be supported by the state, but she needed to be adopted out of the hospital by someone who could understand her situation. My mother was twenty-five years old. She asked my father if he would consider the possibility.

My father came to the hospital to meet Camille, this child who already bore his last name, and he agreed that she was sweet-natured and beautiful. Seeing my mother now, with my own children, I imagine she has always been so sure-handed and easy with infants, but there had to have been the day she realized it. My father must have seen it in her when she showed him Camille: her faith in fragile things, in risky love, her willingness to let the good outweigh the bad and weather the consequences. I cannot imagine what it would be like to have this kind of confidence. I cannot imagine what it would be like to tell her no.

I understand my father's point—they were newlyweds still, had not yet begun to think about children, and here was a baby with problems, a baby who was sure to bring the kind of pain you stood because you had no other choice. Another family ultimately adopted Camille, and the nurses in the clinic would come to get my mother when she returned to the hospital for checkups. She died in the process of her first heart surgery, when my mother was pregnant with me.

I was twenty-five when I had my own daughter. Unexpectedly, there were a lot of people in the delivery room: a student nurse, the regular one, my husband, my father, in the corner, crying, eating the candy I'd been told to pack, and my mother. When my daughter was born, there was a crowd of people watching, and when my mother first saw her, a glimpse from where she stood, she said, "Oh, God, Frank, there's something wrong."

I didn't hear her say this. It wouldn't have mattered if I had; they were handing my daughter to me and I could see her face, could see clearly there was not and never would be a thing wrong with this baby. It wasn't just a confidence; she communicated that to me, as surely as whatever food and breath and blood I had communicated to her while she was still on the inside. This connection lasted through her infancy, until we came to have words to rely on. But, on the day she was born, my mother had been thinking of other babies, had seen a tinge of darkness, and had not been able to stop herself from being a nurse.

Talent is such tidal force.

And my mother's talent is not necessarily one you'd wish for, to be good at helping people who need it and for whom your help might not be enough. That moment in the delivery room is one I turn over in my head even now for what she might have been thinking. It wasn't what she said, or that she was mistaken, or even that, for just a moment, she was scared. It's the fact that she was ready for something to go wrong. She would have known what came next.

My daughter, now, is ten. She is excitable and creative and entirely unselfconscious, and she talks all the time. She talks so very, very much, and is not yet as interested in listening. Sometimes, I think of the look on her face when she was born, when the nurses handed her to me and I knew, *knew,* she was fine, and I miss that solid, inanimate conversation we had, and kept going, for months and months. I think of my mother and Camille, the things she must have known about herself and that baby to have wanted her the way she did. I like the idea that such a connection is not some trick of biology, but only a language you need an ear for.

My daughter's cello teacher wants her to take private lessons. The other day, I watched her playing simple songs: "Fiddle Tune," "Mary Had a Little Lamb." Her face was concentration, plucking, then bowing the songs, her arm held at the angle she'd been taught. Her lips were moving. At first, I thought she was singing the words to the song, then just some of the words, the names of the notes, but then I realized it was some musical expression I couldn't understand. When she finished the song, she laid her cheek across the strings to still the sound. I asked her if Ms. Clarke had taught her to do that, and she said no, she just liked it. The efficiency of the gesture, the natural way she made it, made me wonder if the cello would be my daughter's talent, if someday, we would speak in that.

I know nothing about the cello. I grew up listening to the golden age of country and western music—Johnny Cash, Loretta Lynn, The Statler Brothers—and Motown. My parents did not go to the symphony, and while they insisted on piano lessons for me and my brother and sister for something close to ten years, I remember very little of playing an instrument.

The year I was ten, I took watercolor lessons, ice skating lessons, ballet lessons, tap-dancing, swim team, tennis, golf, and sang in the choir. I played handbells at school, played basketball and softball at church. My mother says if any of us expressed the slightest interest in something, she found the lessons. She took us to practices, to games and meets, paid untold amounts of money, spent unimaginable amounts of time. She says she never could tell what it was that we were going to be good at, and it mattered to her to help us be good at something. Handbells. Tap-dancing, anything.

Of all of this, I still like to swim.

My daughter attends an arts magnet school where they offer her cello lessons; her friends are all violinists. I wanted her to try the cello because I could not imagine living in the same house with someone learning to play the violin, and she acquiesced because all the instruments practice together. This is an arrangement of convenience. Even so, I find myself excited to call the private cello teacher, somehow validated, as though she is nearly grown and elegant and onstage with some kind of universally famous string quartet. It is easy for me to believe she's exceptional. My husband thinks Ms. Clarke probably just needs a better cellist—our daughter is the only one in the fourth grade, hence the solos, the lessons, and perhaps the truer picture.

I ask her what song she is learning now.

"'Batman,'" she says. She's licking the foam from a cup of hot chocolate. "Which is cool, because I have a lot of solos."

"'Batman.'" My husband raises an eyebrow at me.

"Just me and the piano," she says. "The violins kind of come in at the end."

I ask her if she really likes the cello, if she thinks she'll want to play next year, and the answer is yes. But she also wants to learn how to eat with chopsticks, swing all the way around on the parallel bars and to own a hamster. She's never been on a set of parallel bars.

I look at my daughter, her beautiful blue eyes and dark brows, her careful, careless smile. She finishes her hot chocolate and then she disappears into her room, her books, the things she does at her desk with scissors and clay and lists of names of people she makes up, and I won't see her again until dinner. The thing is, she is exceptional; she amazes me daily. Why would I want to believe anything different?

We go to hear "Batman" in the spring performance, a school-wide show that takes place at the local college auditorium. There's singing and dancing and some acting, and when it comes time for the strings to play, the orchestra pit rises on some kind of hydraulic lift so that we can see our children. Stage right is my daughter, composed and focused on Ms. Clarke. She is ready for her solo, and no matter how many times I've heard this song before, in all its TV rerun glory, its unshakable hammering in the brain, I am thrilled when she poises herself to start.

A few weeks after the spring performance, she comes home from school and desperately wants to buy a recorder. A translucent blue soprano recorder with a neck strap. I ask her if Ms. Clarke wants her to learn the recorder.

"No, this is for music class. Everybody's learning. We can play the recorders at school, but they get all hot from where Ms. Poole puts them through the dishwasher."

"Dishwasher?"

"They're still a little wet when we get them."

I can see how this would seem like somebody had spit in them already, nonetheless, what's the point of owning your own recorder? I don't know a single person who plays the recorder outside of elementary school. An inexperienced recorder player seems worse to have around the house than an inexperienced violinist. I look at her face, already making the pleading eyes. She says she'll pay for the recorder with her own money, and I know for a fact my own mother would have bought the recorder for me ten times over, would buy it for her now, would think *who knows what she'll be good at?*

"Why do you want to buy a recorder?" I ask.

"I just do," she says and sometimes there are no other words for it than that.

When I began the manuscript that would become my first novel in college, my mother was supportive, but cautious. She knew I was writing and that making a living being a writer was hard, unlikely, something decades in the making. She worried about what I would do in the meantime. Up until the morning I graduated, she was still saying it was never too late to be a nurse, that nurses always have jobs.

Reading my first novel, I know my mother was confused as to where I'd come up with this stuff. Some of it was borrowed from things she knew: my father and grandfather had vineyards in South Carolina when I was a child, and I used those vineyards as a backdrop to a family story. But who was this aunt who refused to take off her wedding dress, this uncle the narrator had a pretty inappropriate crush on? Who thought these things? Who sounded this way?

I didn't have any real answers for her.

In that first novel, the narrator's mother is nothing like my own: she's fragile-minded, childlike, lives at home with her parents, and throughout the story, she is the kind of character that seems to require a hand at her elbow. I'm not sure why this kind of mother was interesting to me, other than she is the opposite of my own. In my second novel, the mother is paralyzed with grief; in the third, she's been dead for quite some time. Even here, in writing about my true mother, I've cast her in a particular, incomplete light that suits my purposes, that seems smart against the greater point I'm making. I've sifted back through my past to find the things I remember that support this version of her. I ask myself how different this is than making her up altogether, and maybe not so very much. It's what I'm good at, even as I can't articulate why or how or where, exactly, the "want to do it" comes from. When my mother reads this part, I think she knows it's true.

THE BODY REMEMBERS
Lucia Orth

Music and rhythm find their way into the secret places of the soul.
—From *The Republic* by Plato

I

Tonight is the first night of the annual November Leonid meteor showers, and also the anniversary of the night when my daughter Jess was born in Manila—to whom I don't know. She was discovered at dawn on a Sunday morning in mid-November by a young woman who lived in a barrio near the Philippine Army's Camp Crame. I like to think that during those hours Jess spent outdoors, alone, the night sky above her was streaked with meteors, in celebration of her birth and survival.

She would not join our family until almost another year had passed. This week Jess turns twenty. She has always had a hard time during the days leading up to her birthday. I suggest to her that perhaps some part of her remembers those first nights and days. When she came to us she would cry long and inconsolably. Since her earliest years, I tell her that her birth mother was likely a very young girl who could not have taken care of any child. It wasn't Jess herself who had to be abandoned, but the hope of having enough money to buy her formula. (At that time in Manila, thanks to heavy advertising by formula makers, virtually no women breast-fed.) There wouldn't have been enough money for any child's vaccines or shoes, toys or preschool, I tell her. This isn't beyond the truth. There is no legal birth control in the Philippines and the average age of the population is under nineteen; Jess listens to these examples, tangibles that she can understand, logical reasons that a wise young girl might make a hard decision. Once when I repeat this litany, near her fourth birthday, Jess asked, in a worried voice, "Do you think she has enough money for herself?"

The woman (not the birth mother, I try not to use that term very often), I say, would be older now, maybe she got to go to school. I think of Jess being left at the door of someone in the barrio who is known to be good, kind and honest. This would be the type of woman who goes to work at six o'clock on a Sunday morning, a janitress in one of the big office buildings in Manila's financial district, who makes money to support her mother and siblings at home in the provinces. This woman would not sell a baby to a commercial organization to be raised for prostitution, would take the time to find an orphanage or hospital that would take a newborn. And that is what she did.

We adopted Jess about nine months before leaving Manila, after having lived there five years. Before we left, but after the long adoption proceedings had been finalized, I went to see the woman who'd found her. I wanted to thank her. We'd learned her name and address and where she worked from adoption court documents.

I went to where she worked, one of the office buildings in the Makati financial district. She was called into her boss's office, the office of the man who ran the cleaning service in her building. She was nervous, not looking directly at me at first, sitting on the edge of her chair. She spoke a little English. We were soon about to leave the country and move back to Washington, D.C. I also wanted to memorize her features, to try to make sure that she was not the biological mother, although it was clear from the court documents that she was not. I wanted to ask her what she knew or suspected, in case there was any chance Jess would someday want to seek out her birth mother. Her boss had to do some translating; this was too complicated for my rudimentary Tagalog skills. I wondered if I should offer her money, a sort of thank-you, and could not decide if this would be insulting.

"Do you need help," I asked her.

"No, ma'am," she answered.

I showed her Jess's pictures, one with her two older brothers, one with our yellow Labrador, Ranger. "You did a very generous thing," I said. "Thank you, thank you, *salamat*."

"I did want to keep her, but I couldn't," she said. "A neighbor told me to take her to the orphanage in Cavite."

"What was the night like, that you found her, do you remember?" I asked the woman. I remembered we'd had some rain around then; it was cool for Manila, down in the sixties at night.

"It was clear. When I went out that morning at five, it was just getting light, the light was gold, and the morning sky filled with pink clouds, and on the wagon, in front of the door, the newborn baby girl's hair was already dry, and she was sleeping," she said.

II

I went back to the orphanage in the mid-1990s. It had relocated closer in to Metro Manila, in Cubao, Mandaluyong. I was in the Philippines to see old friends and do research for a novel. I took along some photos of Jess to leave with the orphanage, and a gift. In one photo, Jess is wearing a black-and-white checked coat, a black velveteen beret, and holding her impossibly puffy orange cat we named Buko, meaning "Little Coconut" in Tagalog. The woman at the desk said, *"The same labandera, laundry woman, is still with us. Show her the picture and ask if she remembers your little girl."* I went out to the back and in a shaded overhang an old woman, small and brown and wrinkled as tobacco leaves, was hand-washing clothes with a bar of laundry soap. I showed her the picture, told her the date. "Marie, you called her here," I said. That is Jess's middle name now. She remembered. "The little girl shared a crib with a boy, they loved each other, kept each other company, and cried when the other was out of the crib," she said. I hadn't known that. Jess was six years old now. I wondered what had happened to that boy. I gave her a picture of Jess. Then I took a picture of the *labandera,* posed in her blue-and-white striped dress among her buckets, so that I could show it to Jess when I got home. Jess was pleased, I think, that someone remembered her, someone like a *Tita,* or auntie.

Two times, once in fifth grade and again in sixth grade, Jess returned to Manila with her father, my husband. I was concerned on the first visit that she would be looking for her biological mother, judging the faces of all women she met. I shared my worries with a therapist—people are so friendly, she's so friendly, what if she thinks each woman is the one, that she feels some connection and is then disappointed?

But Jess didn't seem to look for a mother. The few times her father took her to areas of extreme poverty, places where she might likely have grown up, she didn't want to stay and look around. She was agitated and anxious to leave.

What would it have been like if we could have had the chance to locate Jess's birth mother? For that young, or very young woman, I would have felt some obligation to do something. We have helped with a former helper's daughter's education through college; it is a pittance compared to here, of course, and I would like to think that we might have made it possible for this girl to get some schooling, have some choices.

Jess was happy we cooked some Filipino food at home, like chicken adobo, and pleased that we listened a lot to the famous Filipino singer, Freddie Aguilar. Perhaps this was enough.

III

When she reached puberty (a word that I used once in a carpool on the way to elementary school, and she told me never to use it in front of her friends again) she struggled. Perhaps it was the realization of what it is to get pregnant, be pregnant, have a child, give a child up. I believe these ideas aren't resolved yet for her. The truth is, things are still unfolding in her life. She's not finished dealing with this, and she may never be.

Once before school, when she was in tenth grade, and after a particularly rough stretch, I took her on my lap, in a rocking chair. Together we looked at a framed picture of Jess that I'd brought from upstairs. It had been taken on her first birthday, when she'd been with us in Manila for only a few weeks. We rocked in the chair. (By the time we adopted her, Jess would not be easily cuddled or held still; it always seemed we hadn't been able to do enough of that with her.)

Now, look at this little girl, unwrapping perhaps her first gift ever—if she messed up, would you just say, Okay, you're bad, you'll never make it, you've done something that can't be fixed. Or, if she were one of your Head Start girls, would you give up on her, I asked Jess.

"No, of course not," Jess said.

"Well, it's the same for you. You get new chances. Be as gentle on yourself as you would when one of your Head Start kids messes up. Why don't you take this picture with you to school today? Put it in your locker, then, whenever you open the door, you just look at her and know you wouldn't be so hard on her."

Jess did this. In fact, the last time I visited her dorm room, she had this same picture out. It travels with her—a small link to a little girl who survived her first night, and first year, under a shower of meteors and a guardian angel.

233

Jess volunteered at our local Head Start for several summers, starting in junior high, and seems to have a special affinity for younger children. This summer she will work as a children's counselor at Ghost Ranch in New Mexico. She is majoring in child psychology.

She must have aspects of both her birth parents that we only sometimes recognize, like her dancing, her laugh. Jess studied ballet for years. Once my husband and I watched as she performed in a main role—at one point, Jess lifted her hand in a sort of quick, palm-out movement. He and I turned to each other in amazement—it was exactly a replica of a Philippine dance movement we simultaneously recognized. She hadn't been taught this. Somehow, the body remembers.

IV

My uncle can name all the stars. He was at our house a few months ago and admired our dark sky, and spoke about the star-finding phrase, "the Arc to Arcturus." I hadn't thought of it since I was a child. My uncle, my father's younger brother by fifteen years, and my elder only by eight years, spent a lot of time at our house when I was young. He was already a scientific type as a teenager. I took great comfort from his company, from his explanations of the stars and the universe and the true origins of man, comparing it unfavorably to the literal doctrine of creation I was given in Lutheran elementary school and at church. It was better to think that we were on our own, that we were part of a huge and continuing spiral of the Milky Way, rather than that God watched over each of us personally and yet overlooked or would not intervene in my family's life. I could go outside when visiting at my grandmother's house, where I often stayed, on a warm summer night, and look up at the stars and know where I was. I could never be lost as long as I could see the night sky. I knew north, the pole star, I could find the Arc to Arcturus, point to the six brightest stars in the sky (Arcturus being the third brightest, after Sirius and Canopus), and knew the planets, which ones were viewable at which time of year, what the characteristics were that made Mars "Mars" and made Venus "Venus." In the winter, I watched for Orion and the Seven Sisters.

We all have our particular wishing star, or guardian star, our pole star, these lunar forms of ice and heat. Some have the whole Milky Way to dream on. My daughter's guardian stars are shooting across the sky each November. I feel deep gratitude for these stars that watched over Jess during her first night on earth.

MY MOTHER'S DATING ADVICE
Quinn Dalton

What lets my heart rest is the image of my daughter—without
a single worry—swinging her pale braids over the sill, then
leaning there against the cool stone wall, waiting
by the window, certain all the heavy things she wished for
would make their way to her, sure she could bear them all
up with no help beyond her own strong body.
  —From "Rapunzel's Mother" by Carolyn Williams-Noren

The Rules

There were some things my mother made clear to me about
dating when I started "going with" my first boyfriend at age
fifteen—a good ten years earlier, it seemed at the time, than my
parents would have preferred. One: a man comes to the door to
collect you rather than honking from his revving car in the driveway.
Two: on a date, the man pays. Three: women don't call men.

Call it "the rules" before *The Rules* book became a national
sensation and convinced otherwise perfectly sane women to buy
egg timers so as not to stay on the phone longer than ten minutes
with a man (whom, of course, they hadn't called).

But I had some problems with the rules. One: the guys I
dated were scared of my parents, who, from my perspective now,
are really nice people, but we're talking about high school guys
here—hence the honking from the driveway. Two: in high school,
we all made $3.35 an hour, so how were guys supposed to pay for
a dinner when I could barely scrounge up weekend matinee
money? Three—and this was the toughest point: I didn't expect
guys to call me. As far as I could tell, I wasn't a girl you called. I

wasn't cute; I wasn't coy. Deep down, I believed a guy could only be won if I said the right things, wore the right things or was just plain inexplicably lucky. He would have to be cajoled. He would have to be called.

In short, guys were *work*.

And that was fine with me. Work was okay. Work I could do. I was, in fact, the embodiment of the Protestant work ethic, fully indoctrinated into the culture of achievement and acquisition.

The problem was that, by the time I was ready to date (or to somehow convince guys to date me), my mother and I had grown wildly suspicious of one another. It was simple: I was convinced that she wanted to ruin my life, and she was convinced that I wanted to ruin my life. And these overlapping paranoias shadowed everything between us, including and especially her reactions toward my attempts at romance.

My parents hated my Roger-Waters-wanna-be boyfriend— let's call him R. They found him rude and sullen. They were right—I knew it at the time—but their reaction of course only made him more attractive to me. No surprise there. What was surprising—and sad to me still—was how much further my attraction to him went. In some fundamental way, I had put my happiness, my whole sense of well-being, into his hands. I couldn't access it myself. If I wasn't with R, I just wasn't quite all there. Some part of me was dormant until this guy handed me the key.

And it wasn't just because I was in love for the first time. Call it more of an overall attitude about the worth of guys as opposed to girls. Hanging with the girls was one thing, but if guys were in the picture, well, then, you were really having fun. (Of course I'm still in frequent touch with several of my closest high school girlfriends after nearly twenty years, through cross-country moves, marriage, divorce, miscarriage and children. Of my high school guy friends—not to mention boyfriends—I am in regular touch with exactly none.) When did I start measuring the success of an evening based on how many guys were involved? I don't know exactly, but I know I did, and not just in high school, but for a long time afterward.

So, you can see how an achiever who didn't understand that love can't be *achieved* and who thought her mom wanted to ruin her life and that guys were somehow worth more than girls was headed for heartbreak.

And there was plenty of it waiting for me.

Five relationships (or seven years, for those of you who measure time that way) after R first sat brooding in my parents' living room, only one thing was clear to me: I'd gotten myself into a nasty pattern. It hadn't been just a couple unlucky relation-ships—I mean, everybody gets burned once or twice. I suspected that the root of my problem was not the inherent flaws of the human male so much as my fear of not having one around to call *boyfriend*. Basically, I was scared of being alone more than I was scared of being heartbroken. I decided my best chance for change was to give up getting serious for a while.

During that time, I did go out on dates, but I came home alone. And I spent a lot of time trying to figure out why I had so little regard for myself when it came to my relationships with men. I had wonderful female friends, and I didn't brag or pout or lie about my feelings to them. So why did I do these things with men?

Mothers, of course, are the default when it comes to blame. But I couldn't blame mine. It wasn't as if she'd advised me to be a doormat. In fact, "Don't be a doormat!" was something I clearly remembered her saying in connection with dating. Call it Rule

Number Four. Also, she'd repeatedly insisted that there was more to life than having a mate. She promised me she would never be one of those mothers who nagged me about when I was going to get married or have babies. She wanted me to have my own life; she often reminded me of my good fortune to be born into one of the first generations of women who didn't need a man to survive.

The problem was, I didn't believe her. I didn't believe her, and I didn't talk to her about it, mostly because I was embarrassed. I didn't want her to know that this was how I'd turned out—a doormat, a girl who wanted love more than anything else. *How had such a strong woman bred such a weak daughter?* I asked myself that a lot when I wasn't writing pages and pages of crappy, not really fictional stories that served mostly to plot all my failed relationships like the jagged lines on a heart monitor.

But I guess all that bad writing had some therapeutic value, because slowly, tentatively, month after month, I began to feel better. After a while, I started to realize that being alone didn't mean I felt horribly lonely.

David worked in the same building as I did. I knew he liked me, had known for months, but for some reason he'd never asked me out. The old me would've tried to make it easier on him, maybe even asked him out. The new me was both more relaxed and more demanding: he was going to have to show some backbone. Eventually, he invited me to lunch, then dinner. On our second date, we went out to a park after dinner and watched the fireflies flash in the trees. We split a six-pack and talked. He said, completely in passing, "You might as well be kind to people, there's not much point in doing anything else." I decided I'd stick around to find out if he meant it.

For me, it was a different way of choosing a man. I wasn't

going to die if it didn't work out, and I wasn't going to beg to be treated well. I knew I could accept the outcome of our next few dates, whatever it might be. That's when I realized I really had changed, and that maybe I was finally ready to be in love like a grown-up.

The following fall, I married David, who turned out to be as much of a sweetheart as he sounded that night in the park. Twelve years later, I'm thirty-seven, and we have two young daughters.

Before we get to the "happy ever after," I must recount a tense moment from early in the wedding planning phase. My parents had not even met David or his family yet; they were coming down the following week. I told my parents I wanted my brother, who is my only sibling, to be my best man. They initially hated this idea—they worried people would think he was gay. On the phone with them, I tried to convince them of their error.

"Look," I finally said. "I think this may be a generational thing."

It was a nice way of saying "outdated" or "totally out of touch." For a moment, I could feel that fifteen-year-old girl straining for independence. I wanted to kiss her on the forehead and laugh. *You thought this would all be over when you turned eighteen? Ha!*

But then my mother spoke. "Honey, I think she's got a point here."

Stunned silence on my end. Giant swig of wine.

If you'd asked me in high school what I thought my parents wanted for me when it came to dating, I would have said they wanted me to have a wonderful time in theory, but in practice they found the whole thing too dangerous, too flawed, better to be avoided altogether.

But as a grown-up, I understood they were still, after all, just trying to protect me. "Thank you," I said to my mom. "Hey, and you know, David likes the idea, too. You're really going to love him. He always calls. He never honks from the driveway."

I was speaking in a code of sorts, trying to let my parents, but especially my mother, know that not only had I chosen well, but I'd done so using, at least in part, her standards. It was the equivalent of putting us on a battleship to sign a truce.

The Rules Revisited

Now that David and I roll our eyes at the boys honking for the teenaged girls next door, my mind has turned to the not-so-distant future, when our daughters get to dating age. I have considered buying a gun, no bullets, just to clean it on the porch. Although this would make my ninety-seven-year-old ex-cowboy grandfather proud, I doubt it will keep our daughters safe or help them weather the heartbreaks they'll inevitably encounter.

In fact, I don't think it's my job to save them from heartbreak. I just want them to be able to recognize it for what it is and have enough self-respect to not stick around for more. Maybe I'll mention that the honking thing is a good minor test of a guy's manners. Not a deal breaker, just a little signal to note. As for paying and calling, my daughters will have their own money and their own phones. And black belts. I think they should have those, too. And most of all, I hope they have the good sense to trust themselves. From what I've seen so far, they're pretty sharp.

But what else? What else can I give them to ensure both their independence and safety? Because I don't want them to feel that I'm trying to trap them, or that I don't trust them, or that, God forbid, I no longer understand the ways of the world. Maybe I should stop worrying about it. Maybe there's no way around that particular generational loop.

As a kid, I thought I'd be a much cooler parent. When my

mother freaked out because my brother was trying to sneak in the pool without wearing his swimmies, I imagined myself as the mother who let the kid take in a gulp or two of water before I fished him out and then, when he'd finished coughing, I'd say (coolly, of course), "See?"

But being cool seems to have lost its value for me these days, mostly because of the primal fear that attends parenting. From the moment your kids can walk, you're running around like the Secret Service trying to protect them from any number of dangers, those you know about and those you don't but can only just imagine, or worry that you'll fail to imagine in time. When I was fifteen and chafing under my mother's constant reminders of all that could go wrong at a lakeside picnic—I could drown, I could get my teeth knocked out by that kid horsing around with an oar, I could get bitten by something, anything—I couldn't understand that the key to her life was that I was alive. *Be careful, be careful, be careful, always and forever. Because without you I might live, but I'll want to be dead.* I know what this feels like now.

And as a girl, I was aware, even before I could put words to it, that these injunctions to be careful weren't just about wearing my seat belt or dressing for the weather. There was another layer to the message, sometimes spoken, sometimes not: Don't be in the wrong place at the wrong time, don't be attacked, don't disappear. It doesn't matter that young males are more likely to die in car accidents or as victims of violent crime. Parents who have sons and daughters tell me they fear for their daughters in a different way than they fear for their sons, and I guess I'd be no exception.

But interestingly, the first pang of fear I felt for my firstborn daughter, which hit me on the first night we brought her home from the hospital, wasn't about survival at all. It was about dating.

242

I was sitting in the rocking chair with her lying along the tops of my thighs, her tiny legs folded against my belly. Nursing was a thing we were still trying to work out, and we were both teary-eyed and exhausted. She drowsed and whimpered, holding on to my index fingers with that iron infant grip, and I studied her red face and tried to imagine what she would look like as a girl, as a young woman. I saw her walking down a hallway of a school, holding her books to her chest, and I burst into tears.

Here she was, a new human being. She did not know about language, or stars, or chocolate or how it felt to have her heart broken. She had a gaze that seemed to start from somewhere far away. Maybe she did know about stars. But how would she know to hold up her chin? How would she know to be gentle with herself, even as she pushed her mind and body to be strong? How would she face being alone?

And how would I not kill anyone who hurt her, or who didn't show her perfect respect? (Yeah, honk, buddy. I'll be right there.)

I think about these things every day. And she's only seven. And I'm trying, in all the ways I can think of, to have conversations about dating that aren't yet conversations about dating.

For example, when she told me that the boy (who is her age) across the street was mean to her when he had another male friend over, I set her up with paints and a popsicle, and it wasn't long before the guys wanted to come over. I set them up, too, and I watched their every move. When I saw something I didn't like, I called them on it. Later, I talked with my daughter about how you can have more fun on your own than you can hanging out with someone who isn't being nice. I also pointed out that when she walked away, they followed. But in the end, what they did didn't matter—whether they came along or stayed—that was their

243

choice. What mattered was that she didn't have to stick around for bad treatment; there was always more fun to be had elsewhere.

And when I heard her saying she wasn't going to be a particular classmate's friend anymore because another girl was now her best friend, I reminded her about how the boy across the street, who has been her friend all of her life, had hurt her feelings. I said we don't abandon our friends, even if we grow closer to one than another. I said that, as time goes on, our friends are the people who stick with us, the people we need.

So goes the conversation that isn't yet a conversation about dating. And about sex? When my younger daughter was born, my older one asked me how the baby had gotten in there in the first place. Fortunately I'd gotten the good advice from a friend who said, "If you try to tell them all about sex at that age they just get bored. Say one thing and then pause and see if they're still listening."

I tried that and then she asked me did we have any cookies. So I just keep saying one thing at a time.

And finally, I guess I'm trying to prepare myself, even now, to share with them the lessons I learned from my own dating experiences. Describing the mechanics of sex is a lot easier than expressing its intricate politics. So I've already started talking with them about kindness, and how there isn't much point in giving— or putting up with—anything else.

A DAY AT THE BEACH
Carolyn Ferrell

Das ist Mutters kleine Suesse, Mutters Goldkind, Mutters Schatz
Mutters kleine suesse Puppe, Mutters Zuckerchen is das!
—Taken from a poem my grandmother wrote on the birth of
  my mother

It's where she loved to be most, the place she adored taking
me complete with carriage and umbrella; later on she'd bring my
sister and brothers (we all arrived in quick succession) whenever
there was a free moment in summer (that didn't happen often in
her life back then). She would have permission to drive my father
to work, and then come home, pack us up and drive the three or
four miles to the Great South Bay, the home of Amityville Beach,
small and fish-fangled, the closest thing to the Baltic Sea beaches
of my mother's childhood: Heikendorf, Moeltenort, and Laboe,
all of which looked out onto the far shore of Kiel, where the
world seemed to be going on without her.

She'd arrived in this place just a few years earlier, after
having run away from home to marry my father, a black G.I., a
transplant from rural black North Carolina who, like the rest of
his family, did not care much for the water. Amityville Beach
lay due south of North Amityville, where in 1962 my father
moved my mother and me from Brooklyn to a neighborhood
of identical capes on a demure cul-de-sac. (The Realtor who
sold them the place guardedly told my mother these were
"colored houses.") And so it was here that my mother, a twenty-
two-year-old girl-woman, began that arduous journey into

245

cleaning, cooking, gardening, babysitting, repairing, consoling, concocting and dreaming. She was glad to leave the roaches and screaming subway trains of Brooklyn. Here in the suburbs, she could live out her dream of being a married woman with children. Being the lone white stranger in a neighborhood where Black Power was lighting certain imaginations, though, had never been part of her dreams.

She had few friends. But she had me.

Bob, my sullen and often antisocial father, left in the early morning for his job as a machinist at a nearby aeronautics factory; he gave my mother a small weekly allowance and expected a clean house, decent meals and grateful disposition in return. During the hours he was at home, he toiled in his basement woodworking shop; for fun, he took us for long drives to arid, tree-filled nature parks on Long Island. He and my mother and I would leave the car for only a few minutes—long enough for my mother to push me in the large carriage over quick gravel paths—then return home. There my mother would place me in a basket on the floor and make dinner. Clean the kitchen. Hold me in her arms. Sweep the floor.

There was the smallest hint of mystery in the house.

In those first years, when I was her new baby girl, my mother spent a lot of time—when she wasn't at chores, when she wasn't kissing my face or tugging at my feet—searching for the letters sent by her mother back in Germany. Always filled with rancor, sometimes with regret, these letters were a rasping balm to my mother's often lonely existence on North Ronald Drive. She would beg my mother to return to Germany; beg her to run away from my father; beg her to remember her roots, the huge estate where she'd been raised, the horses that swept everyone's imaginations. Did my mother remember the equestrian competitions she'd won, the prizes? Did she think of her brothers' futures, how they would fare in the top-notch equestrian world now that she had lowered herself in such a way?

And so on and so forth; the questions were relentless. When my mother stopped answering the letters, huge reels of audio tapes began to appear in the mail. One of my earliest memories is that of my grandmother's voice on the machine, begging my mother for everything.

Was it the beach, with its sand and gentle waves, that saved her from the box of her life? Or was it simply being a mother?

I had such a traumatic pregnancy. I was always fainting, and they didn't find out that my blood count was low until my third pregnancy in 1965. With you I always fainted. I was extremely anemic. Add to that the letters from Mutti that had me in tears all the time. Daddy would carry them around for weeks and hide them in the house. He took care of me then.

I had aches and pains throughout my first pregnancy; then my water broke but I had no real labor. At the hospital they had to induce me, and it was a horrible, long labor, a day and a half. In those days they put you in a room and closed the door.

My father almost never accompanied us to the beach. Almost never to Amityville, almost never to Zach's Bay at Jones Beach (which I grew up calling, thanks to my mother, the "children's beach") almost never to Robert Moses, the "tip of Fire Island," where my mother and I, in later years, would go for long, necessary walks. I would usually be crying over some boy, some romantic misadventure, and she would be all ears, gentle advice. There was something restorative, my mother believed, about the surf crashing in front of us. The air was cleansing. Now and then, I would ask her why my father—whom she'd divorced in 1977, the year we truly embraced full summers at the ocean—so disliked the water. Was it in his blood, passed down from the North Carolina generations, the enslaved ancestors and ship- wrecked Africans? Or was it that the water simply reminded him of my mother's mother, the one who called the military police on him and begged them to end my parents' relationship?

Did she have an answer? Perhaps she had many, I can't remember. When I was a baby, my mother would carefully glide me over the surface of the water, making what she called *swim-swim;* then she'd sit back on her towel and enjoy a piece of bread and cheese; then she'd stretch out in a small square of sun and peek at me in my carriage, which she always brought right onto the sand. Later she would take me in her arms and rest in the sand, dressed in her modest one-piece bathing suit and large Jackie-O head scarf. She'd look out over the Great South Bay as it loomed in front of the ocean. Home was somewhere in front and behind those waves.

The beach was precious balm, wherever she went.

In those days you married young and got pregnant right away. When you were born, I was overjoyed. But my first words to Daddy in the hospital room were: I'll never do it again.

It's not like today. In the hospital you couldn't see the baby; they wanted the mother to rest. They would bring the baby to nurse a day later, and you couldn't even diaper your baby. All I could do was look through the window and watch them feed and diaper the baby.

But I do remember taking you home. Bob held you in the air and said, "It's a miracle, it's a miracle." He was totally taken by you.

And you were such a good baby. But it goes without saying I had no help. Daddy would look at you and hold you occasionally, but that was it. I remember I needed to sleep. A month after you were born, I had a wisdom tooth infection. My breasts got hard, and I couldn't nurse. And you wouldn't take a bottle. You screamed and cried. I had to feed you milk with a teaspoon.

The first baby: a girl, skin as light as sand. My mother was one of the first few immigrants to North Ronald Drive; she barely spoke any English. More than anything, she wanted to be liked by the women in the neighborhood, most of whom worked outside the home at what my father called a "real job." Many of these neighborhood mothers were unmarried, though men lived under their roofs; some, bitter at my mother's seemingly perfect life (her lovely garden, her lovely baby, her overprotective husband), took to calling her *Cinderella* behind her back.

Summers were incredibly hot on Long Island. They called for cold drinks, fans, then air conditioners, cool cars. The mothers on our cul-de-sac tended to smile condescendingly as my mother placed the bed of my carriage on the backseat of my father's station wagon (were there even car seats back then?) and then drove to the beach, even in cloudy weather. The heat was often unbearable. The neighborhood mothers would go back to sitting in their living rooms on plastic slipcovers that stuck like chains to the skin.

But my mother: she was lonely, disheartened. Her own mother's letters never let up, even when my mother bragged about me, the happiest part of her life. In 1963, when I was a year old, my mother decided to invite her mother to America and have her see for herself how much she'd already achieved. Her small garden flourished; her house, though sparsely furnished, was beautifully clean. Plus she was expecting another baby, my sister. Life was not *all* bad in America. Life *had* been difficult in Germany.

My mother was convinced, even as she headed to the City piers with my reluctant, angry father where my grandmother's steamship was docking that her own mother would be won over. Just how could anyone resist the sweet faces of her children?

In 1963, she arrived by boat, and I put this baby in her arms, and that was the end of her racism. She was a real grandma. Even though she and Bob didn't get along.

For instance, when she first came to Amityville and saw the house and garden and a baby, she cried, "Oh my God, what did he get you into?" Of course she was comparing to our old estate in Muessen, and in comparison, the house at 57 North Ronald Drive was nothing. She'd forgotten how, after her divorce, she crammed us into a small house in Heikendorf. She forgot about our kitchen in the basement with all that mold and the lizards in the cabinets. Now she felt I had gone down the social ladder. She talked a lot with my brother Hauke, back in Germany. To marry a black person was, in their eyes, a crime.

But you were the most adorable baby.

When she took me to the beach, people flocked around her and commented on how beautiful her baby was. It was not until later—when she was holding three dark-skinned babies on her lap instead of one—that teenagers would walk by on the sand and call her "nigger-lover."

Do you remember Uncle Bill, Bob's stepfather? The drunk? Well, one day he put it into Bob's mind that you looked too light and that Bob probably wasn't the father. I was so upset that Bob even considered that for a moment. Nowadays I would have kicked my husband out the door if he'd ever ask me such a thing.

But I loved going out with you in the carriage. That was one thing Bob did for me. He got me a beautiful carriage. And I loved putting you in it—the children, the whole neighborhood flocked to see you. But mostly I loved taking you to the beach.

You saved me.

My father was laid off from his machinist job in the seventies, and insisted my mother go out and get work. Her English disqualified her for factory work back then, however, and so he took her over to the community college in Farmingdale, where eventually she would study nursing. Years later, she would become a nurse.

But on the day he first brought her to the college, she had to struggle to remember her social security number.

I idealized motherhood. I just didn't imagine the exhaustion. I always knew I would love it, but I had no one nearby to help. Bob didn't welcome Mutti, so that was out.

After the birth of my fourth child, I had a real break. I went into the bedroom and cried. I said, I can't take it anymore. Four babies,

*no release at anytime. I thought I was going to go out of my mind.
Uncharacteristically, Bob was concerned. For once he didn't yell at
me. He just listened. But that was all.*

*School was the relief for me. Not only social contact, I loved going
to school. Daddy resented it from the first day. But I was there, for
better or worse.*

When I became pregnant with my daughter Karina I was
nearly forty years old—"advanced maternal age," as the doctors
so lovingly put it. The weight I'd gained during my first pregnancy hadn't disappeared, and now, as I grew heavy with Karina,
I felt every bone creak in my body, every muscle stretch itself into
painful oblivion. During my amniocentesis I was told that the
baby exhibited some stigmata for Down syndrome; and because
I'd done the test right before the Christmas holiday, I had to wait
nearly three weeks for my results.

My mother, a full-time ICU nurse, dropped everything to
be with me. To see me back through those doors leading into
motherhood.

I'd had many things she hadn't: a loving husband who offered
unconditional support, a more-or-less healthy bank account, and
a job outside the home that I loved and to which I could return
after the birth. I had friends who were excited for me and who
lived nearby, ready to help; they threw me a baby shower, which
my mother saw as a true luxury (for the first years of my life, she
hand stitched and knit all my clothes); she was overwhelmed by the
generosity. I had boxes of disposable diapers and, for those moments
when breast-feeding became too much, bottles of baby formula.

When people learned I was having a girl, they plied me with
platitudes, even though I was secretly hoping to have another boy

(my reasoning was that if the baby was anything like Ben, I'd be in heaven). It's good to have one of each, they said. Every woman should have a girl and a boy. It's nice to make things even. And so on. My mother said she would've been happy with another boy (even with the lure of all those beautiful girl's clothes at Lord and Taylor, and then the prospect of braiding a little girl's hair, just as she had braided mine so many years ago). Yes, a boy would be just fine.

But then there also was the fact of that female connection which had no tangible explanation—it just *was*.

"I'm glad you're having a girl," my mother secretly confided. "I love Ben with all my heart, but I'm glad you're having a girl."

On the day of my scheduled caesarean section, I had begged my doctor to allow my mother into the operating room, but there was only room for Linwood, my husband. No worries, she assured me: she would wait with Ben and my stepfather, Larry, in the hospital lounge. She would be there. No worries.

When she first came into the hospital room to meet Karina, she kissed the baby and immediately began to braid my hair, which had come undone during the birth. Two fat pigtails on either side of my head. She began to kiss me as she'd done when I was nothing more than a little face looking out from the carriage.

My friends all had their own versions of early life with baby: *I can't take my mother near me for more than a day! My mother and I don't see eye to eye on child-rearing techniques. My mother can't handle her grandchildren for more than a few hours at a time!*

And so on. That was never my experience. Even when my mother and I differed on certain topics: *Why buy the expensive disposable diapers? Pick the baby up when she's crying! Give her a bottle— don't make her wait!* I most always deferred to her. Though I had definite ideas about how I wanted to raise my daughter, I never felt less than grateful for the advice she offered (or in some cases, happily thrust on me). What did I know? And what did the experts know about breast-feeding, napping, nighttime sleeping and colic? Sure, I read many books in the beginning, sought help wherever I could.

But my mother taught me that a mother's wisdom can go a long way.

Two memories: in one, I am sitting on the beach at Overlook, breathing in the deep ocean fragrance of summer as I hold Karina in my arms. She is not yet a month old, but already knows my every move, my thoughts, I believe. (I think: I can't live without you—and she, eyes closed, sends the same thoughts to me.) Though the sun is high, the wind kicks up, forcing us to huddle against the dune. Karina is wrapped in a baby blanket and sunbonnet. Her tiny round hands jut out to touch the edge of my shoulder. It's as if she knows that my first gift to her, besides that of life, is the ocean.

It is so serene, this day. Though there are a few other people on the beach. My mother sits beside me, playing with my son and passing out lunch bagels. In a minute she runs to the water's edge and chases my son in and out of the yawning surf. Seeing her, I yearn for that kind of energy, and suddenly regret having had children so late in life.

It is only a momentary regret. Karina begins to nibble at my skin, and I prepare to nurse her. For everything I don't have, there is, of course, everything I do. Later on I hand her to my mother, who holds Karina to her chest while I dive into the water and swim out as far and close as the waves will take me.

The other memory is more recent. My mother and I are walking arm in arm across Central Park South toward Carnegie Hall. Since her divorce in the late seventies, my mother has taken me to many concerts here. This afternoon's recital is special: the first appearance of Kathleen Battle in New York in over five years. Our excitement is fresh, alive; we walk along, remembering our favorite Schubert lieder from an early album of hers, and wonder what her program will be. Once, at a Battle recital long ago, I caught a glimpse of my mother swaying in her seat, recalling the lyrics of a song she'd rehearsed with a voice teacher when she was a girl in Germany.

My mother and I feel the happiness that comes from walking next to each other in the city. There is so much to remember, to share, to predict. I tell her of Karina's latest kindergarten adventures, of the "hedgehog cake" she and her classmates baked in school, which Karina claimed was "better than Betty Cracker!" My mother laughs—my laugh, as I hear it ring from her throat.

We turn down Seventh Avenue and slow our steps. "You know—" my mother begins "—there really is nothing like having a daughter."

(When I get home later that night, Karina will curl in my arms and ask for another book, another hug. She'll ask me to rub her back, and will fall asleep with her fingers in her mouth as I sit at the edge of her bed. Kathleen Battle's voice still fills my head. And I think of that line from a Sharon Olds poem—which, in my mind I have altered: *When love comes to me and says What do you know, I say This girl…*)

A crowd has already gathered outside of Carnegie Hall when we arrive, breathless and free.

HERE BE DRAGONS
Karen Karbo

Perplexity is the beginning of knowledge.
—From "A Tear and a Smile" by Kahlil Gibran

Not long ago my daughter turned sixteen and asked for a sweet sixteen party. I was surprised. Katherine despises entertaining, for which I blame myself. When she was small and invited friends to sleep over, I taught her to give them the best pillow, the dish with the most ice cream, the choice of which video to watch. As a result, my girl dislikes the effort involved in being what she calls "the hostess with the mostest." Still, for her birthday she wanted a "real" party, held somewhere other than at home, where a professional DJ would spin tunes from her personalized play list. Katherine was determined it should be her best birthday ever, a blowout to end all blowouts. Even so, she's a sensible girl, and has been only mildly damaged by the ludicrous celebrations on *My Super Sweet 16,* the MTV reality show that follows the children of extreme wealth as they plan birthday parties that feature five-thousand-dollar dresses, eight-hundred-dollar manicures (diamond inlays are involved; I don't know how), and at the end of each show, the keys to a luxury car. Katherine's party would be modest, but awesome.

As I pondered what kind of cake to order and for how many, whether we should serve "real food" (read: turkey roll-ups from Costco), and whether helium balloons were festive or just an invitation for someone to channel Donald Duck before collapsing from lack of oxygen, I couldn't shake the thought that once Katherine turned sixteen, I would no longer know what sort of wisdom to pass on to her. In the days before her birthday, I woke up at three in the morning beset by a strange fear: now that she was the same age I was when my own mother died, I would no longer know how to continue raising her. The fact I'd been her mother for sixteen years meant nothing. I'd officially entered terra incognita, that blank, wide-open space on the edge of old maps where cartographers wrote "Here Be Dragons."

My mother was the original hostess with the mostest, the queen of a certain kind of patio party that involved hearty hors d'oeurves, mai tais, tiki torches and a fully dressed grown-up winding up in the pool. She could throw a dinner party for sixteen without forgetting where she left her highball. My own sweet sixteen party was held in our backyard in Whittier. It was March, too early in the year for swimming (in those days heated pools in Southern California were a ridiculous expense no one even considered), but the night was cool and smelled of night-blooming jasmine. I wore a red-and-white checked halter dress. A few boys snuck in a fifth of sloe gin and spiked the Bubble Up. The patio furniture wound up at the bottom of the pool, and someone walked off with the sign my father had posted in the cabana: "We don't swim in your toilet, so please don't pee in our pool." Ha-ha!

The party was technically chaperoned. My parents holed up in their bedroom, propped up against the Danish modern headboard of their California king, watching TV. It was bad enough that they had to be on the planet, much less anywhere in the vicinity of my party. (I have noticed that my daughter and her friends are not embarrassed of their parents the way we were. They allow us into their sphere as if we're their trusted valets. If they didn't, who would do for them?)

Was my sixteenth birthday my best birthday ever, a blowout to end all blowouts? It must have been. November of that year, my mother learned she had an astrocytoma, a rare type of brain cancer, which few people ever survive. My next birthday was the last day I saw her alive; a week later she slid into a coma and died while I was at school.

The strangest thing about the anxiety I experienced as Katherine's birthday approached and the sudden sense that I was parenting without a net, was that I rarely passed down to my girl any of my mother's basic wisdom. Mostly, I would think what my mother would advise and say the opposite. But now there would be no opposite. It would be me, out there with the dragons.

My mother's advice was koanlike and addressed a single subject: how to get a boy. She said that boys liked girls who laugh, but only at their jokes. It was important always to make sure a boy knows you are laughing at his joke and not him. Boys like girls who find them interesting, even if they are boring, and they will be boring, since all they really like to do is talk about themselves. Get good grades, but only good enough to show that you are capable of helping a boy with his homework, but not so good that you appear to be smarter than him. (By my reckoning this meant I could get A's in sissy topics like English and French, but Bs in algebra and chemistry, so I did. Well, in algebra anyway.)

Her favorite book was *The Prophet* by Kahlil Gibran, from which she liked to quote when she was feeling extra philosophical. This was likely to occur while she was cooking dinner, after she'd had a few beers. She would stand at the stove stirring the beef stroganoff, a cigarette smoldering in the ashtray beside the burner and say, apropos a cute boy who'd shown some interest in me for a few days, "*The Prophet* says if you love somebody, let them go, for if they return, they were always yours. And if they don't, they never were." Even now I think back to this and my only response is "huh?"

I'm hard-pressed to think of any instruction my mother offered regarding a possible career, being a single woman in the world, living with roommates, working with colleagues, negotiating a salary, paying bills, saving money, travel, adult love affairs or even marriage itself. She had nothing to say about sex, which made sense because boys were regarded as investment property.

My all-time favorite bit of lunatic counsel was to "use my eyes more." I was fifteen. My mother told me that my failure to land a boyfriend was due to the fact I did not know how to use my eyes. This was one of the simplest tricks in a girl's glittery bag of wiles and why I couldn't master it was a maddening mystery. Using my eyes meant gazing at a boy with adoration, fluttering my eyelashes and glancing down bashfully. I said, "Like this?" and went into such a frenzy of eye-rolling and eyelash-batting I made myself dizzy enough to fall off my stool onto the spotless kitchen floor. I cracked myself up. My mother left the room, her spaghetti sauce simmering madly on the stove.

For decades I wondered what my mother thought she was doing, proffering advice that no one could possibly follow and still appear sane. The lessons she sought to teach me were not really even of the time. She was resolutely middle-aged when she died in 1976, never having received the feminist memo that women needed men like a fish needs a bicycle. The cheeky bons mots of feminism hadn't reached our suburb yet.

My mother's life story was an ancient one. Cinderella-like, Joan Sharkey parlayed her charm into a better berth on the ship, a box seat at the theater. She grew up poor in Ypsilanti, Michigan, the daughter of old Maude Sharkey, who ran a boardinghouse. It was never clear where Maude's husband was; there was a rumor George was hit by a train while coming home drunk. My mother had two less lovely sisters; Lorraine was twenty years older and

Julia was twenty-two years older. They were short and round, un-remarkable. They lacked vision and humor. They married men who worked on the assembly line at Ford Motor Company. My mother, on the other hand, had charm and a head of dark auburn hair that stopped traffic. She was slender, dimpled and crafty. She parlayed all of this into marriage to my father, an educated man with a white-collar job in the design department at Ford. She expected the same for me. She married up, and I would marry further up still. It was how the world worked, or her world anyway.

Then I came along, and like every daughter on earth, I was not the daughter she'd planned on having. She was endlessly frustrated by the fact of me. I inherited her dimples, but in me, her charm had morphed into raucous high spirits that included a love of pranks. I was sarcastic. I had hair that went all over the place. Whereas she was narrow of shoulder and hip and huge of bazoombas, I took after my father, tall and broad-shouldered. At five, I was diagnosed with what was then called "hyperactivity." Ritalin didn't work, but vast amounts of exercise did. I was put on a swim team. My mother was both relieved and horrified. My behavior improved, but in her eyes I became a perpetually sunburned behemoth with shoulders that got wider and stronger by the month. By the time I was in sixth grade, I was five foot eight and weighed 117 pounds. My mother took me to the pediatrician to see if he could help me stop. It seems I was growing just to spite her, to thwart her plans for me.

Every seventy-two hours, a new book on how to be hot, make men do anything you want or marry a millionaire hits the bookshelves. There are a number of bachelor shows, plus an entire series devoted to buying a wedding dress. According to writer and tragic old maid Lori Gottlieb (she's forty and as-of-yet unmarried) writing in the hallowed *The Atlantic Monthly,* as long as someone has a pulse and a penis he's worth marrying. Now landing a man, any man, is as important now as it was when my mother nabbed my father fifty-odd years ago. My mother would have been smirked with irony. It turns out boys are investment property after all. (At least until the current crop of marriageable young women experience the fallout of having "settled," as advised by Ms. Gottlieb.)

Still, for me, as a mother of my generation trying to advise a daughter of this generation, that ship has already sailed. I found out the hard way (is there any other way?) that men are just people: fallible, unpredictable, disappointing, wonderful, *human*. Landing one guarantees nothing. There are a few political wives out there who would back me up on this. Anyway, I can't possibly tell Katherine to use her eyes more—she already knows the story of me falling off the kitchen stool. I can't advise her to be *less* than she is, to dial down her personality or refashion it in the hopes of pleasing anyone, male or female.

For Katherine's life is as different from mine as mine was from my mother's. My mother regarded high school and college as mixers, with term papers. She encouraged me to look "put together" every day as I trudged off to my enormous public high school, because that day Mrs. Quigley might change the seating chart in Civics and I might find myself sitting in front of a new conquest. But Katherine goes to a private, all-girls school. My mother would be appalled to see what a bluestocking I've become, valuing education for education's sake. For Katherine, physics is actually physics, not an excuse to partner up with the star of the swim team while pretending to learn about inertia.

Katherine's opportunity to meet boys is limited to the few dances her school holds a year. She also meets them through the few friends who go to public high school. Boy-girl parties are uncommon. I suspect because it all involves too much effort. It's easier to e-mail like a madwoman, and you can IM and text in your sweatpants while watching re-runs of *CSI: Las Vegas.*

Not long ago, she was invited to a semi-formal dance by a boy she'd known in middle school, who'd gone on to a local co-ed Catholic high school. Katherine and Josh became an item. They texted. They IMed. He called her on her cell. It was like a long-distance relationship, only without the distance. Then two days before the dance, Josh left a voice message saying he couldn't take her to the dance; he was sick and expected to still be sick on the night of the dance, two days away. Katherine and I had already shopped for her dress, her shoes and earrings. It was to be a real date, her first. She was enraged and heartbroken. I didn't know what to tell her.

I wanted to say *fuck him,* but aside from not being able to bring myself to drop the F-bomb in front of my girl, I know she'll say that enough about men as an adult. I said Josh canceled at the last minute because the thought of a real date in the age of hanging out and hooking up was too daunting. I said he chickened out, pure and simple. I put the blame where it belonged, on Josh. Katherine did nothing wrong. I refused to tell her she had been too smart, loud, funny, playful. I would not tell her she needed to learn to sit still. Not that a boy can tell whether you're bouncing your leg while texting.

Had I been even twenty-seven when my mother died and not seventeen, I might have wondered why her advice seemed so maximlike, so unattached to any personal story that told how she arrived at her wisdom. My mother had dictums, but few details. Katherine is the conservator of dozens of silly, convoluted tales of my child—and teen-hood. She's heard them all. We were walking home from the mall, discussing why you never like the boys who like you, and I started in on the story of one of my admirers and she said, "he was the one who used to cruise your house in his purple VW bug! But he would duck down so you couldn't see it was him. But he was the only person you *knew* with a purple VW bug. Like, who else could it be, cruising your house, *not* driving his purple VW?"

I suppose my mother was reluctant to share her stories, because it turns out she had a secret history. My father died a few years ago, and when I was going through his safety deposit box, among the expired passports, car titles and birth and marriage certificates, I came upon a yellowed newspaper clipping from the *Detroit News* Public Notices section. Dated six months before my parents married, it stated that my mother, Joan Mary Rex, had legally changed her last name to Joan Mary Sharkey. I was mystified. Who was Rex?

For several weeks, I was thrilled to think my mother had been married before and that her obsession with my landing the right man was due to the fact that she'd had a secret first marriage to a bad boy she'd run off with against all reason, a boy for whom she couldn't sit still, or bat her eyes or act smart enough-but-not-too-smart, a boy who unmade her and her world. With her heartbreak and humiliation came all her inviolable rules of behavior, her armor for preventing it ever happening again. I thought I had it figured out. I gave the clipping to the husband of my mother's oldest friend, a retired cop who'd become a private investigator, to see if he could track down her ex.

It took the P.I. less than a day to locate my mother's birth certificate, on file in Wayne County, Michigan, a copy of which had not been in my father's deposit box. She was not, in fact, the daughter of old Maude Sharkey, but a very young couple named Calvin and Nora Rex. At the time of my mother's birth, Calvin was eighteen and Nora, sixteen. She listed her occupation as homemaker and he called himself a poet–cabdriver. Maude Sharkey never formally adopted my mother, but took her in as a foster child, thus the last name Rex, my mother's real maiden name, which had never been formally changed. Why she decided to officially change her last name to match that of her foster family only a few months before she married remains a mystery. I suppose she didn't want any more official evidence that she had been a foundling.

From my own perch in the family tree, this knowledge changes nothing, really. It explains why I was so much taller than my cousins and maybe even where my writing gene came from (my grandfather's poignant listing of his occupation as poet, first, then cabdriver). It offers insight into the creation of my mother's weird, inviolable rules, but doesn't change the rules themselves. I'm able to appreciate that her rules were born out of the simple compulsion for security, that even though I was obviously never going to be left as an infant at someone's boarding house (it's still unknown how my mother came into the care of Maude Sharkey), life was still fraught with the possibility of being left to fend for yourself. Still…

Katherine had her party on a rainy night in February. A friend who owned a fitness studio in a beautiful old brick building let us use her space. We arrived two hours early to lock up everything anyone could possibly mess with. I had visions of the rambunctious sloe gin-toting boys at my party, and the kind of mischief they could have had with a collection of ankle weights, dumbbells, yoga mats and exercise balls. What would they ruin? What might they steal?

It turned out we needn't have worried. The fifty kids that showed up were nervous. Each clique stood in a tight circle, shoulder to shoulder. They were like schools of shy fish. They moved to the food table together. They all danced together. I was worried that some of them would hook up and sneak off to the bathroom at the end of the hall. None of them had the courage to venture that far. I was struck by how young her friends seemed, how inexperienced in the ways of socializing. I thought, *Geesh, they really need to get out more,* and could imagine my mother standing there with me, watching, thinking the same thing.

My girl is now sixteen-and-a-half. I don't appear to have a brain tumor (another fear for another essay, that history would repeat itself and my only child would wind up a motherless daughter, like me). Mostly, we get along. I just try to meet Katherine wherever she is on a given day and see what's on her mind. My basic advice is that she should find out who she is and be as true to that person as possible and have faith that other people will find her as lovable as her father and I do. I say that all I want is for her to be the best Katherine there is. I say that everyone has his or her own path. I say that things will get better. Most of all, I avoid pontificating and making proclamations about what guys like or don't like. After all, my mother was bossy and opinionated, and my dad loved her until the day she died.

WHAT I WOULD TELL HER
Rachel Sarah

> I have lived as my daughter's mother,
> the way I had lived as my mother's daughter,
> inside her life.
> —From "Physics" by Sharon Olds

It's impossible for me to tell my mom that she failed me.

Every time I sit down to work on this essay, I shrink. *That sounds too blaming, that sounds too forgiving.* I'll never get it right. One moment, I'm backing away because I want to take care of my mother. The next, I'm lashing out.

Dealing with childhood suffering is complicated. You can carry it around for your life, heavy and secretive. You can blame your parents forever. No matter, it follows you straight into your adult relationships.

My mother likes to tell people that I made her life difficult since the moment she went into labor with me. I was a moody, intense kid. I ruined every family holiday with my antics, she likes to say.

Fortunately, babies have a way of fixing old wounds. Even if it is just temporary. Certainly, my daughter, Mae, helped things out between my mom and me when she glided into this world on April 4, 2000.

My mom's plane was just touching down in New York City—she was en route from the suburbs of Northern California—as I rushed to the birthing center, already nine centimeters dilated. I'm my mother's firstborn, and Mae is her first grandchild. It was the first time in years that my mom and I hugged each other—and held on. This was my picture-perfect fantasy of what a mother-daughter relationship should look like. I wanted to hold on to it.

But "it" didn't last.

When Mae turned seven months old, my boyfriend walked out the door. Our relationship was fragile, layered with his manic depression and my codependency. Around the same time, my mom got a Fulbright to teach English literature in Morocco. She fell in love with the country and she now spends half the year in Rabat, half the year in California.

In the meantime, I moved back to California. My mom had learned how to e-mail, but we barely communicated. I wanted to, but I didn't know how. The year that Mae turned six, my dating memoir, *Single Mom Seeking: Play Dates, Blind Dates, and Other Dispatches from the Dating World,* came out. At first, things were marvelous: I went on the radio, reporters called me for interviews.

Then I got invited to go on ABC's *The View from the Bay* to talk about dating as a single mom. How freaking exciting!

The catch? It was Mae's winter break and she was home from vacation; I had no one else to call upon other than my mother. My mom was excited to come along.

As you can imagine, my thoughts were chasing each other in circles: live TV! What would they ask me? How would I answer?

But there was a deeper worry, too. How would she respond to what I had written about her in the book, a book she herself had not yet read?

When I'd turned *Single Mom Seeking* in to my editor, my mom was hardly mentioned in the book. One of my former writing professors in New York City had offered to read the manuscript, and she called both me and my editor. While she really enjoyed it, she saw a glaring omission in the book: my relationship to my mother.

She said that the "important hole in the story" frustrated her. She was "desperate to understand Rachel's relationship to her own mother."

I was desperate to understand it, too. In one night, I pounded out two paragraphs about my mother and shipped them off. I wasn't dealing directly with my mom about my pain, but I was dealing.

I was doomed to oversimplify and misinterpret. But under the deadline gun and exhausted from the entire process, I sent this page to my editor. It's this one passage, when I explain that my mom left the country on a Fulbright after my daughter was born:

The truth, as we all know, is often layered and complicated. I've never completely forgiven her for coming and going these past six years. Every year, I find myself wishing that she'd be here for Mae's birthday. But she never is…. It's a lifelong disappointment that I feel, and the only way I can forgive her is by becoming what was missing in my own life: the mom I wish I'd had.

Today, I realize that this was *not* about Mae. It was about me. I wanted my mom to be there *for me.* I wanted her to acknowledge *my* birthday. I never heard from my mom when I turned thirty-five. When I turned thirty-six, she sent me an e-mail.

Back at home, after the TV interview, I nervously handed my mom a signed copy of my book, in which I'd written: "I love you." When she sat down and opened it—clearly skimming to find the parts about her—I didn't want to be there. So I went into the other room, where Mae was coloring at my desk.

A book flew over my head and hit the wall. I spun around.

"This is trash," yelled my mom, who'd clearly been aiming to hit me—and missed.

"You are one really sick girl!" she added, before storming off.

Mae, who was now six, held her crayon in midair and stared at me. "What happened?" she asked, looking equally terrified and thrilled.

I didn't answer. I ran after my mom, but she was already in her car, driving away.

Back in the house, I found the phone, and walked out of Mae's earshot. I called my mom and left a message: "I'm truly sorry. I didn't aim to hurt you… I regret that my words were painful. I love you very much."

"Mommy? *What* happened?" Mae said when I came back.

"I wrote something that hurt Gi Gi," I said. "I'm sorry about it now."

Mae, who often astounds me with her maturity, said: "But, Mommy, *everyone* has feelings."

She's right.

But I'd let my mom down. Or, had I really? I'd tried to tell the truth.

Days passed, and my mom hadn't called me back. I e-mailed her, apologizing again. She wrote back:

Hello Rachel,

Anyone can write something vulgar and prurient; it sells well but has no literary merit. My psychologist used the words "teenage purge." Your words on the page hurt people and are destructive to relationships.

Why not consider, the next time, writing a biography of a neglected female author?

I wish I could regain the affection I had for you. It has disappeared, even though I am still your mother and I will always be concerned for your welfare. But that special place in the heart is not there anymore. Maybe it will return someday, next week, next year, I don't know.

I feel the same as (your ex-boyfriend) when he said, "I'm not in love with her anymore."

I burst into tears and called one of my best friends. I told her I couldn't breathe. Today, I wonder: *Who, exactly, is the neglected female author?*

Weeks passed. I was getting geared up for my book tour—San Francisco Bay Area, Seattle, and New York City. My self-esteem was at its lowest.

Now I was supposed to tell the world that I was having the time of my life dating as a single mom. Mae, who's just as emotional as her mom and grandma, picked up on the tension. She was bursting into tears all the time. She was angry.

She started to tape notes to her door: *"I want a new mommy, you're the meanest."*

Great, just great. I had no healthy mother-daughter model; we were doomed to repeat history.

Months passed, and my mom didn't call or write. She had flown abroad and returned again. Then, an e-mail arrived, out of the blue and very businesslike, asking if she could see Mae. Of course, she could.

As I drove out to the suburbs, Mae said: "Mommy, will you tell me about the time that Gi Gi threw your book at you?"

What could I say? I couldn't believe that she'd remembered it.

"Gi Gi was very angry at me, and sometimes when people get angry, they do things without thinking."

In the rearview mirror, she nodded her head, seeming to understand.

On my way to bring Mae to Mom, I knew I wouldn't come inside. I tried my best to hide from Mae how heavy and somber my steps were. I rang the bell, put her bag down on the stairs and gave her a kiss. As soon as the door opened, I walked away.

Were we going to go on this way for the rest of our lives?

Maybe I'm writing this essay because I don't want to go on this way. Maybe, if I apologize, I will correct three decades of wrongs between us. Everything will be right—finally. But that's just my guilt talking.

Seven months after not speaking to each other, my thirty-fifth birthday passed without a word from my mom. Even when we'd lived continents away from each other, she had always called me on my birthday. Not this time.

One night, after a glass of wine, I took a deep breath and called my mom. There was no answer, so I left a message:

Hi, Mom, it's me. I'm calling to apologize again—and also to acknowledge that this silence is really uncomfortable. I don't know what to do or say, I just want to acknowledge how awkward this is.

Her response the next day by e-mail caught me off guard—in the best way. After close to ten months of silence, my mom suggested that we see her therapist together.

I wrote back right away, not quite knowing what I was signing myself up for: my mother's therapist is the same one she has been seeing for two decades, and I vaguely remember being dragged to her office when I was a preteen. I'd refused to go inside. Hopefully I've matured a bit in the past twenty years. Hopefully.

The night before our session, I couldn't sleep. I didn't know what I was going to say. One wish repeated itself over and over: *I want to heal our relationship.*

Still, there was one thorny issue I couldn't avoid: The idea for this very essay had been accepted. I was terrified to tell my mom about this essay. I knew that I could *never* write another word about her without getting her permission first. I felt safe in the therapist's office.

My mother got to the office before me that afternoon, and she sat in the waiting room, on the sofa. I knew better than to try to hug her. She eased the awkwardness by diving into our most-favorite subject: Mae.

My mom: "Did Mae tell you that she swam backstroke across the whole pool on Sunday, all by herself?"

Me: "Really, Mom? All by herself?"

Mae is like a soft, plush ball we toss back and forth between us, never letting it fall. If you didn't know our conflicts, you'd actually think we were having fun. She's probably the only safe topic we can talk about.

But the therapist got us to talk.

And at one point, the therapist directed me to get up and sit in one of the chairs, identical to my mom's. She asked me to scoot my chair close to my mom's, so that we would face each other.

I moved my chair across the room, and my mom moved her chair to meet me halfway. My mom and I were close, our knees almost touching.

"I like your shoes," my mom whispered to me.

I laughed. My mom has always had a silly side, which Mae has inherited, too. I looked at her face.

"See if you can look at Rachel," the therapist said to my mom.

My mom looked up, but her eyes darted to the left, and then to the right.

"Take a deep breath and try again," the therapist said. But my mom couldn't look at me. Her lip was trembling.

The tears welled up in my eyes. I felt so sad, for myself and for her.

Look at me, Mom. I don't know why she seemed so afraid of me. Did she think that I would hurt her again?

I hope that no matter how angry Mae might feel toward me one day, I will always be able to look at her. I lose my cool with my daughter more often than I care to admit—but thanks to my own years of therapy, I have learned to acknowledge her feelings. It's not easy.

As you can see, I've put myself in a bind. Because no matter what I write about my mom, I will upset her. If I write a likeable essay about my mother, will it be enough?

Probably not. She is hurt. It is a hurt that goes beyond me, a hurt that I cannot repair.

So, what would I tell her?

I want to tell her to move closer to me, not further away. The closest relationship I have with my mother is here, on this page. But I need more than that.

INSIDE THE HOUSE AND OUT
Karen Joy Fowler

Slip into your nightgown,
Lie down straight and narrow;
It's time to Hunt the Dragon,
It's time to shoot the Arrow.
—From "Lullaby" by Samuel Yellen in his book
Inside the House and Out

As a small child, my daughter Shannon had two entirely different personalities. Within the family, she was lively, noisy and confident. When I told my friends how incredibly bossy she was, how the family constellation revolved around her, they were frankly disbelieving. The Shannon they saw was a painfully shy child who responded to questions by whispering the answer in my ear. After her first year of nursery school, I asked her what she had liked best. "The curtains," she told me. What least? "The kids."

By the time she made it to first grade, she enjoyed school, mostly because she was good at it. At home she was a fidgeter, but in the classroom she could concentrate on a project for hours. She was small, but athletic. She drew well and was a quick learner.

My routine back then was to walk Shannon from the car to her classroom. She had asked me to, and I enjoyed this bit of time with her—she was usually full of plans for the day. But most of the other mothers said goodbye at the curb, and my daily walk was an irritation to Shannon's teacher, who had told me on a few occasions that it was unnecessary. I had said that I liked walking her in. And that was usually where the conversation ended.

One day at recess Shannon was trying to beat the class record for swinging on the high bars. She had a crowd around her, counting her swings, when the bell rang. In her hurry to finish, she lost her grip and fell, breaking her arm. Her little brother and I picked her up and took her to the emergency room to be casted.

Within a couple of days, her attitude toward school changed. Now she cried every morning and begged to stay home. There was nothing she could do there, she said. She couldn't write or draw or play at recess. All she could do was sit still and sitting still was the thing she hated above all things.

I spoke to her teacher about this, imagining that more thought could perhaps be put into finding things she'd be capable of. Her teacher instantly agreed there was a problem. She'd observed it for herself. Shannon had every mark of a clinical depression, she told me. She arranged a meeting for me with the school psychologist.

To my surprise, when this meeting took place, it appeared not to be about Shannon's depression and her broken arm. It appeared instead to be about my habit of walking her to the door of her classroom. I was not encouraging her independence, the psychologist said, and wasn't this the perfect opportunity to change that? At the same time, Shannon's teacher was telling her that my walking her to the door would have to end. Shannon came home in tears. I felt I'd been ambushed.

"She needs to be kicked out of the nest," Shannon's teacher told me the next day when I went in to object. "She'll never leave if she isn't kicked out." And then, "This isn't up to you. Shannon is yours when she's at home, but she's mine when she's on the school grounds."

I was young for a mother in that place and time and I looked younger than I was. Perhaps this is why my parenting was sometimes criticized by random strangers. I once had a woman at the park ask me if my children's mother knew where I had taken them. But I knew I was a good mother, I knew this, because I was raising my children as I'd been raised and I had the best mother in the world.

My mother was a nursery school teacher with a specialty in child development. I am not afraid of teachers.

My father was a psychologist. I am not afraid of psychologists.

So I went straight to the principal's office to explain that Shannon was always mine and that I would be walking her to her classroom just as long as she and I both wanted it that way.

Trips Taken

I've always felt a strong identification with the female line of my family. My grandmother had four children, three of them girls, the eldest my mother. Grandma told me once that the first time Grandpa asked her to marry him, she said no, she wanted to see the world first. She bought a train ticket from Minnesota to California and he came to the station to ask her again. There she was, with her passage paid for and her bags packed. But she went home with Grandpa. Marry me, he'd said, and *I'll* show you the world.

Which he did, just as soon as she'd raised four children. When I was a little girl, they took a round-the-world cruise. I have her travel diary so I know the trip started inauspiciously. Grandma immediately broke out in hives and had to be confined to her cabin. While she suffered in the dark, Grandpa attended captain's dinners and danced gallantly with widows. Once she left her cabin, she spent the rest of the trip hearing from one woman or another how lucky she was to have married him. It took the Panama Canal to restore her usual good spirits.

My mother also yearned to travel, and also waited until her children, my brother and I, were grown. This may have had something to do with an inconvenient world war. The minute I went to college (I'm the youngest) she and my father left for South America. In preparation, they'd taken two years of night-school Spanish. My mother was better at understanding what was being said; my father was better at answering—together they had it covered. They'd been married more than thirty years, were both in their fifties, but there were places, my mother told me, where they weren't allowed to share a room, because they'd neglected to pack their marriage certificate.

After my grandfather and my father died, my grandmother expressed a great interest in Japan. My mother, my mother's youngest sister, her husband and Grandma all went together. My mother had a wonderful time, my grandmother not so much. When I asked her about the trip, she told me she didn't like rice and she didn't like fish; she'd had a hard time eating. It now appeared that her main motivation had been to have a suit made as she'd done on her original trip east and eventually she realized that it was Hong Kong she'd wished to see, not Japan, at all. Everywhere they went people kept touching her white hair, which she listed as an annoyance, though my mother said she'd actually seemed to like that part quite a lot.

When I was sixteen, my mother used a fund she'd been saving for a new rug to send me on a school trip to Italy. I'm afraid that at sixteen I was more focused on dynamics within the group than on the glories of Italy. There was a lot to gossip about. One girl got engaged to an Italian boy and had to be shipped straight home. The rest of us were pinched and probed, clucked and hissed at whenever we went out. We'd rented rooms in a Perugian convent where the food was very bad—imagine Italy, only with bad food!—and there were bars on the windows to prevent men from climbing into our bedrooms. They would scale the walls and hang from the bars, calling for us until the nuns came and knocked them down with brooms.

Our plane home caught fire and we had to make an emergency landing in Ireland. I was not afraid until after we'd landed. Suddenly strangers were throwing their arms around us. "You had the best pilot in the world," they said. Their voices shook and some of their faces were wet with tears. The best pilot in the world, the man who'd calmly talked to us the whole time we were in the air, making us believe that everything was fine, that everything was under control, was now standing on the tarmac behind us, drinking whiskey straight from the bottle, white as a sheet.

We spent a night in Ireland and then made New York in the middle of the great airline strike of 1966. I had to be flown home first-class, where I was fed frogs' legs, in order to get home at all. All in all, a very agreeable trip.

Later, one summer during college, I went to England and back to Ireland. I traveled part of the time with my brother, and we had many adventures. When I was on my own, I tended simply to go to the movies.

Trips Not Taken

In my dreams, I'm a gutsy person. In the actual world, not so much. Out of high school, I applied to two colleges. One was UC Berkeley. The other was a new program in international studies; the campus was on a ship. Berkeley was by far the cheaper choice, and the new college, the floating college, was not yet accredited, which concerned my father. Berkeley was an easy drive; I could get home any time I wanted to. I had high school friends going to Berkeley.

I honestly can't remember which factor influenced me most, but I made the safe choice. I don't exactly regret it. You seldom get to feel the pleasure of knowing you are in exactly the right place at exactly the right time, but Berkeley between 1968 and 1972 is about as close as I ever came. My professors were brilliant; I got a first-rate education at what was then a cut-rate price.

In my junior year I had a chance to do a year abroad in Norway, a place I still haven't been, a place I still long to go. I said no, because I'd fallen in love with the man I later married. I don't regret this, either, except in a broad why-can-I-only-live-one-life kind of way. Both of these trips not taken became stories that Shannon and her brother were told.

As Shannon grew, her outside personality became more and more like her at-home one and by the sixth grade, the two had fallen into sync with her at-home one. She changed schools that year—entirely her own idea—and found friends who appreciated her energy, her originality. Two of these sixth-grade classmates remain among her closest friends today. In high school, teachers routinely complained to me about her high spirits, which she expressed mainly by nonstop talking during class.

We told Shannon we couldn't afford out-of-state tuition and she went to UC San Diego, about as far away from home as you could get, given that restriction. She called me once during her freshman year to tell me that the other people in her dorm had come from unbelievably *Leave-it-to-Beaver*-ish families. All of their dads went to work and their moms stayed home, she said. Baking cookies. As a feminist, it pained me to point out to her that her dad had also gone to work and her mom had also stayed home. That I had, on occasion, made cookies. "Yes," she said. "But you were openly resentful about it."

I never did push Shannon out of the nest. Instead I apparently complained about the nest at every opportunity.

More Trips Taken

Shannon is now thirty-four years old. So far, she's traveled to sixty-five different countries, has been on every continent including Antarctica. She's lived abroad for months or years—in Costa Rica and Panama; Australia and New Zealand; Ireland and England. Much of the traveling she's done, she's done alone.

Ironically, she's been the one to push me out of the nest. A few years ago, she talked me into visiting Malaysia. On the plane over, I began thumbing through her guidebook. There were warnings of places where Western women had been attacked by mobs. "Did you notice this?" I asked her, and she said she had, but we weren't going to those places. (Though we did end up in a couple of locations where I felt we were not exactly wanted.)

And we were, in fact, attacked, only by monkeys not men. We finished the trip in a nature preserve in Malaysian Borneo. On our way to our room, a troop surrounded us. One large male seized my toilet kit, bit through my toothpaste tube, then threw it and all the other toiletries angrily at me, one at a time. His penis was disturbingly erect. We noticed later that the park was posted with many signs cautioning visitors about Naughty Monkeys.

That night we slept in a room with the lights on; in the dark, rodents of unusual size entered through unseen doorways and rustled through our clothes.

We spent a Christmas together in Spain. Shannon's method of travel involves arriving in a place with no reservations, and then seeing what can be found for cheap. Transportation is usually avoided in favor of walking everywhere. Directions are seldom asked for in favor of finding your own way. When I'm with

Shannon, we sometimes sleep in dodgy places, walk for miles, carrying everything we've packed. Money is spent primarily on museums or concerts or food. Because we've brought so little, dressing-up is not really an option. On a couple of occasions, we've been turned away from seemingly empty restaurants and suspected our clothes were the issue.

Still this method served us well in Spain, until we arrived in Seville on New Year's with no room for the night. We found one vacancy in a place we both agreed was beneath even our flexible standards—was, in fact, out of the question—and then, many exhausting hours later, went back and took it. I have two images of that New Year's Eve: one is of being in the city square in a large, joyful crowd as the clock counted down, sharing champagne from the bottle with strangers, and then watching people smash the empties until the street was with thick with glass. The other is of returning to our lodgings after midnight, walking through the ruined, damp, crumbling hallway past a beautiful young woman eating alone at a candlelit table, a sorrowful look on her face.

Shannon took a job in the Antarctic on the wonderful ship *The Explorer*. I joined her for a couple of weeks and many Antarctic landings. We saw whales bubble-net feeding, leopard seals resting on ice floes, countless, countless penguins. Later I visited her in London for Thanksgiving and the day after, woke to every phone ringing in the house. Friends were calling to tell her *The Explorer* was sinking. We spent the rest of the day glued to our laptops, watching its slow descent on the Internet, worried first of all about the passengers and crew, and then, when they'd been safely rescued, greatly saddened by the final moments of the ship itself. By the time we went to bed that night, *The Explorer* was lying sideways on the water. When we got up the next day, it was gone.

When I look at my grown daughter, I see someone who has chosen to lead a large life. She has enormous energy, imagination and curiosity. She is passionate about the natural world and fascinated by the cultural, political, historical one. Terrible things have happened to her in distant parts of the world. With all my heart, I wish I could erase those things; they've left their mark. (But terrible things have also happened to me, all within an easy drive of home.)

Like her great-grandmother before her, like her grandmother, like her mother, she wished to see the world. Unlike the rest of us, she is actually doing so.

Back in Malaysia, having been attacked by monkeys, threatened by rats, having eaten things from menus we couldn't read and, on the plate, couldn't identify, having walked through forests and villages often uncertain where we were or where we hoped to go, we celebrated Shannon's birthday evening in a karaoke bar in Kuching. We sang "California Dreamin'" and "Leaving on a Jet Plane" to an audience of startlingly talented Japanese businessmen. The quality of our own performance can be inferred from the response. The businessmen told us what a brave performance it had been. They said that we were very brave.

They were half right. I have a very brave daughter. She didn't get that from me.

"DON'T INTERRUPT ME UNLESS YOUR EYES ARE BLEEDING" AND OTHER MOMENTS OF MOTHERHOOD
Susan Wiggs

And above all, watch with glittering eyes the whole world around you because the greatest secrets are always hidden in the most unlikely places. Those who don't believe in magic will never find it.
—From *The Minpins* by Roald Dahl

What kind of mother would tell her five-year-old, "Don't interrupt me unless your eyes are bleeding"?

Probably, a parenting book will advise you that it's not a good idea to threaten a child. Yet I, with my fancy-schmanzy advanced degree (in education, no less) and my years in the classroom, was heard to utter this and other such soul-damaging warnings. More than once. To this day, I still wonder if my daughter bears hidden emotional scars.

The reason I made this statement to Elizabeth is that it worked. She quit asking for a juice box, game of Chutes & Ladders, help with making a cave for her trolls, practice jumping rope, advice on cleaning Sharpie Marker off the refrigerator door, or any of the myriad concerns of a five-year-old. And I—then a young mother, teacher and newly published author—did indeed get my writing done for the day in a state of blissful silence. Every work-at-home writer with kids can relate to this moment—being on deadline, caught up in the white heat of creation and desperate to get the story out of your head and down on paper.

Much later, I emerged from my creative fog to the acute

sensation of Something Wrong. The house was Too Quiet. Anyone who has ever raised a child knows the peculiar quality of a too-quiet house. There is nothing peaceful about it. This eerie vacuum of silence is the deafening sound of impending doom. Most days, our house rang with the clamor of doors slamming, Nickelodeon turned up loud and left on, "Chopsticks" on the piano complete with made-up lyrics, and a running stream of dialogue from my only child, who had a lifelong habit of narrating everything she did. Silence was Not Normal.

In a mother's imagination, the world can come to an end in a split second. That's the amount of time that passes between the realization that you haven't heard a peep out of your child for far too long, and the gut-deep knowledge that said child is lying blue-faced on the kitchen floor, suspended with her dungarees caught on the jungle gym or drowned in the birdbath. In that split second, you suffer the tortures of the damned, imagining the calamities your helpless offspring has endured while you weren't paying attention.

After a panicked search of the house, I found Elizabeth busily putting the finishing touches on a drawing of a girl with curly yellow hair and bright red teardrops of blood streaming from her eyes.

Oops.

And not only had she created a devastatingly literal picture of my parenting; she had published a book of her own. I could only hope it wasn't *Mommy Dearest*. While I was struggling with a few pages of my novel, my preliterate child had written a story, then illustrated and self-published it as a book.

Did I melt to the floor with remorse? Ply her with Gummi Bears and extra hours of bedtime stories? No, I puffed up like a tick with pride. Why? Because I felt like a patron of the arts. What can I say? That's the way I roll.

I love my daughter—my heart, my only child—to distraction.

From the moment she was born, I regarded her as a magical creature, a fairy child given to me by supernatural forces. Some women talk about the pain and terror of childbirth. I remember none of this. I just recall the dizzying joy of holding her, of knowing that I had made this miracle and that she was mine.

But sometimes, I just needed her to be quiet and I didn't always tell her diplomatically.

Elizabeth made her book out of typing paper and the cardboard from a cereal box, stapling it all together. She'd included a copyright page and a title page. The story, written in random letters strung together, was sophisticated beyond her years, giving me a glimpse of a gifted, budding writer. If I'd spent the past two hours guiding and abetting her play, would she ever have created such a thing? Was I right? Was I wrong?

When you're in the moment, you don't judge.

I'm not recommending child neglect here. But I do think being overly attentive has its hazards, as well. I doubt you'll read this in any child-rearing book, but I believe there is immeasurable value in showing a child your determination and passion for your art. The smartest, most intuitive creature in the world is a small child. When you shout a warning about bleeding eyes or hair on fire at her, she understands what you're really saying. And I didn't just tell Elizabeth about the bleeding eyes. I told her other things, too. Like the fact that there are fairies in the yard. *Don't let people tell you those glittering, zooming creatures are dragonflies. They're fairies. Believe it.* And that when you're in an airplane, you might be flying over a map. And that you'll never be bored if you keep stories in your head. As far as I knew, the art and craft of writing held no mystique for my daughter. It was simply the Thing Mom Did when she was "working." So I thought, anyway. Then one day, when Elizabeth was about eight—third grade, a watershed year for a writer because that's when she switches in school from manuscript printing to cursive writing—she parked herself beside me as I wrote. By this age, she was capable of sitting still for whole minutes at a time.

I write the first draft of my stories in longhand, using a particular fountain pen with a clear barrel so you can see the ink cartridge inside. After my daughter watched for a while, she asked, "Where do all the words and paragraphs come from?"

Without thinking, I replied, "They're all here, up inside this pen."

She studied the pen closely. "I think I'd like to borrow it."

This is one of the best things a child does: reminds the grown-up to believe in the magic.

My mom was my first patron of the arts. Once I had a child, my own mother turned into a goddess. Her IQ shot up a good fifty points. It's impossible to talk about the way I raised my daughter without reflecting on the way my mother raised me. So much of what I know of raising a child, I learned from my parents. The rest, I learned from my daughter.

Mom was a girl of the early sixties, in pedal pushers and Keds and a middy blouse. She wore red lipstick and a kerchief, and she smoked Parliament cigarettes. In college, she dreamed of becoming a meteorologist, although her very traditional parents didn't love the idea, and she became a teacher instead. I wonder if she thinks she settled. Did this make her determined to nurture her own children's dreams? My mother was my first writing teacher. As a toddler, I used to scribble drawings on church collection envelopes and bank deposit slips, and Mom would write the words I dictated. These stories all seemed to be about a child up a tree, with scary things coming after her. To this day, that's pretty much what all my books are about.

When I was six years old, I came down with pneumonia in the dead of winter. We lived in western New York, repository of the worst lake-effect snows in the country, and due to the pneumonia, I was not allowed to go outside. My mother no doubt tired of endless readings of *The Poky Little Puppy, Go Dog. Go!, Mike Mulligan and His Steam Shovel* and *Yertle the Turtle*. She showed me how to knit and taught me to play selections from *The Cat in the Hat Songbook* on piano. Finally, she taught me to type.

We had an old manual typewriter with a spooled ribbon that smelled of musty ink, and an inspiring complement of round glass keys arranged like a toothy smile. It was an antique even then (the midsixties) and had a curious, irresistible charm. The typeface was an odd sans serif lettering I later learned was called "Futura." From the moment I sat down in front of this typewriter, feet dangling from my chair, eyes wide with wonder, I was overcome by the feeling that magic was about to happen.

Mom and I sat side by side at the Formica kitchen table. It was yellow, with a pattern of overlapping boomerangs, and I had to sit on a stack of Grolier encyclopedias so I could reach the keyboard with the proper posture. My mother was very methodical in showing me the way to touch-type. She started with the four fingers of the left hand: *ASDF*. Again and again I typed those letters in various combinations: *FADS. SAD. AS. AD. FA,* until I could type them with my eyes closed. We moved on to the right hand. We added one letter at a time until I'd memorized the location of every letter on the keyboard. She showed me the shift key and how it could transform a keystroke into something entirely different. She gave me a tour of the exotic symbols above the numerals, taught me the meaning of the mystical ampersand.

I recovered from the pneumonia before I learned to touch-type the top row of numbers and symbols, and to this day, I'm not able to use them without looking. But the lessons of those dark winter days became part of my blood and bone. Something in me awakened—a realization that publishing is the way a story finds its voice. When typed words appeared in print on white paper, my stories were transformed into printed pages. To an emerging writer, this is the moment the world shifts.

It's doubtful that when my mother sat down with a bored, restless, slightly feverish child, she meant to foster a future writer. She was probably just trying to minimize the whining and earn some peace and quiet.

But it was also her instinct, and her mothering style, to nurture creativity in a variety of fashions. She believed in artistic expression in all its forms, from knitting to making pancakes in the shape of animals. When we were very small, my sister and I used to lie awake in the bedroom we shared and shout downstairs to our mother to play the piano for us. Invariably—and, I now realize, with remarkable good humor—she would oblige, playing our old upright piano and singing us to sleep, the strains of Brahms'"Lullaby" and "Here We Go Looby Loo" winding up the stairs and into the darkening bedroom with its gabled windows and angled shadows lying across the wooden floor.

Of all the arts, music was the thing that came most naturally to my mother. She believes in singing several times a day, with gusto and confidence. She gives equal value to "Little Brown Jug" as she does to an aria from *Cosi fan Tutte*.

When it was my turn to be the mom, I passed on the same lesson. Learn to play an instrument, preferably piano, but anything will do, even a slide whistle or harmonica. Sing a lot. Fill the silence with singing. All songs are good. We had one of those enormous stereos that stacked the LPs above the turntable, dropping each down and playing it in turn. This is how I came to know every note in the "William Tell Overture," "Bippity Boppity Boo," *Peter and the Wolf* and *The Sound of Music.*

A generation later, Elizabeth and I sang and danced our way through Disney videos, Raffi albums, the Allman Brothers and Rush on cassette tapes. Sometimes my husband would come home after work to find the two of us still in our jammies, having turned the dining room into a tent city made of blankets staked to the floor with stacks of books. Sometimes we played, sometimes I wrote. This is the balancing act of the working mother. When you're home with a small child, you get to play all the time. But remember, a child doesn't see playing as play. It's simply the thing they do, from the moment they wake up until the moment they fall asleep. So don't be surprised if your adored, lavishly played-with child grows up and tells you she doesn't remember you playing with her. Ever.

That five-year-old is twenty-four now. I'm not sure what part of the eighties she'll associate with her childhood. The big hair? Leg warmers? Please, God, not the shoulder pads. She just got engaged to be married. She's a gifted, natural writer. In her lifetime, she's interrupted me many times. To date, her eyes have never bled. So far, so good.

ABOUT THE CONTRIBUTORS

Julianna Baggott is the author of five novels—*Girl Talk, The Miss America Family, The Madam, Which Brings Me to You,* cowritten with Steve Almond, and *My Husband's Sweethearts,* published under the pen name Bridget Asher. She has also written three books of poems, including *This Country of Mothers, Lizzie Borden in Love* and *Compulsions of Silkworms and Bees.* Under the pen name N. E. Bode—*The Anybodies* trilogy, *The Slippery Map,* the prequel to *Mr. Magorium's Wonder Emporium,* and *The Prince of Fenway Park.* She lives with her husband writer David G. W. Scott and their four kids, and teaches at Florida State University's Creative Writing Program. Along with her husband, Baggott is a cofounder of the nonprofit organization Kids in Need: Books in Deed.

Gayle Brandeis is the author of *Fruitflesh: Seeds of Inspiration for Women Who Write, Dictionary Poems, The Book of Dead Birds: A Novel,* which won Barbara Kingsolver's Bellwether Prize for Fiction in Support of a Literature of Social Change, and *Self Storage: A Novel.* In 2004, *The Writer Magazine* named her a Writer Who Makes a Difference. Gayle is on the national staff of the grassroots organization CODEPINK: Women for Peace, and is a founding member of the Women Creating Peace Collective. Mother to two teenagers, Gayle lives, writes and teaches in Riverside, California.

Katherine Center is the author of two novels, *Everyone Is Beautiful* and *The Bright Side of Disaster,* and she has two more forthcoming. She started writing fiction in the sixth grade, when she penned the tale of how all five members of Duran Duran fell in love with her and she was forced to pick one. Later, she graduated from Vassar College, where she won the Vassar College Fiction Prize, and earned a Master's in fiction from the University of Houston's Creative Writing Program. She now lives in her home state of Texas with her husband and her two feisty little kids—a daughter and a son. For more about Katherine (or to find out which member of Duran Duran was the lucky winner), please see her Web site: katherinecenter.com.

Amanda Coyne has an MFA in creative writing from the University of Iowa. Her work has appeared in such publications as *Harper's Magazine, The New York Times Magazine, Bust* and *Jane*. She has read original essays on NPR's *All Things Considered*, PRI's *This American Life* and is coauthor of the book, *Alaska Then and Now*, published in 2008 by Thunder Bay Press. She moved to Alaska to write for the *Anchorage Press*, Alaska's alternative newsweekly. Currently, she teaches writing at Alaska Pacific University and is freelancing for local and national publications.

Catherine Crawford edited the book *If You Really Want To Hear About It: Writers on J. D. Salinger and His Work*. She is a freelance writer and a columnist for the gaming and parenting Web site, What They Play (whattheyplay.com). Catherine lives in Brooklyn with her husband, two daughters and one large tub.

Quinn Dalton is the author of a novel, *High Strung*, and two short story collections, *Bulletproof Girl* and *Stories from the Afterlife*. Her stories and essays have appeared in numerous literary magazines and anthologies. Visit her online at quinndalton.com.

Calla Devlin's fiction has appeared in anthologies and literary journals including *Five Fingers Review, Watchword* and *Square Lake.* She lives in San Francisco with her family.

Anne Marie Feld's work has appeared in the *New York Times,* and a weekly journal chronicling her pregnancy with her daughter appeared on *Babycenter.* Her essays have also appeared in the anthologies *Mommy Wars* and *Modern Love.* She lives in San Francisco with her husband and two children, where she spends much of her time preparing pasta with butter sauce and talking about fairies and firefighters.

Carolyn Ferrell is the author of the story collection *Don't Erase Me,* which won the Art Seidenbaum Prize of the *Los Angeles Times* Book Awards. Her stories have been anthologized in *This Is Not Chick Lit: Original Stories by America's Best Women Writers,* edited by Elizabeth Merrick and *The Best American Short Stories of the Century,* edited by John Updike. A recipient of a National Endowment for the Arts fellowship, Ferrell teaches at Sarah Lawrence College and lives with her husband and two children in the Bronx.

Ann Fisher-Wirth's third book of poems, *Carta Marina,* will appear from Wings Press in 2009. She is the author of *Blue Window* and *Five Terraces* and of two chapbooks, *The Trinket Poems* and *Walking Wu Wei's Scroll.* With Laura-Gray Street, she is coediting *Earth's Body,* an international anthology of ecopoetry. Her awards include a Malahat Review Long Poem Prize, the Rita Dove Poetry Award, a Poetry Award from the Mississippi Institute of Arts and Letters and two Poetry Fellowships from the Mississippi Arts Commission. She has had Fulbrights to Switzerland and Sweden, and has served as President of ASLE (Association for the Study of Literature and Environment). She teaches at the University of Mississippi.

Karen Joy Fowler is the author of five novels and two short story collections. Her first novel, *Sarah Canary,* won the Commonwealth medal for best first novel by a Californian. *Sister Noon* was a finalist for the Pen Faulkner award and *The Jane Austen Book Club* was a *New York Times* bestseller. A new novel, *Wit's End,* was published in April 2008.

Emily Franklin is the author of two novels for adults, *The Girls' Almanac* and *Liner Notes,* as well as over a dozen books for teens. She edited the anthologies *It's a Wonderful Lie: 26 Truths about Life in Your Twenties* and *How to Spell Chanukah: 18 Writers Celebrate 8 Nights of Lights.* She is coeditor of *Before: Short Stories about Pregnancy from Our Top Writers.* Her next book, *Too Many Cooks: A Mother's Memoir of Tasting, Testing, and Discovery in the Kitchen* will be published by Hyperion in May 2009. Visit her at emilyfranklin.com.

Ayun Halliday is the sole staff member of the quarterly zine *The East Village Inky* and the author of *No Touch Monkey! And Other Travel Lessons Learned Too Late, Dirty Sugar Cookies: Culinary Observations, Questionable Taste, The Big Rumpus* and *Job Hopper.* Her first children's book, *Always Lots of Heinies at the Zoo,* will be published in Spring 2009.

Mary Haug grew up on a ranch in central South Dakota and writes nonfiction about her sense of place and her family. She has been published in *Peril and Promise: Writings from South Dakota and*

Beyond; Homefront; One House, Many Skies; Crazy Woman Creek: Women Rewrite the American West; South Dakota Magazine; and Radio Works. She also edited The Woster Brothers' Brand. She is grateful to her husband, Ken, for forty years of love and support and grateful for her daughter, Maura, who has redefined the model for mothers and daughters.

Kaui Hart Hemmings is the author of House of Thieves, a collection of stories, and The Descendants, her first novel, a New York Times Editor's Choice. The Descendants is now out in paperback. Visit her at kauiharthemmings.com or partywithaninfant.blogspot.com.

Ann Hood is the author most recently of a memoir, Comfort: A Journey Through Grief; the bestselling novel, The Knitting Circle; and the Young Adult novel, How I Saved My Father's Life (And Ruined Everything Else). Her short stories and essays have appeared in many publications, including the New York Times, the Paris Review, Bon Appetit, Traveler, O and Food and Wine. She lives in Providence, Rhode Island.

Karen Karbo is the author of three novels—Trespassers Welcome Here, The Diamond Lane and Motherhood Made a Man Out of Me— all of which were named New York Times Notable Books. The Stuff of Life, about caring for her father during the last year of his life, was a People Magazine Critic's Choice, a selection of the Satellite Sisters Radio Book Club, a winner of the Oregon Book Award for Creative Nonfiction, and also a Times Notable Book. Karen's most recent title is How to Hepburn: Lessons on Living from Kate the Great, a contemporary reassessment of one of America's greatest icons.

Sheila Kohler is the author of six novels and three collections of stories. Her work has been anthologized in the Best American and O'Henry Prize Stories and she has won the Willa Cather prize. Her latest novel is *Bluebird or the Invention of Happiness,* based on the life of Lucy Dillon. Her novel, *Cracks,* is now being filmed with Jordan Scott and Ridley Scott as directors. Eva Green plays Miss G.

Ericka Lutz's award-winning short stories and personal essays are widely anthologized. Her essays appear in *Child of Mine, Literary Mama, Toddler* and *France: A Love Story.* Her short stories have appeared in numerous anthologies and journals. She is the author of seven nonfiction books including *On the Go with Baby* and *The Complete Idiot's Guide to Stepparenting.* A founding editor at Literary Mama, Ericka currently writes their popular monthly column, "Red Diaper Dharma."

Joyce Maynard is the author of eleven books, including the novel *To Die For* and the memoir *At Home in the World,* translated into eleven languages. She divides her time between Mill Valley, California, and Guatemala, where she runs The Lake Atitlan Writing Workshop. Visit her at joycemaynard.com.

Elise Miller's first novel, *Star Craving Mad* is available in the United States, Japan and Indonesia. She lives outside Philadelphia with her husband and two children.

Jacquelyn Mitchard, whose first novel, *The Deep End of the Ocean,* was named by *USA TODAY* as one of the ten most influential novels of the past twenty-five years, is the author of thirteen works of fiction, a frequent contributor to *Parade* magazine, and will write *Ladies' Home Journal*'s column about motherhood for 2009. She lives near Madison, Wisconsin, with her husband and seven children.

Catherine Newman, author of the award-winning memoir *Waiting for Birdy,* is a contributing editor at *FamilyFun* and *Wondertime* magazines, and a regular contributor to *O, The Oprah Magazine.* She writes a weekly parenting column, "The Dalai Mama," at wondertime.com, and wrote "Bringing Up Ben and Birdy" on babycenter.com. Her work has been published in numerous magazines and anthologies, including the *New York Times* bestselling *The Bitch in the House.* She lives in Massachusetts with her family.

Katrina Onstad's writing on film and culture has appeared in the *New York Times, Elle,* the *Guardian* and *Salon,* earning her National Magazine Award nominations in both the United States and Canada. Currently, Katrina is a columnist with *Chatelaine* magazine and a film critic at CBC.ca. Her first novel, *How Happy to Be,* was published in 2006, and a follow-up is forthcoming. Katrina lives in Toronto with her partner and two children.

Lucia Orth lived in Manila for five years, working for a nonprofit organization. She has also lived in London, Beijing and Washington, and traveled extensively in Asia. She graduated from Notre Dame Law School, and currently teaches in the Indigenous and American Studies Department at Haskell Indian Nations University in Lawrence, Kansas. She and her husband live on a ninety-acre farm. They have three children. Her first novel, *Baby Jesus Pawn Shop,* which is set in Manila, was published in November 2008. Her Web site is luciaorth.com.

Barbara Rushkoff's first writing job was interviewing MC Hammer. Since then, she has written for *Index, Rolling Stone* and *People* and started the seminal zine, *Plotz* (plotzworld.com). Author of the book *Jewish Holiday Fun, For You!*, she is currently working on a book of short stories. She lives with her husband and daughter in New York.

Rachel Sarah brashly describes her dating blunders in her book, *Single Mom Seeking: Play Dates, Blind Dates, and Other Dispatches from the Dating World.* On her site, singlemomseeking.com, she writes about love, sex and what's in between. Rachel has written for *Family Circle, Pregnancy, American Baby* and *Lifetime TV.* She lives in the San Francisco Bay Area with her eight-year-old.

Laurie Gwen Shapiro is the author of three novels for adults including *The Unexpected Salami,* an ALA Notable book, and the bestseller *The Matzo Ball Heiress.* She has also written two books for young adults. Laurie is also a filmmaker, and co-directed the documentary *Keep the River on Your Right: A Modern Cannibal Tale,* for which she shared an Independent Spirit Award with her brother David Shapiro. She was coproducer and shares a Film By credit on the documentary *Finishing Heaven* (HBO, 2009), and with Conor McCourt, has coproduced two Cinemax documentaries about her former high school English teacher (and former big-time crush) Frank McCourt. Drop her a line at LaurieGwenShapiro.com.

Tara Bray Smith was born and raised in Hawaii. She is the author of *West of Then: A Mother, a Daughter, and a Journey Past Paradise,* a memoir, and *Betwixt,* a novel for young adults. She lives and writes in New York City and Düsseldorf, Germany, with her husband, Thomas Struth.

Ellen Sussman's *Dirty Words: A Literary Encyclopedia Of Sex* was published by Bloomsbury in 2008. Her anthology, *Bad Girls: 26 Writers Misbehave,* became a *New York Times* Editors Choice and a *San Francisco Chronicle* Bestseller. She is the author of the novel, *On a Night Like This* also a *San Francisco Chronicle* Bestseller. It has been translated into six languages. Her Web site is ellensussman.com.

Heather Swain is an award-winning author of two novels, *Eliot's Banana* and *Luscious Lemon* (chosen as the best novel of 2005 by the Indiana State Library) and the editor of the anthology *Before: Short Stories About Pregnancy from Our Top Writers.* Her short stories, personal essays and nonfiction articles have appeared in anthologies, literary journals and magazines such as Salon.com, *American Baby* and *Other Voices.* Her first young adult novel, *Me, My Elf and I* will be published in Spring 2009. She lives in a crooked house in Brooklyn with her husband, their children and a dog. Her mother visits often.

Ashley Warlick is the author of three novels, *Seek the Living, The Summer After June* and *The Distance From The Heart of Things,* all published by Houghton Mifflin. She is the youngest winner of the Houghton Mifflin Literary Fellowship, a founding member of the advisory board for the Novello Festival Press and a book columnist for several newspapers. In 2006, she received a fellowship in literature from the National Endowment for the Arts. She teaches in the MFA program at Queens University in Charlotte, North Carolina, and at the South Carolina Governor's School for the Arts and Humanities.

Susan Wiggs's life is all about family, friends…and fiction. She lives at the water's edge on an island in Puget Sound, and she commutes to her writers' group in a seventeen-foot motorboat. Her novels have been translated into more than two dozen languages and have made national bestseller lists, including the *USA TODAY, Washington Post* and *New York Times* lists. The author is a former teacher, a Harvard graduate, an avid hiker, an amateur photographer, a good skier and terrible golfer, yet her favorite form of exercise is curling up with a good book. Readers can learn more on the Web at susanwiggs.com and on her lively blog at susanwiggs.wordpress.com.

Sara Woster contributed essays to the anthologies *Greece, A Love Story* and *The May Queen.* Her paintings and animation have been shown throughout the world including exhibits in Amsterdam, London, Japan and New York. She is a graduate of The New School Writing Program. Her nonfiction journal of images and words, *Babe in the Woods,* the true account of having a baby in northern Minnesota in less than modern conditions, can be viewed on her Web site sarawoster.com. Woster is finishing up her novel, *Survival Skills,* as well. She lives in Brooklyn with her husband and daughter.

ACKNOWLEDGMENTS

My heartfelt gratitude to my guardian agent, Emmanuelle Alspaugh. Her dedication, support and enthusiasm have been an incredible blessing. A big thank-you to Wendy Sherman and Michelle Brower at Wendy Sherman Associates.

Thank you to the brilliant Ann Leslie Tuttle, a consummate pro and crackerjack editor. It has been a great pleasure working with such an insightful and gifted wordsmith.

Thanks to Tara Kelly for her lovely cover design.

Words are not enough for Kimberley Askew, my dearest friend and confidante. She is truly a remarkable woman, my trusted editor-in-arms, and an endless source of inspiration.

To my brave contributors willing to bare all for their art and their audience, you humble me with your courage and unbelievable talent.

I offer my love and devotion to my family: Don and Debbie Richesin, David and Marianne Warwick, Orson and Yvonne Burlingame, Jackson Blaine and Ruth Richesin, Colin and Wendy Dodd, and Whitney and Ginette King.

Thanks to the good people and staff at Playdate Café in San Anselmo, California—especially our fearless leader and creative genius Susannah Rose Woods.

To Elizabeth Hodel: Thank you for lovingly caring for my daughter on such short notice.

For the past decade I have shared my life with Joel Warwick. There is never a dull moment. I marvel at his intelligence and passion every day.

Lastly, I must thank the inspiration for this anthology, my mother and daughter, for whom I owe my life and my future.

CREDITS & PERMISSIONS

Essays

"The Mother Load" © Jacquelyn Mitchard, 2009

"Things to Remember Not to Forget" © Katherine Center, 2009

"Radical Promises" © Anne Marie Feld, 2009

"The Heart Speaks" by Sheila Kohler originally appeared as "Can You Hear Me?" in the May 2004 issue of *O, The Oprah Magazine.*

"Garden Variety Mothering" © Catherine Newman, 2009

"My Mother at Fifty" by Joyce Maynard originally appeared in the October 2005 issue of *Homemakers Magazine.*

"Beyond the Family Party Face" © Ericka Lutz, 2009

"Mother-Daughter Therapy: An Essay on Neurotic Contemporary Parenting" © Julianna Baggott, 2009

"Cutting the Purse Strings" © Heather Swain, 2009

"A Willing Sacrifice" © Mary Haug, 2009

"The Whole Point of Motherhood" © Barbara Rushkoff, 2009

"In The Offing" © Tara Bray Smith, 2009

"Poison Pens" © Gayle Brandeis, 2009

ABOUT THE EDITOR

Andrea N. Richesin is the editor of *The May Queen* (Tarcher/Penguin, 2006) which was excerpted and praised in the *New York Times*, the *San Francisco Chronicle, Redbook, Cosmopolitan, Bust, Daily Candy* and *Babble*. As a follow-up to *Because I Love Her*, she is editing a forthcoming father-daughter anthology (Harlequin, May, 2010). She has worked for Thomson Publishing in London, *Red Herring* and *Edutopia* magazines, and McCann-Erickson in San Francisco. Visit her at nickirichesin.com.